The social effects of unemployment in Teesside

Katharine Nicholas

Manchester University Press

Published by Manchester University Press,
Oxford Road, Manchester, M13 9PL, UK
27 South Main Street, Wolfeboro, NH 03894-2069, USA

British Library cataloguing in publication data
Nicholas, Katharine
 The social effects of unemployment in
 Teesside, 1919–1939.
 1. Unemployment—Social aspects—
 England—Teesside (Yorkshire)—History
 —20th century 2. Teesside (Yorkshire)—
 Social conditions
 I. Title
 306'.36   HD5766.T3/

Library of Congress cataloging in publication data applied for

ISBN 0 7190 1772 6 *cased*

Photoset by Wilmaset, Birkenhead, Wirral
Printed in Great Britain by
Billing & Sons Ltd, Worcester

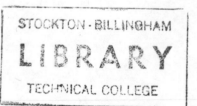

Contents

Figures and tables

Acknowledgements

There are many people who helped me with the research and writing of this book and I should like to thank them.

Invaluable assistance in the research was given to me by the staff of Cleveland County Archive Department and Durham County Archive Department, the librarians of Darlington and Newcastle Public Libraries; the University Libraries of Newcastle and Bristol, the Bodleian Library and the Library of Teesside Polytechnic. I am grateful for the co-operation of the Durham Health Authority, Middlesbrough and Stockton Conservative Associations, the Labour Party, and British Steel, all of whom allowed me to consult their records. Mrs and Miss Davies, the daughter and granddaughter of Arthur Shepherd, the Darlington MP, talked to me and gave access to documents in their possession. The dieticians of North Tees Hospital and Dr Pugh of Sedgefield, in County Durham, generously gave up their time to provide invaluable help and guidance in nutritional analysis. The *North Eastern Daily Gazette* and the *Darlington and Stockton Times* advertised on my behalf for interviewees, and of course I owe a very special debt of gratitude to all those Teesside people who gave up their time so willingly and hospitably to tell me about their lives between the wars.

In the writing of the book continual support and assistance was given by David Taylor of Teesside Polytechnic and John Stevenson of Sheffield University. Both read the manuscript and provided many valuable suggestions. Finally, it was the advice and encouragement of the editor, Alec MacAulay, who helped to bring the project to completion.

Introduction

The aim of this study is to examine the social effects of unemployment during the years 1919–1939 in three Teesside towns: Middlesbrough, Stockton-on-Tees and Darlington. Unemployment was one of the greatest social problems of the inter-war years and Teesside was one of the areas which suffered seriously and persistently from the depression. A wealth of contemporary study was produced on the subject, and on various related problems of poverty, but to date there has been little historical research into the subject. Only two pieces of original research have tackled the question, and the standard works on the social history of the inter-war years draw their information chiefly from the contemporary investigations, without considering the mass of original source material available. It is the purpose of this study to re-examine those problems which concerned contemporaries in the context of all the information which is now available to the historian: the effects of unemployment on living standards, on health and nutrition, on levels of crime, on political attitudes and behaviour, and on those communities and individuals which were affected by it.

The value of this task of re-examination is crucial. For example, on the question of the effects of unemployment on crime, it is essential for the historian to be able to examine in detail the whole pattern of crime figures for Teesside and England in the inter-war period, and consider these alongside the comments and information of those people who were living at the time, rather than to rely on the latter only. On the question of health, it is important both to consider the contemporary debate on standards of health and to take into account new information and discussion on the problem of unemployment and health. When assessing standards of nutrition of the unemployed it is useful to consider these in the light of modern nutritional standards, as well as taking account of calculations made by people in a time when nutritional science was still in its infancy. These advantages of distance and more complete information apply to every chapter of the thesis.

This is the first oral history of unemployment. Several of the contemporary surveys relied heavily on material from interviews, and this is a historical study to complement these.[1] Part 2 of Chapter 4 and Chapter 7 rely greatly on oral testimony, which was one of the most important sources for the thesis. In some cases the author used the interviews to ask again the sort of questions posed by contemporary investigators, and in others to ask new questions. The contributions of those people who were the children of unemployed men, which was necessarily absent from the contemporary surveys, are especially important here.

Oral testimony is now a well established historical source, and frequently used in studies of recent history. Interviews have been a useful source for historians long before the easy availability of tape-recordings; in English history the practice goes back at least as far as Bede, and the use of material based on interviews (such as the work of Booth and Rowntree) has been widespread.[2] As with every other historical source, interviews present problems of interpretation. They are similar to those involved in using written memoirs. It is important to judge how truthful a person is, how well informed, now good is his memory. The historian must also judge whether the informant has a particular standpoint or view of the world, or even temperament which might colour his attitude to any subject, and whether the passing years may have coloured the informant's attitudes. In short, the information given by an interviewee will not be fact, but a guide to facts, as is the case with so many historical sources. The best guide to the problems of interviewing is probably given by Paul Thompson in the first edition of *Oral History* which discusses them in some detail.[3] However, the value of interview material must also be stressed. In some ways interviews with elderly people are likely to be of more use than written memoirs. They are not so often made self-consciously as an attempt to present a particular view of the past. Also, as Thompson pointed out,

Many social pressures against openness diminish in retrospect and the last years of life for many people are a time of reflection and special candour. Nor is loss of memory nearly as serious as is often believed. Memory loss is in fact often concentrated during and immediately after the perception of an event. There are numerous old people who retain a remarkably full and accurate memory of their earlier years.[4]

Their most important advantage, of course, is that these people can give information about their personal experiences and attitudes which is completely unavailable elsewhere. In this study the information which interviewees could give about the experience of living through the depression on Teesside was invaluable and otherwise quite unobtainable.

Apart from the general difficulties of relying on interview material there will be particular problems which result from the individual sample. In this study many of the interviewees offered their help after seeing posters or articles in local newspapers about the author's work. Some were found as the result of personal contacts, and often one interviewee suggested another. A few were simply known to the author. Others were deliberately sought; most of those people who were actively involved in politics were found after an approach to local political associations. (Mr and Mrs Chilvers were the two who did not come into this category.) The author conducted formal interviews with fifty people, and had informal conversations with many more who remembered the inter-war years on Teesside. The chief limitation of this sample is that it tended to produce people who were either more intelligent than the average, or who came from 'respectable' homes. The latter category comprises those people who practiced a high standard of household management; who tended not to spend a large proportion of their income on items which were not strictly necessary; who valued hard work and had a strong sense of responsibility to their families. For this reason the impression given by informants of standards of household management, and indeed general ability to cope with the problems of depression, is such as to present a picture, which although by no means rosy, was much brighter than for the less intelligent, less fortunate in family circumstances, and less provident. These people are less likely to reply to newspaper articles, or to be willing to talk if approached. Indeed the chances of the 'respectable' people living to be elderly are probably much greater. Some of the people interviewed had not come from respectable homes, and many others had lived near families with poor standards of management; but descriptions of these people by others, even close neighbours, still lack the real value which comes from a personal account.

This does not mean that the interviewees were especially pri-
vileged people. They had nearly all lived in areas where unemployed
men were the rule rather than the exception, and usually in working
class districts of their town. A disproportionate number were people
who had had a better education than the average (gone to grammar
school or perhaps further education) and these people may have had
a more detached view of the depression, in retrospect. But the
majority of the interviewees were ordinary people who had worked
for most of their lives for one of the area's major employers – ICI or
the steelworks. One or two came from the middle classes, and spoke
of helping the unemployed. Nor were they at all similar people. They
included people of very different temperaments, attitudes to life,
different political attitudes, and experiences. A few wished to tell a
story with a particular point, like the man whose main concern was
to talk of the injustice of the Means Test, but most offered to talk
simply out of a desire to help, combined with a natural interest in
talking about their youth.[5] They included men who had been
unemployed (but only one woman), the wives of unemployed men,
and their children. Often the children of unemployed men had also
been out of work themselves.

The other main limitation of the sample was inevitable; it was the
fact that most interviewees had been young people in the inter-war
years. A few could remember the twenties clearly, but most could
only talk about the thirties. This was a major disadvantage, especially as other parts of the study showed that conditions for the
unemployed were very different in the twenties than the thirties.
Also, of course, the stories of people who were already middle-aged
or old when the depression began are lost. It was not possible to talk
to anyone who had lived his early years through a time when
Teesside was a relatively prosperous area, in the late nineteenth and
early twentieth centuries, worked then and then become unemployed. It was left to their children to tell their stories for them. All
these problems are mentioned where appropriate in the text.

The people interviewed were not, therefore, a comprehensive or
representative sample of Teesside people of the inter-war years. This
was not possible and so was not intended. They are, though, a rich
source of extremely useful information.

As people were encouraged to talk, the interviews were not carried
out according to any strictly predetermined pattern. However, the
author did have a list of basic areas of interest, and questions on these

were put to most people at some point in the interview. They were as follows:

1. Questions about the family background, and occupation of the interviewee.
2. Questions about the unemployment of the interviewee, or his/her relative – how long they were out of work and when.
3. Their attitudes to unemployment.
4. The attitude of the family, if any.
5. How unemployed men spent their time.
6. Whether there was any source of help for the unemployed and their families.
7. Whether unemployment affected people's attitude to religion or politics.
8. What people ate, and how they managed the household budget.
9. Whether unemployed people left Teesside.

Questions about crime were not put in the first interviews, but so many people volunteered information about the subject it was included in the list. Many other questions were put to individual people about their own experiences, and most people spoke about many aspects of Teesside life.

In an attempt not to ask leading questions, inquiries were almost always neutrally phrased. For example, the question 'How did you feel about being out of work?' would be put instead of 'Were you unhappy about being unemployed?'

Teesside was chosen as an example of one of the depressed areas which suffered from very heavy unemployment in the inter-war years, but one which had not been studied before, by either contemporaries (with the exception of McGonigle in Stockton) or historians. Three towns, Middlesbrough, Stockton-on-Tees and Darlington were chosen to represent the area. They were broadly similar in that they were centres of industry, but each had its own individual characteristics, which meant that they both complement each other and provide comparisons within the individual subject studied.

The problem of studying the effect of unemployment raises a number of methodological problems, and these are discussed as they arise. The most important, which affects every topic examined in the thesis, is the problem of how to isolate the effects of unemployment from any other social or economic factor which may cause an observed reaction. For example, if the crime rate rose in an area of high unemployment, the rise may not have been as a result of unemployment, for many other social and economic factors influence criminal behaviour. Even if it seems reasonable to attribute the rise in crime in part to unemployment, it may be difficult to assess the relative importance of this as against any other factor, This problem is most acute in the areas of health, crime and politics and it is discussed at some length in each case, but it is basic to every topic studied. Each chapter will therefore not merely examine reactions which may be effects of unemployment but attempt to put them into the context of other social and economic factors in inter-war Teesside.

The other chief methodological problems arise from the difficulties of using various types of source material. Information has been drawn from a wide range of sources, and each has its own drawbacks. Whilst all of these have been discussed in the relevant chapters, it is important to stress the need to tackle these difficulties. For example, the figures of people registered as unemployed are by no means a correct representation of those people actually out of work. The problems of interpreting crime figures are well-known, and they can never provide more than an approximate guide to the actual number of people who break the law. In the case of each question tackled the value of the sources had to be rigorously considered.

There were also problems caused by gaps in the documentation of a particular subject. This was most serious in the case of a variety of records relating to Darlington. Far fewer of the minutes of committees of the local authority in Darlington actually survive, and those that do were often less detailed than those of Middlesbrough or Stockton. Also the response of interviewees was much poorer in Darlington than in the other two towns. This made comparisons between the three towns difficult in those areas where information for Darlington was scarce, and thus an important part of the study was hampered. For this reason some chapters take the form of a comparative study of the three towns, and others draw information from all three to make a more general study of the subject concerned. This approach is possible because the three towns are broadly similar in character, although, even so, local differences are pointed out.

On occasions the constraints of the subject meant that some interesting lines of research were not developed. The question of the comparative standard of living of the employed and unemployed of

Teesside was not considered in great depth, because the purpose of the section was to examine living standards amongst the unemployed, and the wage-rates of the employed were only used to provide a comparison, to set the incomes of the unemployed in context. There is a considerable amount of material available on local wage rates, which, if researched fully, would add to those comparisons already made; but this would require a full study of its own.

Another large area which could not be considered fully in this study was the question of newspaper reactions to unemployment. The main reactions of the local press are commented on in Chapter 6, but there were also in these newspapers many fleeting references to unemployment in its different aspects which were curious or contradictory, but which contributed little to this study. Also, as is pointed out in Chapter 6, one local newspaper rarely mentioned the subject of unemployment at all. A full study of press reactions to unemployment, including newspapers from larger areas than Teesside, might come to some interesting conclusions on the whole question of press reaction to the problem, which could in turn throw more light on the question of the response of the whole community to a problem such as unemployment.

Other areas of study provided not too much information but too little. One of these was the effects of unemployment on religious attitudes. Some interesting comments were made about these by some interviewees (see Chapter 6) but the whole question proved elusive. As clergymen of all denominations tend to move from an area every few years, and few stay in their last parish after they retire, it proved difficult to find such men who had worked in Teesside during the inter-war years. Also church records shed little light on the social questions of the day. Figures for church and chapel attendance are available for the nation as a whole, but not for a small area like Teesside.[6] There is some information concerning the problems of the unemployed which exists but was not available to the author. Harold Macmillan records in his autobiography that he had kept all his correspondence from the time when he was an MP in Stockton in the thirties, and that the majority of his letters were from unemployed men with some practical problem which they hoped their MP could solve.[7] Unfortunately all Macmillan's papers can at present be seen only by his official biographer. Also, the question of the extent to which

charitable help affected and aided the unemployed is one where the
information is more tantalising than substantial. Some judgements
have been made on this question in Chapter 6, but they are based
on scattered information (mostly from newspapers) which contain
little detail. Such evidence as there is suggests that this is an
important area, and further detail would have added greatly to the
subject of the community response to unemployment.

Nonetheless, much interesting information about the questions
posed was available. Despite some disappointing gaps, in general
the subjects considered are well-documented, and most of the
sources consulted were rich in interesting and useful material.
Whilst their ι   is always limited because of difficulties of
interpretation they all have considerable positive value. In the case
of each question considered it has been possible to draw some
useful conclusions.

Middlesbrough, Stockton-on-Tees and Darlington before 1919

From the mid-nineteenth century onwards Teesside was one of
Britain's most important centres of industry. Three of the country's
old staple industries, shipbuilding, iron and steel, and heavy
engineering dominated the local economy. Table 1, which shows
the distribution of the workforce in each of the three towns under
study, illustrates this. These figures, which are taken from the
census of population, do not show the numbers of men working in
any particular industry but they clearly show the preponderance of
workers in heavy industry. Of the three towns, Middlesbrough, in
1921, had the smallest proportion of 'metal workers', thirty-five
per cent of the total. A further thirteen per cent were classified as
general labourers, many of whom would also work in the same
industry. Fourteen per cent of the workforce were involved in
transport and communications, an important adjunct to the iron
and steel trade. Office workers, a category which would also
contain many people who worked for iron and steel firms, were the
fourth largest occupational group, accounting for six per cent of the
total. Few other groups accounted for even as much as one per cent
of the whole. Similar patterns can be seen in Stockton and
Darlington. In both these towns 'metal workers' accounted for
thirty-nine per cent of the workforce in 1921, and no other group
more than five per cent of the whole.

Table 1 *Distribution of male employment on Teesside, 1921*

Total number of occupied males over 12 years of age	
Middlesbrough	13,687
Stockton-on-Tees	21,589
Darlington	21,364

Chief occupational groups	Middlesbrough		Stockton		Darlington	
	No.	% of whole	No.	% of whole	No.	% of whole
Metal workers	15,180	35	8,493	39	8,295	39
Men involved in transport and communications	6,253	14	1,993	9	2,212	10
General labourers	5,937	13	3,609	17	940	4
Men involved in commerce, finance and insurance (incl. clerks)	2,742	6	1,570	7	1,686	7

Source: 1921 and 1931 Census.

Each town, however, had experienced a different pattern of development and exhibited its own particular characteristics. Middlesbrough, the largest of the three (see Table 2), was an iron and steel town, a product of the latter half of the nineteenth century. It had seen a dramatic growth in those years: in 1831 only 154 people lived in a small village there, but by 1841 it had grown to a town of about 6,000 people. This rapid growth continued: in 1861 Middlesbrough's population was 19,000 people, and it was 105,000 by 1911. This growth was the result of the development of

Table 2 *Population of Middlesbrough, Stockton-on-Tees and Darlington, 1921 and 1931*

Town	1921	1931
Middlesbrough	131,070	139,274
Stockton-on-Tees	64,126	67,722
Darlington	65,842	71,835

Source: 1921 and 1931 Census.

the iron and steel industry in the area. During the years 1840–80 many small iron and steel firms grew up in Middlesbrough, and by 1914 a process of self-rationalisation had merged them into two: Dorman Long and Bolcrow Vaughan. By this time Dorman Long had acquired a world-wide reputation for producing iron and steel for the shipbuilding industry and the structural steel trade. During the competitive years of the nineteenth century Bolcrow Vaughan's chief strength had been the diversity of its production.[8] These two firms were the town's chief employers; but as Middlesbrough was also a port there was usually dock work available as well, and some of its men chose to go to sea.

By comparison, Stockton-on-Tees was an old, established town. It was already a major shipbuilding centre in the eighteenth century, and by 1914 it was one of Britain's most important centres of industry. In the nineteenth century British shipbuilding had a strong predominance in world trade: in 1892 it produced eighty-two per cent of all merchant shipping launched. The North East accounted for forty-two per cent of world production, and the share of the yards on the river Tees was about nine per cent.[9] It is fair to say that in 1914 Teesside was one of the world's most important shipbuilding centres. In 1914 there were two shipbuilders in Stockton, the Ropner Shipbuilding and Repairing Company, and Smith's Dock and Co. Heavy engineering was Stockton's other main industry, much of it being marine engineering geared to the shipbuilding trades.

Darlington was an old market town, and it kept its importance as a centre for agricultural produce from North Yorkshire even when it grew after the development of the railways, and became a centre for heavy engineering. Most of her engineering works were in some way connected with the railways, either making or repairing engines or engine accessories, but marine engines and even sewing needles were produced there.

These different backgrounds and industries shaped the characters of the three towns. Middlesbrough was a large, new industrial town, a product of the late nineteenth century boom in the iron and steel industry. The centre had been planned, and the rows of houses built in an orderly grid system, but the outlying districts consisted of houses quickly built in response to the large influx of population which had come some forty to fifty years previously. Many of them were shoddily built and they had quickly deteriorated.

Although during the nineteenth century it had been possible to earn high wages in the steelworks, the living conditions in the town were poor. Stockton was equally industrial in character, but because it had grown more slowly, had fewer environmental problems, whereas Darlington was described even in 1931 by one of its medical officers of health as being more like a town from the salubrious south than the industrial north.[10]

The type of work available in each town also influenced its character. Whilst all three towns were chiefly populated by industrial workers, there was more work available for the casual labourer in Stockton and Middlesbrough than in Darlington, whose workforce consisted chiefly of skilled artisans.

The Problem of Unemployment between the Wars

For most of the inter-war years, after the initial boom of the years 1919–21, Britain suffered levels of unemployment unknown in her history. Since the great depression of 1815–20 there were never fewer than one million people out of work, and at the depths of the depression, in 1933, there were three million people registered as unemployed. Although unemployment had been a fairly regular feature of the trade cycle in the nineteenth century economy, and at times large numbers of workers were thrown out of work, the size, and more importantly the duration of inter-war unemployment made it into a new kind of problem.[11]

These unprecedentedly high levels were caused mostly by an unhappy mixture of structural and cyclical unemployment. Of the two, structural unemployment was more important, because it was this which accounted for the persistance of the problem. During the inter-war years there was a marked structural decline in the staple export industries of Britain, which had been a crucial part of Britain's economy in the nineteenth century. Before the First World War one in four of British workers was employed in one of these staple industries: coal, shipbuilding, cotton manufacture, heavy engineering, and iron and steel. These had been generally prosperous, although in the last years of the century they had faced growing competition from similar industries in Europe, the United States of America and Japan. There is also some evidence that standards of organisation, management and technology in these industries were slipping behind those of their foreign competitors.

The extent of the decline of the staple industries before 1914 is the subject of considerable debate, and it is not useful to this section to enter into this debate, but only to point out that there were signs before the First World War of incipient difficulties in these industries.[12]

During, and immediately after the First World War some of these staple industries, such as iron and steel, coal and shipbuilding, expanded their capacity to meet the needs of the war and then the post-war boom. Their resources would have been unnecessarily unwieldy for even a normal peace-time economy let alone the severe slump of the early 1920s. There was also an accelerated structural decline, due to the fact that in many cases there was a permanent decline in demand for their goods, due, in part to changes in consumer needs. As increased use was made of steel, the demand for pig iron (a traditional British export) fell, and as the speed and carrying capacity of ships was increased fewer were needed, while the large fall in the demand for coal reflected the increasing use of alternative sources of energy. The other reason for the drop in demand for British goods was that after the war her industrial rivals emerged stronger than before. During the war Britain had been deflected from normal production, and so had given her competitors an ideal opportunity to expand and capture new markets. After 1914 the United States and Japan, in particular, were formidable rivals in the production of steel, and textiles.

Another major problem to face the staple industries, as well as the whole British economy, was the two severe cyclical downturns of 1921–23 and 1930–33 caused by massive worldwide slumps. In these years levels of unemployment rose all over the country, but again the staple industries were the worst hit because their normally high levels of exports made them especially vulnerable. Steel production fell from 9.6 million tons in 1929 to 5.2 millions in 1931, and the shipbuilding industry launched only 133,000 tons in 1933, compared with a minimum of 1 million tons during every year of the 1920s.[13]

Of all the old export industries the worst hit were shipbuilding, coal, and cotton, which were faced with a permanent decline in demand. There was also a fall off in the demand for pig iron, but this was partly compensated for by the increased call for steel. In fact the total output of the iron and steel industry did increase during the inter-war years, but this increase was not sufficient to use the industry's excess capacity, nor to compensate for the dislocation and the changes which were taking place. Similarly engineering had mixed fortunes: while there was a decline in the demand for some types of engineering, especially marine engineering which had been dependent on shipbuilding, other products came to the fore.

Other problems were more definitely home based. The over-commitment of the early twenties was based on an over-optimistic assessment of future demands. There were also inefficiencies of management, organisation and technology which exacerbated their problems. British firms were often smaller, and therefore had higher production costs than their rivals. In many cases there seems to have been a reluctance to accept new developments; for example the shipbuilding trade was slow to switch from the production of steam to diesel engines, thus losing potential customers, and the iron and steel industry similarly slow to change from acid to basic steel production. An added difficulty, not of industry's making, was the fact that after the return to the Gold Standard in 1925 the currency was over-valued, which over-priced British goods, although this state of affairs eased with the 'cheap money' policy of the 1930s, after the devolution of the pound in 1931.

The cyclical downturns of the early twenties and early thirties caused unemployment rates to rise in all parts of the United

Table 3 *Unemployment rates in selected depressed areas, 1933*

Town	% of insured workforce
Saltburn	91
Jarrow	77
Cleator Moor	64
Stornoway	70
Wishaw	60
Clydebank	54
Taffs Well	82
Pontycymer	72
Merthyr	68
Abertillery	66

Source: Glyn and Oxborrow, *Inter-War Britain*, p. 153.

Kingdom. But the structural unemployment in the old staple industries resulted in the areas which depended on them becoming depressed for the whole of the inter-war years. The areas with persistent unemployment were mostly fairly isolated, geographically: South Wales, industrial Scotland, parts of Lancashire, Tyneside, Teesside and County Durham. Table 3 shows the very high rates of unemployment in the depressed areas in the depths of the depression: the ten towns in this table all had over fifty per cent of their insured workforce (less than the real total) out of work. Table 4 shows how the depressed areas were still suffering when other parts of the country were enjoying something of an economic upturn. The growth of new industries in the Midlands and South created new jobs and new wealth in these areas, and the gap between prosperous and depressed areas increased as the thirties continued.

Table 4 *Percentage of insured workers unemployed in various towns, 1934*

Town	% of unemployed insured workers	Town	% of unemployed insured workers
Jarrow	67·8	Coventry	5·1
Maryport	57·0	Oxford	5·1
Merthyr	61·9	Luton	7·7
Motherwell	37·4	St Albans	3·9

Source: J. Stevenson and C. Cook, *The Slump*, p. 57.

These continuously high levels of unemployment brought with them many problems. Long-term unemployment was one of the most serious. The Pilgrim Trust found in Rhondda Urban District that only twenty-three per cent of men who had been out of work in 1932 had found work by 1936.[14] In the more prosperous town of Deptford the figure was sixty-two per cent.[15] The chances of young people leaving school, and of those who were paid off at eighteen, finding work were slender, but the worst affected age group were those men aged between fifty and sixty-five.[16] Those who were young enough often left the depressed areas, leaving them depopulated. Twenty-eight per cent of the population of the Rhondda left for other parts of the country between 1921 and 1935. The depressed areas faced financial ruin and many social problems. J. B. Priestley visited Stockton in 1933, and described it as being 'like a theatre which is kept open merely for the sale of drinks in the bars and chocolates in the corridors'.[17]

The Problem of Unemployment in Middlesbrough, Stockton-on-Tees and Darlington

The patterns described in the previous section can be seen in miniature in these three towns. Although the years before the First World War were still prosperous ones for the Teesside industries, in common with most of the old staple industries of Britain they faced fierce competition from abroad. This was particularly true of the iron and steel trade, and although the Middlesbrough firms did amalgamate to meet increasing competition there is some evidence that their standards of management and technology were slipping behind those of their competitors.[18] During the First World War iron and steel production was stepped up to cope with the demands of the armed services and afterwards the industry faced the depression with a capital commitment which was unrealistic for the needs even of a healthy peace-time economy. Bolckow Vaughan found it very difficult to adjust to post-war circumstances: during the 1920s it never operated above fifty per cent capacity, and then it was badly hit by the thirties depression. It merged with Dorman Long in the 1930s. Dorman Long survived better through the difficult years of the 1920s by turning to structural engineering. In 1924 the firm made the steel for the Sidney Harbour Bridge, which provided much needed work. Inevitably, though, it was hit by the depression, and in the worst years operated at thirty per cent capacity. A long campaign of rationalisation and re-organisation, which was begun in 1931 helped the firm to better fortunes at the end of the decade.[19] However, Middlesbrough's main engineering firm, Richardson Westgarth, which was very dependent on the fortunes of ship-building, shut down altogether in 1930.

The acute troubles of shipbuilding affected the North-East to an even greater extent than the country at large. The 67,000 tons launched in 1934 represented only 14.5 per cent of the national total, as compared with 42 per cent in 1892.[20] Production of ships on the River Tees sank from the record level of 1920 to about a fifth of this three years later (see Table 5).

Table 5 *Production of ships on the River Tees, 1920–3*

Year	Gross tonnage
1920	200,000
1921	130,000
1922	46,000
1923	43,000

Source: G. A. North, *Teesside economic heritage*, p. 67.

By the end of the 1920s both of Stockton's shipyards had closed down, and they remained closed throughout the inter-war years. Blairs marine engineering firm closed in 1931, although another Stockton firm, Pease and Co., which concentrated on structural engineering, survived and expanded.[22] This one success story apart, Stockton was hit by the almost total decline of her chief sources of wealth and occupation. It was not until the chemical industry near Billingham (which eventually became ICI) began to achieve sustained success during the mid thirties that the town's fortunes began to revive.

On the whole, Darlington's industry survived better than that of Middlesbrough and Stockton. This reflected the mixed fortunes of heavy engineering country-wide. Some of Darlington's old established firms changed their products to suit new conditions. Darlington Rolling Mills and Co. developed special light steel sections for metal windows and the motor industry. Whessoe, one of the oldest of the town's engineering firms, manufactured gas holders and storage tanks for oil refinery plants. All firms, of course, were affected by the depression, and some failed and were taken over by companies outside the region.[23]

Although they were the worst hit by the depression, Stockton and Middlesbrough did see a recovery from the mid thirties onwards as a result of the growth of the chemical industry on Teesside. A number of small chemical firms were established on Teesside during and after the First World War, and in 1926 two of the larger ones decided to merge and create a British chemical firm which would rival the large and successful ones of Germany. The new firm was called Imperial Chemicals Incorporated, its name reflecting the intention to produce chemical to serve the whole of the British Empire. It was one of the success stories of the inter-war years, and was of enormous importance to Teesside. Although, founded in

1926, its development was halted by the depression, and it was not completed until 1935. After this time it became one of the major employers of the region.

Chapter 1

The extent of unemployment in Middlesbrough, Stockton-on-Tees and Darlington

Problems involved in calculating unemployment

There are a number of problems involved in calculating the numbers of people unemployed in Britain during the inter-war years. The most basic of these is to find a precise definition of unemployment, because any attempt at doing so involves some arbitrary assumptions. This is because every definition of unemployment is made according to the standards and expectations of a particular society and these are rarely clear-cut. For example, in inter-war Britain no housewife could ever be recognised as unemployed, even if for some reason she lost her work. Nor were people over seventy ever considered to be unemployed, because at this age they were entitled to an old age pension, and so someone aged more than seventy who had been working but had lost his job was not out of work. Contemporary studies of unemployment were also concerned about 'grey areas'. They discussed whether people who had become out of work and had subsequently lost interest in having a job could really be considered to be unemployed.[1] For the purposes of this study all those who have no jobs, but are able-bodied and of reasonable intelligence, below retirement age and who would normally expect to work for a wage of some kind will be regarded as unemployed. Inevitably this is an imprecise definition, and certainly it is an arbitrary one, but the reason for using it is that it is in line with the main assumptions made about unemployment in a modern industrial state. Problems, and grey areas, such as the case of people over retirement age who had lost their jobs, will be discussed where appropriate.

The official statistics, which have been used both by contemporaries and by historians, were not intended to conform with the definition set out previously. In fact they were not strictly speaking statistics of unemployment at all, but rather a calculation of the number of people, including most of the unemployed, who were registered with the Labour Exchange together with (during the 1920s) the numbers of those who were receiving parish relief because they were unemployed and destitute. Since these numbers were mostly made up of those people who were entitled to some kind of relief, it is necessary to give a brief explanation of the relief system.

Before the First World War relief was given either by the local Board of Guardians, who gave outdoor relief to unemployed people with no other source of income, or under the provisions of the 1911 Unemployment Act. This act covered those involved in the shipbuilding, engineering and building trades. It was a contributory scheme, which provided state benefits for a limited period for people from those industries who were unemployed, and who had paid a sufficient number of contributions. Such people registered at the Labour Exchange, and collected their benefit there. Soon after the war a form of benefit was also paid to ex-servicemen and civilians who had been displaced by the end of war production. This was called the out of work donation, and was non-contributory. It was paid by the government as a recognition of the status of people who had helped in the war, to keep them from the indignity of applying for parish relief, but also to relieve the burden which was placed on local rates by large numbers of unemployed people applying for relief.[2]

In 1920 there was a new Unemployment Insurance Act, which extended the scheme of unemployment insurance to the greater part of the British workforce, excepting only the self-employed, civil servants, agricultural labourers, and those who earned more than £250 a year. Those who were not covered by the Act still had recourse to the Guardians if they became unemployed and destitute.

The 1920 scheme formed the basis for relief until 1934, but various adjustments were made to it. It soon became evident that many people were going to be unemployed long after their insurance money ran out, and the scheme was extended to give 'dole money', still distributed by the Labour Exchange to those people whose period of benefit had expired. However, uncovenanted benefit, as it was called was not given as soon as ordinary benefit ran out. An act of 1921 allowed for two periods of dole of sixteen weeks each (often they were extended) with two gaps of two or five weeks in between. During the 'gap' people had to turn to the

Guardians, which resulted in a large number of people being cared for alternately by local and national government. This unwieldy system was abolished in 1924, when incovenanted benefit was made a statutory right.

A significant move towards centralisation of the system (at least as far as the compilation of statistics was concerned) was achieved in 1931, when the Boards of Guardians were abolished, and all benefit was funded by central government. After this change the only figures available were those from the Labour Exchange. These also became a better estimate of the extent of unemployment in 1934 when youths between the ages of fourteen and sixteen were included in the insurance scheme, and again in 1937 when agricultural labourers were included. Domestic servants were included in 1938.

The most serious drawback in using unemployment figures collected by national government (which are the ones used by contemporaries and historians) is the fact that, in general, only insured workers were included. During the 1920s some of the uninsured unemployed were included amongst figures kept by the local Board of Guardians, but these are not always available, and are not reliable as a count of those who slipped through the insurance net. Each Board had considerable local autonomy, and hence its own criteria for granting relief, so that many people may have been disallowed benefit on various grounds. Also, because of the stigma attached to receiving parish relief people who could be supported by relatives or savings would do this to avoid going to the Guardians.

In 1931, after the abolition of the Board of Guardians, there were 19·5 million people in the UK counted by the census as being gainfully occupied, 12·5 million of whom were insured against unemployment.[3] Most government estimates of unemployment rates during the inter-war period were based on figures for the insured unemployed; with the result that the numbers given are always an underestimate. The percentage figures, however, are usually over-stated because the percentage rate among the unin-sured unemployed was normally lower than amongst the insured.[4]

However, it is not even the case that official figures are an exact account of the insured workers without a job. The criterion for including a person in the statistics was that he was registered at the Labour Exchange. Some uninsured workers who were looking for work might register at the exchange, and some employed people who wished to change their job might do the same. Also, not all insured unemployed were automatically registered, because the count was made from the number of books lodged at the Exchange. Some people might take their cards away even though they were without work, especially if they received no benefit and had little confidence in the likelihood of the Exchange finding them a job. Cards were thrown away if nothing was heard of a man for eight weeks, although he might be out of work but travelling around. Conversely, a man might have found a job before those eight weeks had elapsed and failed to notify the Exchange.

The official unemployment figures, therefore, were a count of those who were caught by the official net. W. Garside described the count of the unemployed as 'a count of the individuals who, having regard to the law and administrative practice of the time had sufficient motive to record themselves at the Employment Exchange as out of work'.[5] It would seem though, that any unemployed person who had any hopes of ever receiving benefit had a very strong motive to do this. Any significant underrecording would most likely be because a large number of unemployed people were not entitled to benefit. At different times during the inter-war years changes of regulation were introduced which included or excluded different categories of people. The list of changes (Table 6) on administrative practices shows the effects on the unemployment totals.

All these problems (Table 6) apply to all unemployed people, but there are especial difficulties involved in any attempt to discover the extent of unemployment amongst women and juveniles. As it was more difficult for them to obtain benefit, in both cases the official figures seriously underestimate the extent of unemployment in these two groups. The chief area of employment for women was domestic service, an occupation which did not come under the insurance system until 1938. It is very probable that many married women did not bother to register for benefit, and their chances of doing so were reduced after the 1931 Anomalies Act, which said that a married woman could only receive unemployment benefit if she had paid enough insurance contributions before marriage: any paid after marriage were not valid. Faced with these difficulties it is impossible to judge how many unemployed women there were, or even to estimate a margin of error in the statistics, only to note that they are likely to be seriously understated.

Table 6 *Changes in administrative practices affecting unemployment benefit, 1924–38*

February 1924
Removal of certain restrictions on grant of uncovenanted persons with no other means of support. Abolition of the 'gap'.
+ 13,500 persons
August 1924
Relaxation of certain conditions of benefit.
+ 70,000 persons
August 1925
Restoration of special conditions of extended benefit.
− 40,000 persons
January 1928
Persons of 65 and over cease to be insured under the act.
(This had the effect of slightly raising the rate of unemployment because a smaller proportion of people over 65 were unemployed.)
April 1928
Relaxation of certain conditions.
+ 40,000 people
May 1928
Health cards franked at Labour Exchanges.
+ 25,000 people
March 1930
The end of the not genuinely seeking work clause.
+ 60,000 people
October 1931–May 1932
Restrictions in benefit.
− 180,000–190,000 people
January and February 1935
Changes in regulations
+ 20,000 people
September 1937
Changes in the method of counting.
− 50,000 people
April 1938
Extension of scheme. 240,000 people aged 14–64 included.

Source: W. R. Garside, *The Measurement of Unemployment. Methods and Sources in Great Britain 1850–1979*, London, 1980.

The extent of juvenile unemployment is even more difficult to estimate.[6] Before 1934 no young person under the age of sixteen was eligible for benefit, although most of them would hope to start full-time work at fourteen. Therefore before 1934 there is no way of estimating the extent of unemployment amongst people of these ages: roughly half of all juveniles. Even amongst those who were over sixteen, there was a lower tendency to work in insurable occupations; many worked at temporary jobs, (such as errand boys) especially in times of depression. Although it is difficult to judge the extent of unemployment amongst women and juveniles from the official figures, the problem of female and juvenile unemployment must be considered, because of their inherent importance, and other information on these questions will be used whenever possible.

An enumeration of the deficiencies of the inter-war unemployment statistics should not, though, obscure their usefulness. The reservations expressed about the figures are not sufficient to call into question their entire value, only to show that they should be viewed critically. In the case of adult males they are a real help towards an understanding of the extent of the problem. A large majority of men did work in insured trades, and the numbers of uninsured are available and so the figures for insured unemployment are a good basis for judging the extent of unemployment.[7] Of course the fact that the figures of registered unemployed do not exactly reflect the rate of insured unemployed must be borne in mind, but as has already been said, there were strong motives for people to register at the Employment Exchange. As the relationship between the insured and uninsured unemployed was roughly constant, the figures of registered unemployed do show unemployment trends.[8]

There are also limitations in the inter-war unemployment figures which are quite unconnected with the system of collection. Government statistics where published in the form of the total number of books lodged on the last day of each month, divided only into numbers of men, women and juveniles. It was a simple counting of heads system which gives little idea of the make-up of the unemployed. The ages of unemployed people were not recorded, nor was it possible to tell for how long any person remained unemployed. This means that important questions like the age structure of the unemployed, or the average unemployment expectancy of different categories of people (men, women, juveniles, the skilled and unskilled, people in different industries) cannot be answered from the statistics. Some independent contemporary surveys considered these questions, and some special government surveys did the same. These will be referred to where useful, and the general conclusions of similar postwar studies, based on more precise information will be taken into account. Oral testimony can often confirm general impressions in this area, and all these sources will be used to tackle these questions.

Another very important omission in the official statistics is a record of short-time working. The *Ministry of Labour Gazette* did give some figures for short-time working in selected industries, but unfortunately the main industries of Teesside were not included in these. The only other possible source of information is the records of local firms or union branches but these are not always exact. It is generally assumed that short-term working will increase as unemployment rises, but in the case of a severely depressed town where the main firms are shut down altogether this will not apply. In the absence of official or local statistics only local knowledge can provide any clues in this area.

The extent of unemployment in Middlesbrough, Stockton and Darlington

The unemployment statistics available for Teesside are a better than average reflection of the true state of unemployment, because most Teesside people worked in insurable trades. The census figures for 1921 show that in each of the three towns under study less than five per cent of men did not work in insured trades. In the case of Middlesbrough, and to a lesser extent Darlington, it is possible to supplement the figures of the 1920s with statistics from the Boards of Guardians, which include some uninsured people, and more importantly people in the 'gap' between insurance payments. The Middlesbrough Guardians' figures before 1924, (when the gap was abolished) show that between seven and nine per cent of those receiving some form of relief were not listed amongst the registered unemployed, and after 1924 the figure was normally around two or three per cent. Therefore in Middlesbrough, these figures give the best estimate of the real extent of unemployment, and the Stockton ones, where there are no Guardians' figures available, are the most understated. However, in the case of each of the three towns, both the numbers and the percentages given will be an understatement of the true level. In the case of the numerical total this is because of the system of counting, as outlined in the first section of the chapter, and in the latter because the percentages given for Teesside are a percentage of all workers, not of all insured workers.[9] Therefore

while the national figures underestimate the absolute number, and
overestimate the percentage of unemployment, the Teesside figures
understate both.

Table 7 *Numbers unemployed in Middlesbrough, and the UK yearly
average, 1919–39*

Year	Labour exchange figures (Middlesbrough)	% of work-force	Able-bodied unemployed (Middlesbrough)	% of both figures	% of insured work-force (UK)
1919	n.a.	n.a.	n.a.	n.a.	n.a.
1920	n.a.	n.a.	1,762	n.a.	3·9
1921	3,620	26	3,680	33	16·9
1922	9,000	17	5,024	26	14·3
1923	n.a.	n.a.		n.a.	11·7
1924	10,317	19·5	4,333	23	10·3
1925	11,476	21·7	1,635	24	11·3
1926	18,201	34·5	1,233	40	12·5
1927	8,014	15·2	2,973	20	9·7
1928	8,089	12·5	2,429	17	10·8
1929	6,631	24·7	1,161	14	10·4
1930	13,031	37	678	37	16·1
1931	19,543	41	n.a.		21·3
1932	21,683	39	2,022	45	22·1
1933	21,071	31	2,151	44	19·9
1934	16,458	29			16·7
1935	15,347	22			15·5
1936	11,929	17			13·1
1937	9,193				10·8
1938	11,831	22			12·9
1939	10,875	20			10·5

Source: Compiled from figures in the *Ministry of Labour Gazette*,
Minutes of Middlesbrough Guardians, and Glyn & Oxborrow, *Inter-War
Britain*, p. 145.

The unemployment figures for Middlesbrough during the
inter-war years are given in Table 7.[10] This table also gives the
national unemployment rates, and the comparison makes it
possible to see the extent to which Middlesbrough was hit by the
depression. For most of the inter-war period unemployment was
around twice the national average, which in real terms would be
more than double the average, although there was a comparatively
good recovery at the end of the twenties. In the slumps of the early

twenties and early thirties there were extremely high levels of unemployment in the town; in 1932 an average of forty-five per cent of people were recorded as being out of work. The year of the General Strike, 1926, was also bad, with an average of 40 per cent of the whole labour force out of work. Although these levels of unemployment were by no means the highest in the country, they do represent a town working well below capacity during the whole period, with at times nearly half of the entire working population recorded as unemployed.

Most of Middlesbrough's registered unemployment was accounted for by men, because they formed around 80 per cent of the town's full-time workforce, and it was those industries which employed chiefly men which suffered most during the depression. The slump years saw very high rates of male unemployment: forty-eight per cent in 1922, fifty per cent in 1926, and over fifty per cent in the years from 1930 to 1933. Although there was the usual pattern of recovery at the end of each decade of the inter-war period, by the end of the thirties there were still nearly a quarter of all adult males without a job.

Registered unemployment of women suggested that at times female unemployment was also very high. In the years of the thirties depression, registered unemployment of women was around thirty-five per cent of the female workforce. In better years this figure dropped to a more modest 10 per cent, but it is important to remember that these figures are considerably understated.[11] While women's jobs were probably not so endangered by the depression as mens' it is clear that it was not easy for women who normally had full-time jobs (these women formed nearly twenty per cent of the work-force) to find work in inter-war Middlesbrough. There were strong social pressures against women working in times of depression, married women especially were liable to be the first to be paid off when a firm was in difficulties, and of course the general depression affected womens' work in a similar way to mens'.

Many women, though, and especially married women, did part-time work: domestic cleaning, working in laundries, taking in washing or sewing, selling home-made food. These jobs were female preserves, and no unemployed man would consider doing them. These people are not necessarily included amongst either the employed or the unemployed (especially if they worked at home) but oral evidence strongly suggests that these women were likely to be able to continue working during the depression. The demand for the kind of work they did continued through the lean years, because it was consumer-orientated casual work which commanded low wages.

The percentage of juveniles who were registered as unemployed was small, except in the worst years of the depression. Of course this is almost certainly a great underestimate of the true case. Indeed the chief use of these figures is to show how many young people were eligible for benefit; although the rise in the early thirties does give an indication of the probable severity of the situation. However, it was true that a smaller proportion of young people were out of work than adults. Youths under eighteen were likely to get low paid casual work, which they would lose when they could command higher wages. The Carnegie Trust, in its study of unemployed young people found that in Glasgow and Cardiff the year of maximum employment was fifteen, and in Liverpool it was sixteen.[12] Oral evidence for Middlesbrough suggests that this town was no exception. The typical experience of those inter-viewees who had been young men in the inter-war years was that they worked intermittently until they were laid off at eighteen or twenty-one. As one man put it 'boys of fourteen kept the family going'.[13]

One insight into the extent of unemployment not given by the employment statistics is given by the list of casuals relieved in the Middlesbrough workhouse. Casuals were people (almost always adult men) who travelled round the country, and because they had no home could be temporarily sheltered in the workhouse. In normal times casuals would be tramps, or unemployables, and only a handful would be recorded, but in times of depression their numbers rose sharply. This suggests that many of them were travelling to look for work, or were people (probably casual labourers) who were pushed by the pressures of employment into a lifestyle yet more basic than their previous one.

In Table 8 the figures for the depressed years of the thirties are missing, but it is clear that in those of the twenties vagrancy increased tremendously. In 1921 the figure was nearly eight times as great as in 1920, and it was twenty-two times as great in 1922. Throughout the twenties the figure never dropped to anywhere near the 1920 level, although there were far fewer in the late thirties. There is very little other information about these people, and so it

Table 8 *Number of casuals relieved in the Middlesbrough workhouse, 1913–26 (weekly average)*

1913	1920	1921	1922	1923	1924	1925	1926	1927	1928	1929	1937	1938	1939
	188[a]	1,475	4,250	1,213	n.a.	448	552	573	571	401	91[a]	98	89

Note: From incomplete set of figures.
Source: Minutes of Middlesbrough Guardians.

would be very easy to forget their existence: these figures show that they were a problem of considerable proportions.

The statistics in Figure 1 are in the form of yearly averages of unemployment, giving the trends throughout the inter-war period, but concealing seasonal variation. Figure 2 shows that during most of the period the Middlesbrough unemployment pattern followed the normal pattern of less employment in the winter, and more in the summer, when certain trades, such as building, were more active. In relatively good years unemployment would rise by about two thousand in the winter quarter, and fall by a similar number in the spring. An indication of the severity of the slump was that in bad years this seasonal fluctuation was levelled out, and sometimes even reversed, by a cyclical one.

As will be evident from the seasonal nature of certain occupations unemployment was not a new feature of Teesside life. Although Middlesbrough had been a generally prosperous town before 1919 its citizens had known seasonal variations in employment, as well as the vagaries of the trade cycle. It is difficult to estimate the extent of unemployment in the town before the First World War. The 'Third Winter of Unemployment' in its case study of Middlesbrough in 1922 said that before the war 'unemployment, save of a casual nature was almost unknown', although they qualify this by saying 'some of the conditions of work at the blastfurnaces are not conducive to thrift, and thus even a moderate depression brought considerale hardship'.[14] It seems likely, though, that the authors of this study were misled by an impression of the town's prosperity, and so underestimated the extent of unemployment in pre-war days. A. A. Hall, in his study of living standards on Teesside in the latter part of the nineteenth century suggested that not only was there a large amount of casual employment (with periods of unemployment for the casual workers) but also that cyclical unemployment affected all kinds of workers, including those in skilled and specialised jobs.[15] On the basis of his evidence it would appear that the experience of unemployment was by no means unknown to large numbers of Middlesbrough's population. The differences of the post-war situation were, of course, the exceptionally high numbers of people out of work, and the persistence of unemployment, which meant that many people were out of work for a year or more, and became long-term unemployed.[16]

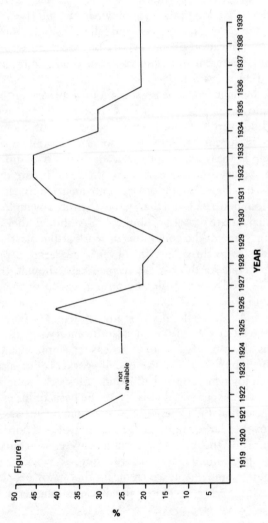

Figure 1 Registered unemployed in Middlesbrough as % of total work-force, 1921–39

Figure 2

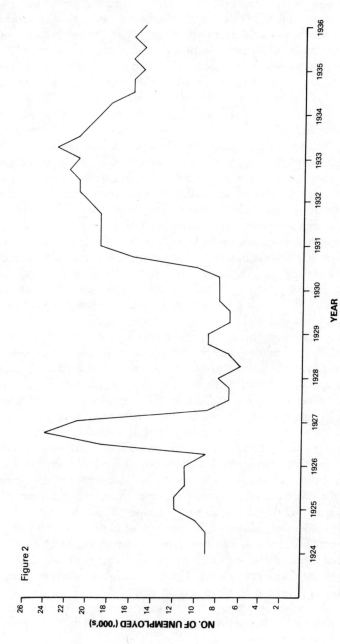

Figure 2 Middlesbrough: seasonal variations in unemployment, 1924–36

Because of the 'snapshot' nature of the unemployment statistics, it is not possible to tell the length of time any one person remained out of work, but it is clear that in towns like Middlesbrough one of the most significant features of the depression was the substantial number of people who remained out of work for several years. The Pilgrim Trust, in their extensive and detailed survey of unemployment in 1936 concluded that long-term unemployment was one of the most serious effects of the depression, and that towns with persistent high unemployment had large numbers of long-term unemployed. In 1936 they found that in Crook, County Durham, seventy-one per cent of the unemployed had been out of work for five years or more. The figure for the Rhondda Valley was forty-five per cent and Liverpool twenty-three per cent. The incidence of this type of long-term unemployment is likely to have been less in Middlesbrough than in Crook or the Rhondda, because both these towns relied solely on one industry which had become virtually defunct. Middlesbrough had slightly more industrial diversity, and did experience something of a recovery during the later thirties. However, it is probable that its long-term unemployment was greater than that of Liverpool, which did not experience the very severe slumps at the beginning of each decade of the inter-war years. Even assuming that the Middlesbrough rate was as low as that of Liverpool, there would still have been around 2,000 men who had been out of work for five years or more among a total adult male work-force of 36,000. Oral evidence from Middlesbrough interviewees confirms the impression that it was a common experience for men to be out of a job for at least a year and often much more. Many interviewees spoke of some people that they knew well who had been out of work for several years, even if this had not happened to them. Long-term unemployment chiefly affected two categories of men: those over fifty, and the young untrained man in his early twenties. The older man was the most vulnerable. Men over fifty were most unlikely to find another job when high levels of unemployment persisted, and they were forced into a form of early retirement. Young men over eighteen were caught in a gap between being cheap labour and experienced workers. Young men were usually sacked from their first job at eighteen, when in prosperous years they would then get a job in the ironworks, but when jobs were scarce and labour plentiful preference there was always given to men with experience. Conversely, men in middle years had the best chance of finding work. In 1931 unemployment across the country was thirteen per cent for men between the ages of 25–44 but 22·6 per cent for men between 55–64.[17]

Post-war studies of unemployment, based on more detailed statistics, show that these trends are normal in relatively good years, and become exaggerated in times of depression.

Another category of people who normally find it more difficult to find work are those with physical or mental handicaps. In time of high unemployment, when the search for a job becomes fiercely competitive one interviewee described men 'queuing up for a little whisper of a job' which meant that only the fittest and most able were able to find work.[18] The Pilgrim Trust found that many long-term unemployed had minor physical defects (such as a stammer, or short stature) which meant that although they were perfectly competent to work they were always at a disadvantage against more 'normal' competitors. One of the interviewees of this study, an intelligent and obviously healthy man, told how he was always turned down for jobs in the iron works because he was too short. Long-term unemployment also tended to reduce people's health and working efficiency, (certainly most employers believed that it did) so that any man who remained out of work for a long time became less and less likely to get a job.

If normal tendencies, to the disadvantage of certain categories of people in the employment market, were exaggerated by the depression, it was nonetheless true that throughout the inter-war years many people on Teesside became unemployed. In some cases they stayed without a job for long periods, even though they were able bodied, intelligent, healthy and keen to work, and had some training in local trades.

Unfortunately there are no records of the extent of short-time working in Middlesbrough, and so it is impossible to quantify the extent of this problem. *The Ministry of Labour Gazette*, in its general reports of the employment situation in the country, frequently mentioned that there was a good deal of short-time working in the engineering industries, and to a lesser extent in the iron and steel industry. Short-time working certainly added in good measure to the difficulties of the Depression, but the precise contribution cannot be estimated.

Figure 3

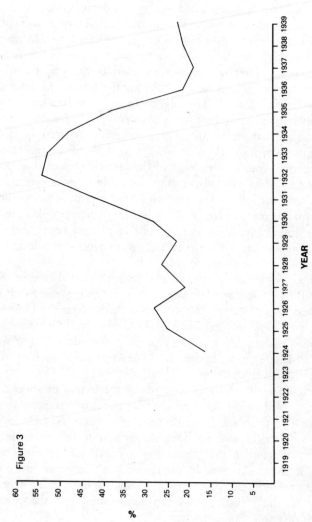

Figure 3 Registered unemployed in Stockton-on-Tees as % of total work-
force, 1924–39

Table 9 *Numbers unemployed in Stockton-on-Tees, 1919–39 (yearly averages)*

Year	Labour Exchange figures	% of total work-force
1919	n.a.	
1920	n.a.	
1921	n.a.	
1922	(6,730 men)	(32% men)
1923	(5,062 men)	(23% men)
1924	5,491	19%
1925	8,015	28%
1926	9,235	32%
1927	5,431	18%
1928	4,813	16%
1929	4,144	14%
1930	7,644	26%
1931	11,922	41%
1932	14,070	48%
1933	13,124	45%
1934	9,875	34%
1935	9,826	34%
1936	8,009	27%
1937	5,878	20%
1938	6,379	22%
1939	5,901	20%

Source: Compiled from the *Ministry of Labour Gazette*, 1922–39.

The employment situation in Stockton-on-Tees was in many respects, broadly similar to that of Middlesbrough, and many of the remarks made about that town also apply in Stockton. The chief difference was that Stockton was affected to an even greater extent by the thirties depression, because of the closure of the shipyards and Blairs Engineering Company. Figure 3 and Table 9 show that Stockton, during the worst years, had one of the highest unemployment rates in the country. In 1932 fifty-four per cent of the whole work-force was registered as unemployed. It is important to remember that these figures are an underestimate to understand the impact of the depression on this town. The very end of the period saw a stronger recovery in Stockton than in Middlesbrough, because Stockton benefited more from the development of ICI in nearby Billingham.

As in the case of Middlesbrough, the greatest part of unemployment was accounted for by adult males. In 1932 registered male

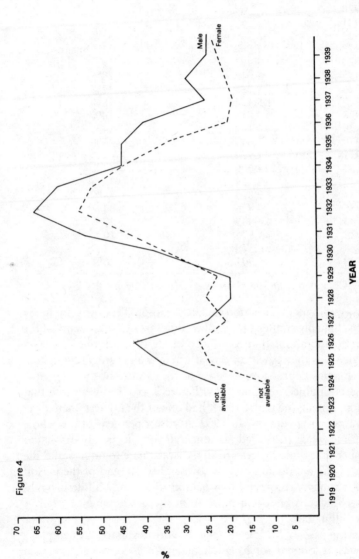

Figure 4 Registered male unemployed as % of total male work-force and registered female unemployed as % of total female work-force in Stockton-on-Tees, 1924–39

unemployment reached sixty-seven per cent of the male workforce, and it was not until 1936 that the figure fell below forty per cent. Registered female unemployment was also remarkably high, reaching fifty-four per cent of the female workforce in 1932 (see Figure 4). According to these figures the employment prospects for women who habitually worked in insurable occupations were nearly as bad as those for men. The real situation may have been almost equality of disadvantage. Registered juvenile unemployment was again lower than adult unemployment for the whole of the period, but in the early thirties it was still over fifty per cent, indicating that in these years it was exceptionally difficult for any person to get a job. Women and juveniles were still, though, more likely to find work of a casual nature.

The pattern of quarterly variations in unemployment also shows the overwhelming effect that the depression had on the local economy (see Figure 5). For most of the period the normal tendency of seasonal variations in employment was overridden by cyclical and structural conditions. An inevitable result of these conditions was a considerable number of long-term unemployed. The findings of the Pilgrim Trust about the extent of long-term unemployment in areas affected by the depression in a similar way to Stockton, are a useful guide to the possible extent. In 1936 they found that in Crook seventy-one per cent of those unemployed had been out of work for five years or more, and the figure in the Rhondda Valley was forty-five per cent. Although Stockton did not suffer the complete shut-down of industry of Crook, its situation was similar to that of the Rhondda Valley.[19] In view of the very severe depression in this town it is possible that short-time working was less of a problem than it would be in a more prosperous town, but those of Stockton's engineering firms which did not close down almost certainly put some of their workforce on short time working at times, which compounded an already difficult situation.

Darlington is a rather different case from Stockton or Middlesbrough (see Table 10). Although its main firms were hit by the depression, they all continued working (sometimes below full capacity) and so continued to provide employment. The unemployment figures for Darlington show that it was in the rather unusual position of having an unemployment rate close to the national average for the whole inter-war period (see Figure 6).[21] This still meant, however, that it suffered high rates of unemployment. At its

Figure 5

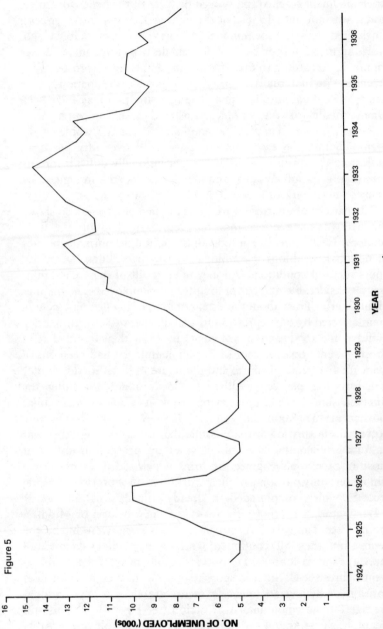

Figure 5 Stockton-on-Tees: seasonal variations in unemployment, 1924–36

Table 10 *Numbers unemployed in Darlington, 1919–39 (yearly averages)*

Year	Labour Exchange figures	% of total work force	Numbers of able-bodied unemployed	% of both figures
1919				
1920				
1921				
1922		15	192	
1923			1,538	
1924	2,117	7	1,793	12
1925	2,578	8	668	10
1926	4,095	13	966	16
1927	2,833	9	1,205	13
1928	2,270	7	1,175	11
1929	2,323	7	870	10
1930	3,627	11	731	14
1931	5,704	18	125	18
1932	6,893	22		
1933	7,539	24		
1934	5,263	17		
1935	4,710	15		
1936	3,691	12		
1937	2,798	9		
1938	2,767	9		
1939	2,433	8		

Sources: Compiled from the *Ministry of Labour Gazette*, 1922–1939, and figures in Darlington MOH Reports.

worst male unemployment was about a third of the male workforce, a low figure by the standards of Middlesbrough and Stockton, but still a serious one (see Figure 7). Official figures for unemployment of women were only a few per cent less than the rate for men, which shows again that the unemployment prospects for those women who normally expected to work full-time (at least those in insurable occupations) were as bad as those for men.

As the depression in Darlington was less severe, and more importantly less protracted than that of the other two towns, fewer men would have been long-term unemployed. Oral evidence (much less strong in the case of Darlington because fewer interviewees came forward from this town) also suggests that in the slump years it was common for men to be out of work for at least a year.

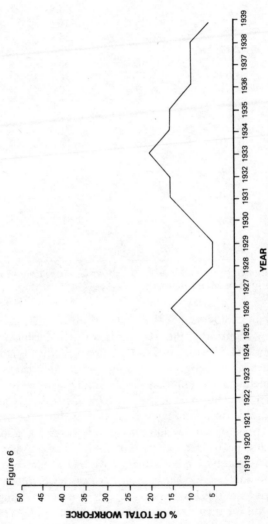

Figure 6 Registered unemployed in Darlington as % of total work-force, 1924–39

Figure 7

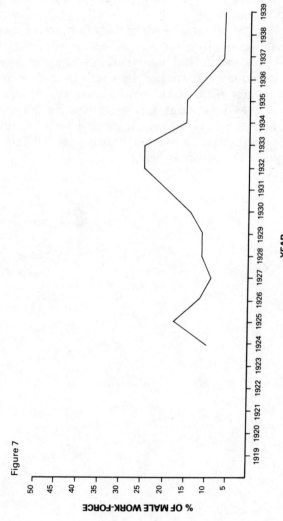

Figure 7 Registered male unemployed in Darlington as % of total work-force, 1924–39

A more common problem for Darlington workers is likely to have been short-term working. Reports in the *Ministry of Labour Gazette* continually single out the engineering industry as one where short-time working was prevalent. It seems probable, on this evidence, that short-time working was more common in Darlington than Stockton, where many firms closed down altogether; in fact the extent of this is the most important caveat against the general impression of this town as one which escaped the worst consequences of the depression.

The unemployment figures for each of these three towns shows them to be examples of places suffering serious depression during the inter-war years. Stockton had one of the highest unemployment rates of the country; it was towns like this which aroused so much contemporary interest and concern, which created the idea of the 'Hungry Thirties'. Middlesbrough survived better, but not much better, and Darlington was also a town hit by depression, but it provides an interesting contrast to the other two because the effects of the depression were less acute there.

Chapter 2

Living standards of the unemployed

Incomes and the cost of living

One of the inevitable effects of unemployment was the need to live on a low income, and many of the effects of unemployment are in some way connected with this. The object of this chapter is to consider the incomes of different categories of unemployed people within the context of (i) the level of wages on Teesside, and (ii) the local cost of living. The first is important to show how great a change occurred in a person's finances when he became unemployed; and also illuminates the experience of unemployment, which is in part influenced by the discrepancy of income between the unemployed person and his employed neighbours. The second considers the all-important question of how well it was possible to manage on unemployment relief.

The income of an unemployed person could vary quite considerably according to what form of relief they received. People from insured industries, who had paid sufficient contributions, could claim Unemployment Benefit for a fixed period until they had drawn their full entitlement. Others had to rely on money given on a non-contributory basis to people who were destitute. In the 1920s this came from the local Board of Guardians, who were supported by the rates. The rates of relief given by the Guardians varied quite considerably from area to area, according to their resources and generosity. In the 1930s the funding for non-contributory relief came from central government, but it was still administered by a local body, the Public Assistance Committee. These committees had a degree of local autonomy, and rates of relief still varied from area to area.

An exception to these schemes, until March 1921, was an additional source of relief given by the government to ex-service-men and some civilians who had done war work. This out of work donation, as it was called, was non-contributory and was provided so that people who had been involved in war did not have to face the said stigma of applying to the Guardians for relief, and also to relieve a burden which would otherwise have fallen on local rate-payers.

The scales of unemployment benefit and out of work donations were fixed nationally, but Boards of Guardians and Public Assistance Committees had a degree of local autonomy, and within certain limits fixed their own scales.[1] Local scales are only extant for Middlesbrough. The national rates are given in Table 11, and the local rates for Middlesbrough in Tables 12 and 13.

Until 1924, the non-contributory parish relief provided more money for any man with a wife and family than the insurance scheme. The latter did not include dependants' allowances, because at its inception it was intended only to provide a supplement to savings which would tide someone over a temporary period of unemployment.[2] Unemployed men with families in receipt of standard benefit would have had to go to the Guardians, or to

Table 11 *Scales of benefit under Unemployment Insurance Acts, 1919–39 (in shillings)*

	Single men	Single women	Wife	Child	Family of four
December 1919	11	11	0	0	11
December 1920	15	12	0	0	15
March 1921	20	16	0	0	16
June 1921	15	12	0	0	15
November 1921	15	12	5	1	22
August 1924	18	15	5	2	27
April 1928	17	15	7	2	28
March 1930	17	17	9	2	30
October 1931	15	13	8	2	27
April 1934	17	17	9	2	30
May 1934	17	17	9	3	32

Out of work donation

Man	29
Woman	25
First child	6
Other children	3

Source: 1921 and 1931 Census

Table 12 *Able-bodied relief scales of Middlesbrough Board of Guardians, 1921–6 (s d)*

Scale (pre-1922)		Scale (July 1922)	
Single persons	10	Single persons	15
Single persons in lodgings	16	Single persons in lodgings	16
Man and wife	20	Single persons living at home	10
Man, wife and 1 child	25	Man and wife	20
Man, wife and 2 children	30	Man, wife and 1 child	25
Man, wife and 3 children	35	Man, wife and 2 children	29
Man, wife and 4 children	40	Man, wife and 3 children	33
Man, wife and 5 children	45	Man, wife and 4 children	36
Man, wife and 6 or more		Man, wife and 5 children	38
children	50	Man, wife and 6 children	40
		Man, wife and 7 children	42

Scale (September 1922)		
Single persons	12 6	12 6
Single persons in lodgings	16	10
Single persons living at home	10	10
Man and wife	20	20
Man, wife and 1 child	24	25
Man, wife and 2 children	27	29
Man, wife and 3 children	30	33
Man, wife and 4 children	33	36
Man, wife and 5 children	33	38
Man, wife and 6 children	35	40
Man, wife and 7 children	35	42

Scale (1926)	
Single persons	10/12
Man and wife	20
Man, wife and 1 child	24
Man, wife and 2 children	27
Man, wife and 3 children	29
Man, wife and 4 children	31
Man, wife and 5 children	33
Man, wife and 6 children	35

Half given in money and half in kind.

Source: Compiled from Middlesbrough Board of Guardians Minutes.

Table 13 *Public Assistance Committee scales in Middlesbrough 1931, 1936 and 1937 (in shillings)*

	1931	1936	1937
Single man	12s 6d	17	17
Single man living at home	10	17	17
Man and wife	20	26	26
First child	4	2	3
Subsequent children (maximum of six)	2	2	3

Source: Compiled from Minutes of Middlesbrough Public Assistance Committee.

relatives for extra financial support. Out of work donation, though, was fixed at a higher rate than either UB or parish relief, and did give dependant's allowances. This was because it was based on the system of allowances to dependants which had been established during the war. When out of work donation was abolished in March 1921 the principle of giving allowances to dependants was established, and it was recognised as being cheaper than raising all benefits, and more acceptable than placing a large burden on ratepayers, and so was included in the new Unemployment Insurance Act.[3]

After 1924 the idea that Unemployment Benefit should be the most remunerative was established on Teesside, and the Middlesbrough Guardians' scales were brought into line so that those whose insurance money had run out should not be getting more than those in receipt of UB. This principle was maintained until the late thirties when Middlesbrough PAC scales were adjusted so that men with large families were as well off receiving PAC money as unemployment benefit. Both scales were fixed on the principle of less eligibility, (by which no relief should be greater than a possible wage) although this principle was undermined in the thirties when wages in the depressed areas fell to such an extent that relief money sometimes provided more money than employment.[4]

Not all unemployed people automatically received the full relief to which they were nominally entitled, and the figures given in Tables 11–13 are the maximum possible relief. Unemployment Benefit was not means tested because it was an insurance scheme, nor was the special out of work donation. However, both parish relief and PAC money were. The Middlesbrough Guardians had a fixed rule that the savings or any extra income of a claimant would be counted against any relief given. Apart from this the exact amount given to the claimant was decided by the local relief committee, and the generosity of its actions depended on which individuals were members of the committee.[5] Public Assistance money was subject to strict rules which included a family means test whereby members of the family were expected to support an unemployed relative. Two-thirds of the income of a parent (including pension money) were taken into account, as was three-quarters of a child's income. Under this system it was common for relief to be disallowed in the case of a young person whose father was working, or a parent with employed children.

During the 1920s most of the Teesside unemployed received money from the Government. Most of them normally worked in insured industries and so qualified for either standard or extended benefit, while some of them would have qualified for out of work donation. It is not possible to say exactly how many qualified for the higher rates of out of work donation, but they would have been predominantly the young men who had fought in the war. The Middlesbrough Guardians' figures show that about 3–5 per cent of the town's unemployed in the twenties were not eligible for UB or transitional benefit, (see Chapter 1) although these included men who had from time to time to go to the Guardians for relief in the 'gap' between the payment of insurance benefit and that of 'incovenanted' benefit.

In the thirties a much larger proportion of people were excluded from the UB scale, for all those who had been out of work for more than six months had to accept money from the PAC. Again, it is impossible to calculate what proportion of the unemployed were eligible for UB and what proportion received PAC money, but in view of the heavy depression in the town it is likely that a large proportion received the lower PAC scale.

Family size and composition made a great difference to how well it was possible to manage on relief. Even though relief did give dependants allowances, they were small, and large families were undoubtedly the poorest. In this respect they followed the normal pattern of working class families, except that the poorest of all were those families where several adults were all out of work but living in one family. In this case a family which would normally have been at its most prosperous stage, with father and children all contributing to the family income, were encountering the greatest hardship of all the unemployed. Often in these cases the children left home.

Although unemployment relief was means tested, some out of work families did manage to add to their income in different ways. It was common practice to take in lodgers, something which increased in the twenties when the local housing shortage intensified.[6] Some help to the family budget could be given from food grown on allotments – Stockton's Medical Officer of Health believed that this food made a very significant addition to the diet of unemployed families. Oral testimony tells of people killing pigeons and rabbits from the nearby countryside for food, or stealing vegetables from local farmers. Interviewees also described quite a few cases of individual entrepreneurial attempts:

He (father) used to have football tickets printed, and he used to sell maybe twenty or thirty, and probably make himself a couple of shillings at the end of the week, with a lot of work taking them round and paying out . . . the man next door to us, he'd hardly any schooling, but he learned to play the clarinet which he bought in a secondhand shop for a couple of coppers and he used to go round various pubs and play it.[7]

A more significant contribution to the family income sometimes came from the mother doing some kind of part-time work; taking in washing or sewing, selling home-made food, doing domestic cleaning or other traditionally female jobs. According to Lady Bell, in her study of Edwardian Middlesbrough, this was common even when there was plenty of employment, and the oral evidence of this study suggests that in times of unemployment the mother's job could becor : very important.[8] One interviewee described her mother thus: 'She was just an ordinary housewife, bringing up a large family, and she just had to take whatever was going to earn a little money.'[9]

Young teenage children, who were able to get low-paid casual work, could also help to boost the family income in the same way, and sometimes even very young children might help by, ıor example, collecting firewood to sell.

All these factors in determining family income also affected the employed. Again, family size and composition were two of the most important, especially as wages were not adjusted according to family size. The family of the employed man followed the traditional working-class pattern of stages of poverty and relative affluence: a young childless couple would be fairly well off, but a family with a number of young children would be poor, once the children started to earn (assuming that they did) the family became relatively affluent, but the parents would become poor once they were too old to earn, if their children left home.[10] Like the unemployed, they might look for supplements to their income. More important than any other variable, though, could be short-time working. If a man who nominally earned £2 a week lost a day's earnings he would lose 6s 6d or 16·5 per cent of a week's earnings. The same man would only earn £1 7s if he worked a three-day week. Unfortunately it is very difficult to make a precise estimate of how great an effect short-time working had on the earnings of the Teesside unemployed, but the extent of short-time working in the iron and steel industries and engineering certainly did have an effect on earnings.[11] Piece-workers were most vulnerable to its effects. One of the people interviewed, a retired businessman with an excellent memory for figures, told me about a joiner he knew who kept a record of his take-home pay each week during the thirties, and at the end of each year calculated his average weekly wage.

He found that his most prosperous years in that decade had been 1938 and 1939, when he had earned an average weekly wage of £2 0s 8d and £2 0s 4d respectively.[12] The rates for northeastern joiners given in the *Ministry of Labour Gazette* indicate that a man working a full week as a joiner would earn over £3 per week. No other interviewee was able to give as precise an example as this, but others agreed that in many cases during the thirties a man would earn little more when he was working than he could get in relief, which confirms this impression.

Even without short-time working, the information available about wages on Teesside suggests that in this area, as in other depressed parts of Britain, standard wages were lower than the national average.[13] In the thirties the average wage of the British workman was about £3 per week, but that of the Teesside man about a pound less.[14] All those interviewees who ventured an opinion about the average wage on Teesside in the thirties (few had an accurate memory of the twenties) suggested that it was about £2 or less, and that £3 per week was definitely a good wage.

This is backed up by such information about wages in the region as is available in the *Ministry of Labour Gazette*. This publication listed North-Eastern rates for iron and steel workers, dock workers and furniture makers. The latter two were relatively small employers in the region, although even so the local rates were lower than the national average.[15] As an example of an iron and steel workers' wage, Table 14 gives the rates for a full week for a northeastern blastfurnaceman. A blastfurnaceman was not a skilled worker, but would be earning more than a labourer; he was earning in the middle range of wages for iron and steel men.

Table 14 *Wages of a northeastern blastfurnaceman: rate for full week, 1926–38*

Year	Rate of pay per full week	Wage per week
1926	6s per shift + 12%	£2 0s 0d
1928	6s per shift + 10%	£1 19s 5d
1928	6s per shift + 9%	£1 18s 6d
1934	6s per shift + 6·5%	£1 18s 0d
1936	6s per shift + 11·5%	£2 0s 0d
1936	6s per shift + 12·0%	£2 0s 0d
1937	6s per shift + 13.5%	£2 1s 0d
1937	6s per shift + 18·25%	£2 2s 0d
1937	6s per shift + 35%	£2 8s 0d
1937	6s per shift + 41·75%	£2 11s 0d
1938	6s per shift + 46·75%	£2 13s 0d
1938	6s per shift + 49·5%	£2 14s 0d
1938	6s per shift + 51·75%	£2 14s 6d
1938	6s per shift + 49·75%	£2 14s 0d
1938	6s per shift + 47·75%	£2 13s 0d

Source: Compiled from *Ministry of Labour Gazette* 1926–1938.

How these wages compared with rates of unemployment relief is shown in Table 15.

In the case of the family with two children, the one with a working father had a significant advantage over the one with an unemployed parent, provided that he was able to work a full week. This gap was especially large during the twenties and late thirties, when an employed man could get about 10s more, or a third again, than the unemployed man, but it narrowed during the thirties depression. The family with five children would have a much smaller difference of income, and for the years of the thirties the difference between Unemployment Benefit money and being in work was only a shilling or two. A family of six children would be

Table 15 *Weekly income of a family of four, employed and unemployed, 1920–38*

	1920	1926	1930	1936	1938
Family of blastfurnaceman in full employment	£3	£2 0s 5d	£1 18s 6d	£2	£2 14s
Out of work donation	£2 1s				
Family in receipt of unemployment benefit	15s	£1 7s	£1 10s	£1 12s	£1 12s
Family in receipt of relief from Parish or PAC (Middlesbrough)	30s	£1 7s	£1 7s	£1 10s	£1 12s

Weekly income of a family of seven, employed and unemployed

	1920	1926	1930	1936	1938
Family of blastfurnaceman in full employment	£3	£2 0s 5d	£1 18s 6d	£2	£2 14s
Out of work donation	£2 10s				
Family in receipt of unemployment benefit	15s	£1 13s	£1 16s	£1 16s	£2 9s
Family in receipt of relief from Parish or PAC	£2 5s	£1 13s	£1 13s	£1 16s	£2 1s

Sources: The *Labour Gazette*; *Minutes of Middlesbrough Board of Guardians*; *Minutes of Middlesbrough PAC Committee.*

no better off with an employed father in those years. Short-time working could drastically alter this picture. In the thirties depression, when there was a small gap between employed and unemployed families, the loss of one day's earnings would bring the income of the employed family of four to within a few shillings of the unemployed family, whereas the employed family of seven would then have less than their unemployed counterparts. It must be remembered that these figures are based on the rates for a man earning in the medium range of Teesside incomes. The financial advantages of having a job to a labourer with a family could be negligible during the thirties, even if he worked a full week. This bears a strong similarity with the findings of the Pilgrim Trust: 'We give details which suggest that for a semi-skilled worker in one district of Wales, for which a special analysis was carried out, the difference between Unemployment Assistance and possible wage is probably negligible if a man has three or more children.'[16]

The only local contemporary survey of incomes was done by
McGonigle and Kirby in 1936, which came up with significantly
different results from the ones of this study.[17] They found that in a
Stockton council estate 369 families with an unemployed father
had an average weekly income of 29s 2d (adjusted according to
family size) while 408 families with employed fathers had an
average weekly income of 51s 6d per week: over £1 per week more.

This is partly accountable for by the fact that in 1936 wages
were beginning to rise after a few very depressed years, but also
because McGonigle's survey was of families living in a particular
area; it was not a representative sample of incomes. Those people
who chose to move to a council estate (where rents were
comparatively high) were probably those of the employed who
earned a higher than average income. Others, and these will have
included all the unemployed who were there, went because of
official encouragement, after the 'slum clearance' schemes of the
thirties.

The evidence of this study suggests that the financial experience
of the Teesside unemployed was quite different from that of their
employed counterparts in the 1920s and 1930s. During the
twenties, especially in the first slump of the twenties, the unemployed were at a considerable financial disadvantage as against the
employed. This changed in the thirties. In this decade the
experience of the unemployed family and the employed were very
similar in as much as they had similar incomes. This is in
accordance with contemporary studies of incomes in the depressed
areas. This probably distinguishes the experience of the Teesside
unemployed, and those of other depressed areas, from those in
relatively prosperous parts of Britain. For example, Herbert Tout,
in his study of Bristol, found unemployment to be a major cause
of poverty.[18] In the thirties, the unemployed of Teesside were not
isolated by their financial position. This is borne out by oral
evidence. Several interviewees said that a man got little more
money by working, although they usually felt that it was
preferable to unemployment:

My father went back to sea, because he was so, you know, depressed. He
didn't get much more money going to sea, but he went . . . When they
went to sea it was £8 5s a month (about £2 a week) and they had to keep
their family out of that and they had to take, oh, their own straw bed and
things like that.[19]

In contrast, the unemployed of the twenties were at a strong disadvantage. This will be considered further in the next section.

The standard of living – quantative assessment

A knowledge of the level of incomes provides a very limited insight into the financial position of the unemployed, unless it is linked to a cost of living index. To achieve this a local budget has been constructed, and it has been costed according to Teesside prices.

The budget constructed for this study is a list only of food items in a week's expenditure, and the cost of living index has been based on this. This is because although there is sufficient local information to cost food items over the whole period, this is not the case with rent, household goods, heating and clothing. Information about expenditure on these items, though, is available in the cost of living survey done in 1936 by McGonigle and Kirby. This was a study of 141 Stockton families, constructed in great detail and with extreme care, and one of the authors had a good deal of local knowledge with which to verify the findings. The budget done by McGonigle and Kirby was not one of unemployed as such although the survey included both these categories; the findings are grouped according to income levels. Groups I and II represent the typical budgets of the unemployed, because the income of Group III was above maximum relief. In one item only is there likely to be an unrepresentative assessment of cost: because the study deals with people living in council houses the rents quoted are likely to be unrepresentatively high. In McGonigle's study 7s is quoted as being the average rent of the poorest families, whereas oral evidence suggests that during the thirties rent of a house could be as little as 3s and the norm being between 4–7s for a two bedroomed house.

The construction of the food budget was based almost entirely on oral evidence. This exercise was making greater demands on the oral evidence collected than in almost any other part of the study, because a greater degree of precision of memory was expected of informants than in most other topics discussed. However most people appear to have eaten a limited diet, concentrating on a few cheap foods, with family meals following a similar pattern week after week; and so it was easy for people to state what they used to eat. Some informants had had the job, as children, of doing the shopping, and could list those items which were unfailingly bought

each week. In some cases interviewees could remember the exact
quantities bought each week, for example many families seem to
have bought a standard amount of flour and yeast regularly. Other
foods were bought according to price; such as vegetables in
standard twopenny bags. Others, such as meat and fish were more
variable, but an average amount has been quoted in the specimen
budget.

The foods which seem to have been most universal amongst the
people interviewed were home baked bread, suet puddings, stew
and dumplings (made from cheap cuts of meat, or a sheep's head,
and vegetables) and vegetable dishes such as pan haggarty; a
mixture of potatoes, onions and cheese. Most people agreed that
unemployed people ate margarine not butter, and condensed milk
was more frequently used than fresh. Less frequently mentioned,
but still recurrently so, were cheap fish; herrings or kippers, bacon,
cooked pies, mushy peas, fish and chips, lentil soup, rabbit pie and
faggots. Some people insisted that they never ate ready cooked
food, but clearly many families did rely on fish and chips or pies
and peas as an occasional treat, and it seems that a number of
people who did not themselves figure amongst the interviewees
lived almost entirely on ready cooked food and bread and dripping.
From this evidence it was possible to construct a specimen budget,
which was then verified with certain of the informants who had
clear and detailed memories, who could confirm that the budget for
this study was one that their family might well have eaten and who
could suggest what were appropriate quantities for a family of five,
comprising two adults and three children.

The major disadvantage of the specimen budget is that it is not
representative of the whole working class community of Teesside.
Most of the people interviewed came from the 'respectable' part of
the community, who always tried to provide the most economical
food that their money and ingenuity allowed. It seems that a
substantial minority of people ate more expensive, ready cooked
foods, and presumably less of them. It omits altogether alcohol, and
while some parents were either teetotallers, or denied themselves in
times of financial stringency, many others drank in varying
amounts from moderate to excessive, but unfortunately it is
extremely difficult to judge what an average consumption of
alcohol might be. The budget is also based on the assumption that
other expenditure would be similar to that shown in Table 16, that

Table 16 *Average weekly budget of 121 Stockton families, 1936 (adjusted according to family size)*

Group I	(46 families)	with a net income of between	25s–35s
Group II	(40 families)	with a net income of between	35s–45s
Group III	(31 families)	with a net income of between	45s–55s
Group IV	(17 families)	with a net income of between	55s–65s
Group V	(7 families)	with a net income of between	70s–80s

Mean rent paid[a]

	s d	% net income
Group I	7 10½	25·27
Group II	9 2½	23
Group III	10 0	20
Group IV	11 9¼	19·98
Group V	15 3¼	20·20
	10 10	21·73

Fuel and light

	s d	% net income
Group I	3 5½	11
Group II	3 11½	10
Group III	4 11½	10
Group IV	5 7¼	9·5
Group V	6 2	8
	4 9¾	9·70

Insurances and medical attention

Group I	4d per head
Group II	4½d per head
Group III	4¾d per head
Group IV	7d per head
Group V	6d per head
	6¾d per head

Note: [a] This was on a local authority housing estate.

Table 16 *continued.*
Average weekly budget of 121 Stockton families (adjusted according to family size) in 1936

Cost of household utensils and cleaning materials

Group I	10*d*
Group II	1*s* 7¾*d*
Group III	1*s* 8¾*d*
Group IV	2*s* 6*d*
Group V	2*s* 10*d*

Cost of clothing and boots

Group I	2*s* 8¼*d*	7*d* per head
Group II	3*s* 9¼*d*	8½*d* per head
Group III	5*s* 5¼*d*	10½*d* per head
Group IV	6*s* 10*d*	1*s* 5*d* per head
Group V	9*s* 8¼*d*	1*s* 9½*d* per head
		1*s* 1*d* per head

Hire purchase

Group I	2½*d*
Group II	5¼*d*
Group III	1*s* 6¼*d*
Group IV	3*s*
Group V	3*s* 5*d*

Amount not spent on food		*Amount left*	
	£ s d		£ s d
Group I	19 0¾		13 5
Group II	1 3 7¼		16 10
Group III	1 6 7½		1 1 9
Group IV	1 5 9½		1 5 2
Group V	1 4 1¼		1 12 7

Source: G.C.M. McGonigle & J. Kirby, *Poverty and Public Health,* London, 1937.

is to say nothing was spent on smoking or gambling. Both these activities were cheap, but they were both widespread, and oral evidence suggests that although both may only have cost the average person a few pence per week, they were a regular expense for very many people. The budget would also be only typical of a week when no domestic difficulties necessitated the spending of money on anything other than food, rent, basic and cheap necessities and insurance money. The need to replace any large household item, or to care for any sick member of the family, or any other thing incurring extra expense would probably mean that less was spent on food. The budget errs then on the side of generosity, and whilst it is fairly representative of a certain type of people it is not in any way 'average' and shows a 'good' and not a 'bad' week.

After constructing the budget it is necessary to cost it. Prices were found from three main sources. The first of these was again oral testimony, which is useful for certain items, when the food and its price stay together in a person's mind − a 'twopennyworth of potstuff' being one of the most common examples. Other information came from advertisements in local newspapers. It was common for local newspapers to carry advertisements from shops such as the Co-op or Hintons, to give local prices. This was particularly common during the early twenties when prices began to fall steadily, and shop managers were keen to advertise the fact. A third invaluable source of information was the records of a local grocer, Pybus Brothers, which provided the prices for a large range of goods in the mid and late thirties. Unfortunately it is not possible to say how Pybus Brothers' prices compared with other shops in the district, although their order books show that they had a number of fairly well off middle-class customers, and so it is probable that they were not the cheapest of shops.[20]

The specimen budget shown in Table 17 shows that the cost of food for a family of five with an unemployed breadwinner was 13s 7d. This had to be provided from 32s maximum unemployment benefit, or (as was the case for most of the Teesside unemployed) 29s Public Assistance. This is a little more than a third of their income, and according to McGonigle's estimate of other necessary expenses was a realistic proportion of income to spend on food. The same budget was costed for every other year of the inter-war period, except 1928 for which information on prices is scarce,

Table 17 *Standard budget to feed a Teesside family of five, 1930*

	s	d
Meat	2	0
Vegetables		10
Margarine		6
Eggs		6
Flour	4	4
Yeast		3
Baking Powder		2
Sugar		$7\frac{1}{2}$
Tea		$8\frac{1}{2}$
Milk (condensed)		7
Jam		$7\frac{1}{2}$
Dripping		6
Fish		8
Cocoa		$6\frac{1}{2}$
Currants		6
Suet		2
Biscuits (broken)		6
Total	13	7

and this is shown in Table 18 and 19, as a table of prices and a cost of living index.

The most important thing shown by the cost of living index is the high cost of living in the 1920s, and its sharp fall in the 1930s. The fact that the cost of living fell in England in the 1930s has been observed before, but rarely related to the position of the unemployed who lived in very straightened circumstances in the early 1920s. The standard budget of 1930 would have cost nearly 22s per week in 1920. This was about three quarters of the income of a family of five on maximum relief; a quite urnealistic amount to spend on food especially as rents in the twenties were likely to have been higher than those quoted for the thirties, because overcrowding pushed up prices.[21] A family with out of work donation would have fared better, but even so would have had to spend about half of its income on food. In contrast, the family of an employed man receiving £3 per week could reasonably afford to pay 22s for food. The cost of living dropped steadily during the twenties, and reached its lowest in the years 1931–2, after which it rose gradually, although it did not reach the levels of the twenties again.

The evidence of the cost of living index suggests that during the nineteen twenties a family with an unemployed breadwinner would have been suffering severe hardship. This is an important reminder of their position, because the great contemporary concern about the plight of the unemployed of the thirties leaves the twenties as the forgotten decade of the inter-war years. The position of the unemployed of the twenties was probably similar to that of those out of work in Edwardian and late nineteenth century Britain; before depressed wages and prices levelled off the most marked financial differences between the employed and the unemployed, and before much development of social services, or much public awareness of their position.[22]

The fact that the standard of living of the unemployed was lower in the 1920s is borne out by oral evidence. Not many of those interviewed had a clear memory of the twenties, but those who did affirmed that there had been more poverty then. Several people noted that there had been more barefoot children in the twenties; this being a standard guide as to the extent of hardship, and one which almost certainly indicated that other privations were also more common. One Stockton man, who remembered his father's unemployment in the twenties and the early thirties, as well as his own in the early thirties, was in a particularly good position to make this comparison:

Well, we normally think of the thirties as being the great depression days. Now my memory, possibly because I was younger at the time was of the engineers' lockout of 1922 . . . at the end of the period I have the recollection of possibly the finest feed of my life, and I can still taste it now, pink salmon.

The interviewee does suggest that his extreme youth might have made him more aware of his family's problems, but most people suggested that in their early childhood they tended to take difficulties for granted, the problems of depression falling more heavily on adults. If a child could observe the difference, it was likely to be quite marked.

The standard of living – qualitative assessment

The purpose of this section is to assess the nutritional value of the standard budget previously shown, so as to measure the standard of living not only in strict quantitative terms but also in qualitative

Table 18 *Budget for an unemployed family of five per week, 1920–38*

Cost	1920		1922		1924		1926		1928		1930		1932		1934		1936		1938	
Year	s	d	s	d	s	d	s	d	s	d	s	d	s	d	s	d	s	d	s	d
Meat	3	0	3	0	2	6	2	6			2	0	2	0	2	0	2	1	2	4
Vegetables	1	0	1	0	1	0	1	0				10		10		10		10		11
Margarine	2	0		9		9		8				6		6		6		6		6
Eggs		6		6		6		6				6		6		8	1	0	1	0
Flour	4	10	4	10	4	6	4	6			4	4	4	1	4	1	4	8	4	9
Yeast		6		6		4		4				3		3		3		3		3
Baking pwdr		2		2		2		2				2		2		2		2		2
Sugar	3	4		6	1	6	1	1			7½		7		7		7		7	
Tea	1	0	1	0	1	0	1	0			8½		8½		11		11		1	0
Milk		10		9½		9½		7½				7		7		7		8		8
Jam		9		9		6		6				4		4		4		4		4
Dripping		6		6		6		6				4		4		5		5		5
Lentils		8		8		8		8				5		5		8		8		8
Fish		6		6		6		6				8		8		4		4		4
Cocoa		6½		6½		6½		6½				4		4		4		4		4
Dried fruit		6		5		3		3				4		4		4		3		3
Suet		6		6		6		6				4		4		4		4		4
Biscuits		4		4		3		3				2		2		2		2		3
Total	**27**	**11½**	**19**	**3**	**18**	**4**	**16**	**8½**			**13**	**5**	**13**	**3**	**13**	**7½**	**14**	**4**	**14**	**7½**

Source: Compiled from information in: local newspapers, Pabus Brothers Records, and oral evidence.

Table 19 *Price index, 1920–38 (in old pence)*

Year	1920	1922	1924	1926	1928	1930	1932	1934	1936	1938
Meat	150	150	125	125		100	100	100	116	116
Vegetables	120	120	120	120		100	100	100	100	110
Margarine	200	150	150	153		100	100	100	100	100
Eggs	400	300	200	200		100	100	135	200	200
Flour	111	111	103	103		100	95	95	107	110
Yeast	200	200	133	133		100	100	100	100	100
Baking pwdr	100	100	100	100		100	100	100	100	100
Sugar	533	240	240	173		100	93	93	100	120
Tea	141	141	141	141		100	100	129	129	141
Milk	143	136	107	107		100	100	100	100	141
Jam	120	120	120	100		100	100	100	100	100
Dripping	150	150	150	150		100	100	100	100	100
Lentils	120	120	120	120		100	100	100	100	100
Fish	100	100	100	100		100	100	100	100	100
Cocoa	162	162	162	162		100	100	100	100	100
Dried fruit	150	125	75	75		100	100	100	87	87
Suet	150	150	150	150		100	100	100	100	100
Biscuits	200	200	150	150		100	100	100	100	150
Total	180	154	136	130		100	99	103	108	115

Source: Compiled from information in: local newspapers, Pybus Brothers Records, and oral evidence.

terms: to show not only how much food Teesside people could afford but also how nutritious it was. This is a task which is often left undone by historians who discuss the standard of living question, but is a very important aspect of the subject. Those historians of the inter-war years who have considered the question of nutritional standards amongst the unemployed refer only to light shed on the question by the contemporary debate on nutrition, which was conducted at a time when nutritional science was very new, and some theories or standards held during the inter-war years are no longer accepted by modern nutritionists. In this section the standard budget for Teesside is subjected to a nutritional analysis in accordance with present-day standards.

In the contemporary debate on standards of nutrition the question of whether it was possible to be adequately fed on unemployment relief was one which exercised the minds of the social investigators. Some observers believed that the relief scales were adequate, and others felt that any poor nutrition amongst the unemployed was more likely to be the result of inadequate education than inadequate food.[23] George Orwell quoted a newspaper article of the 1930s which claimed that by eating a diet chiefly composed of vegetables and wholemeal bread, with cheese as the main source of first class protein, it was possible to give an adult a balanced diet for 3s 11d per week.[24] These kind of claims came under attack from the extensive studies of two eminent men: B. S. Rowntree and J. B. Orr.[25] Boyd Orr, in his nationwide survey of nutrition found that although some groups of people ate a diet which was less than excellent, not because of insufficient money but through ignorance or personal choice, the poor (who included the unemployed) suffered insufficiencies of diet which were wholly due to lack of means. B. S. Rowntree in his second study of York reached similar conclusions. He found that seventy-two per cent of all the unemployed living in York were living below the minimum standard of nutrition set by the BMA in 1933, and attributed this almost entirely to their poverty. He wrote 'many working class families in York are not getting enough to eat, and this is due not to lack of knowledge but lack of means'. He found that young children and nursing mothers were especially at risk of malnutrition. Although he did no formal study along the lines of Boyd Orr or Rowntree, McGonigle, the Medical Officer of Health for Stockton, who had a special interest in nutrition, was convinced that malnutrition caused by poverty and not mis-management was the cause of a great deal of ill-health amongst the unemployed of Stockton and their families.[26]

As many factors determined the level of incomes of the unemployed, so did they influence the nutritional standards of out of work people. Family size was certainly one of the most important of these; as larger families were poorer they were almost certainly worse fed. Personal factors were also important, and any failure on the part of parents to budget stringently and deny themselves luxuries would result in poor nutrition for the family. The competence of the mother as a manager and housekeeper was also of paramount importance, as contemporary studies testify.[27] These things were borne out by interviewees. As one might expect those people from large families remember much more in the way of hardship than those from small ones; indeed only children of an unemployed father could remember no problems in getting enough food. Competence of the housewife was also commented on as being a matter of great importance. One woman, a teenager in the 1930s, whose mother had come from a middle class family but had married a steelworker said, 'I've seen us just eat turnip, mashed turnip, with a bit of bread, and you put it on your bread . . . if you got a Yorkshire pudding that was your dinner.'[28] Her mother was not trained by long experience to use the cheapest of foods and fed the family on ready cooked foods when money was available. Although a rather exceptional case, there were other families who fared the same for different reasons.

In contrast to this, many interviewees do not remember the thirties as a time when they felt seriously short of food. Many people said that they 'never went hungry', and suggested that their families' diet had, in fact, been a good one because they ate few luxury foods, such as sweets. Many praised the standard of food provided by their mother or wife, which may in part be attributed to family loyalty, but the foods cited do seem to bear this out. Although many contemporary studies of working class diet suggest that vegetables were rarely bought, on Teesside they were valued as a cheap and filling food. Stew, made from vegetables and cheap meat, usually a sheep's head, was the most commonly mentioned food, suet was a common 'filler' and many people made good use of cheap fish, and pulses. Most bread was home-made. Cheapness and variety in diet was achieved by constant watchfulness on the part of the housewife. One man said of the housewives of Middlesbrough in the thirties 'people were quite expert in improvising with regard to food'.[29] Another, an insurance agent in poor parts of Middlesbrough, said, 'they seemed to manage all right. They would have to go out shopping a lot keener than before, but they were always keen shoppers before then.'[30] Indeed the types of foods mentioned by interviewees as being commonplace amongst the respectable Teesside unemployed are reminiscent of those discovered by Elizabeth Roberts, in her study of living standards in Barrow and Lancaster in Edwardian England, from which she concluded that standards of nutrition in working class diets were high.[31] In the light of this it is important to look at a nutritional analysis of the standard 1930 budget given previously.

The nutritional analysis shown in Table 20 is based on the standard budget of this study. The total weekly budget of one adult has been calculated in terms of its calorific and food value, according to the standards presently accepted by the British Ministry of Health, and then divided by seven to give the amount consumed daily. This is then compared with the daily recommended intake for an adult (see Table 21). These findings were examined by the dieticians of North Tees General Hospital, Cleveland, who provided the author with considerable help in this project. The Teesside budget is sufficient in calories for most categories of adult, and sufficient in iron (because of the amount of offal consumed) but slightly deficient in every other category. The dieticians of North Tees hospital advised that this diet, although nominally deficient, was not seriously lacking in any category of food. Few people, they suggested, are likely to eat a diet which fulfils all ideal requirements. However, certain categories of people would not be adequately fed by this diet: nursing and pregnant mothers would be undernourished, as would very active men or teenage boys, who would suffer a deficiency of calories. In view of the fact that these categories include a large number of people, and especially that the health of pregnant and nursing mothers is very important for the well-being of their children, these findings show that a significant number of these Teesside people who lived on the standard budget of an unemployed family were likely to have been underfed.

These findings, though, do bear out the evidence of oral testimony, that a good housewife, aided by the low cost of living in

Table 20 *Nutritional analysis of Teesside budget of the 1930s*

Food	Total weight(s)	Calories	Protein (g)	Thiamin (mg)	Riboflavin (mg)	Nicotinic acid (mg)	Ascorbic acid (mg)	Vitamin D (mg)	Calcium (mg)	Iron (mg)
Sheep's head	50	25	2·32	0·05	0·12	1·05	8·5	Tr	5·5	0·7
Liver	100	79	24·8	0·18	2·14	11·2	15	1·13	11	17·8
Heart	50	118	8·5	0·24	0·45	3·45	3·5	0	12·5	2·45
Most meat	100	232	16·8	0·04	0·3	5·2	0	Tr	12	2·8
Fish (Herring)	100	234	23·1	Tr	0·88	4·0	0	25	39	1·0
Potatoes	700	560	9·8	0·77	0·28	8·4	80	0	56	35
Lentils	100	99	7·6	0·11	0·04	0·4	Tr	0	13	24
Sugar	250	985	Tr	0	Tr	0	Tr	0	130	0·36
Milk (condensed)	100	322	8·3	0·08	0·48	0·22	0	0	132·5	0·05
Fats (marg. or dripping)	350	4,586·75	Tr	Tr	Tr	Tr	0	Tr	7	Tr
Dried fruit	50	121·5	0·85	0·05	0·15	0·6	1·5	0	47·3	0·8
Suet	200	1,790	0·009	Tr	Tr	0·006	0·015	Tr	6	0·4
Eggs	100	147	12·3	0·09	0·07	0·07	0	1·75	52	2
Turnip	100	14	0·7	0·03	0·03	0·04	17	0	55	0·4
Swede	100	18	0·04	0·04	0·04	0·08	17	0	42	0·3
Carrot	100	23	0·9	0·06	0·06	0·8	6	0	48	0·6
Cabbage	100	7	1·1	0·06	0·06	0·3	40	0	30	0·5
Flour	2500	8,750	245	2·5	10·5	17·5	0	0	375*	37·5*
Total divided by 7		2,587	51·7	0·62	2·24	7·6	26·9	3·98	153	18

Source: Standards from McCanse and Widowson, 'The Composition of Foods', HMSO, 1978.

Table 21 *Recommended daily amounts of food energy and some nutrients for population groups in the UK*

Age range[a] years	Occupational category	Energy[b] (MJ)	Energy[b] (Kcal)	Protein[c] (g)	Thiamin (mg)	Riboflavin (mg)
Boys						
under 1					0·3	0·4
1		5·0	1200	30	0·5	0·6
2		5·75	1400	35	0·6	0·7
3–4		6·5	1560	39	0·6	0·8
5–6		7·25	1740	43	0·7	0·9
7–8		8·25	1980	49	0·8	1·0
9–11		9·5	2280	57	0·9	1·2
12–14		11·0	2640	66	1·1	1·4
15–17		12·0	2880	72	1·2	1·7
Girls						
under 1					0·3	0·4
1		4·5	1100	27	0·4	0·6
2		5·5	1300	32	0·5	0·7
3–4		6·25	1500	37	0·6	0·8
5–6		7·0	1680	42	0·7	0·9
7–8		8·0	1900	47	0·8	1·0
9–11		8·5	2050	51	0·8	1·2
12–14		9·0	2150	53	0·9	1·4
15–17		9·0	2150	53	0·9	1·7
Men						
18–34	Sedentary	10·5	2510	63	1·0	1·6
	Moderately active	12·0	2900	72	1·2	1·6
	Very active	14·0	3350	84	1·3	1·6
35–64	Sedentary	10·0	2400	60	1·0	1·6
	Moderately active	11·5	2750	69	1·1	1·6
	Very active	14·0	3350	84	1·3	1·6
65–74 }	Assuming a	10·0	2400	60	1·0	1·6
75+ }	sedentary life	9·0	2150	54	0·9	1·6
Women						
18–54	Most occupations	9·0	2150	54	0·9	1·3
	very active	10·5	2500	62	1·0	1·3
55–74 }	Assuming a	8·0	1900	47	0·8	1·3
75+ }	sedentary life	7·0	1680	42	0·7	1·3
Pregnancy		10·0	2400	60	1·0	1·6
Lactation		11·5	2750	69	1·1	1·8

Notes:

(a) Since the recommendations are average amounts, the figures for each age range represent the amounts recommended at the middle of the range. Within each age range, younger children will need less, and older children more, than the amount recommended.

(b) Megajoules (10^4 joules). Calculated from the relation 1 kilocalorie = 4·184 kilojoules, that is to say, 1 megajoule = 240 kilocalories.

(c) Recommended amounts have been calculated as 10% of the recommendations for energy.

(d) 1 nicotinic acid equivalent = 1 mg available nicotinic acid or 60 mg tryptophan.

(e) No information is available about requirements of children for folate. Graded amounts are recommended between the figure shown for infants under 1 year, which is based upon the average folate content of mature human milk, and the 300 µg daily which is suggested for adults.

Nicotinic acid equivalent (mg)[d]	Total folate[e] (μg)	Ascorbic acid (mg)	Vitamin A retinol equivalents (μg[f])	Vitamin D[g] cholecalciferol (μg)	Calcium (mg)	Iron (mg)
5	50	20	450	7·5	600	6
7	100	20	300	10	600	7
8	100	20	300	10	600	7
9	100	20	300	10	600	8
10	200	20	300	(g)	600	10
11	200	20	400	(g)	600	10
14	200	25	575	(g)	700	12
16	300	25	725	(g)	700	12
19	300	30	750	(g)	600	12
5	50	20	450	7·5	600	6
7	100	20	300	10	600	7
8	100	20	300	10	600	7
9	100	20	300	10	600	8
10	200	20	300	(g)	600	10
11	200	20	400	(g)	600	10
14	300	25	575	(g)	700	12[i]
16	300	25	725	(g)	700	12[i]
19	300	30	750	(g)	600	12[i]
18	300	30	750	(g)	500	10
18	300	30	750	(g)	500	10
18	300	30	750	(g)	500	10
18	300	30	750	(g)	500	10
18	300	30	750	(g)	500	10
18	300	30	750	(g)	500	10
18	300	30	750	(g)	500	10
18	300	30	750	(g)	500	10
15	300	30	750	(g)	500	12[i]
15	300	30	750	(g)	500	12[i]
15	300	30	750	(g)	500	10
15	300	30	750	(g)	500	10
18	500	60	750	(g)	1200[h]	13
21	400	60	1200	10	1200	15

(f) 1 retinol equivalent = 1 μg retinol or 6 μgβ carotene or 12 μg other biologically active carotenoids.

(g) No dietary sources may be necessary for children and adults who are sufficiently exposed to sunlight, but during the winter children and adolescents should receive 10 μg (400 i.u.) daily by supplementation. Adults with inadequate exposure to sunlight, for example those who are housebound, may also need a supplement of 10 μg daily.

(h) For the third trimester only.

(i) This intake may not be sufficient for 10% of girls and women with large menstrual losses.

Source: A. W. Goode, J. P. Howard and S. Woods, Clinical Nutrition and Dietetics for Nurses, Hodder & Stoughton, 1985, pp. 177–8.

the early thirties could manage to feed an average sized family an adequate diet: providing that all conditions previously discussed were favourable. This is a slightly more optimistic picture than those presented by Rowntree and Boyd Orr, and McGonigle. This is partly because their standards were higher than those issued by the British Government today; the early nutritionists slightly exaggerated the need for certain foods, especially protein, as Table 22 shows.

Table 22 *Recommended daily amounts of energy and nutrients for a moderately active adult male in the 1930s and 1980s*

	BMA, 1933	League of Nations minimum standards, 1936	Ministry of Health, 1985
Calories	3,400	3,400	2,750
Protein (g)	100·0	100·0	69·0
Calcium (g)	not quoted	0·5	0·5
Phosphorus (g)	not quoted	1·0	–
Iron (mg)	not quoted	10·0	10·0

Sources: B. S. Rowntree, *Poverty and Progress*, 1941, pp. 174; 183; DHSS Report No. 19.

Another probable explanation for the more optimistic picture presented by the study is the fact that the low cost of living on Teesside made it easier for its inhabitants to buy a nutritious diet than those of Rowntree's study in York. These two facts, though, do not altogether dispense with the concerns of the contemporary social investigators. According to the nutritional analysis, pregnant women and nursing mothers were likely to be underfed (probably with adverse effects on their children) as were members of large families if they were living at home. The families of the long term unemployed were also likely to be at risk. After a long period of unemployment all savings would be used up, and occasional unexpected demands on the budget would be met from the budget for food. In this case individual family fortunes would be of great importance.

Whereas it was possible for the unemployed of the thirties to manage, for most of the time, to provide a reasonably good diet for all but special categories of people, this was clearly not the case in the twenties. The cost of living index shows that the unemployed of the twenties must have been able to buy much less food than those of the thirties, and therefore they will have been less well nourished. Because it is not possible to do a similar nutritional analysis for the twenties budget, it is not easy to say how much worse their diet was. It is probable that rather than eating a fundamentally different diet in those years, people simply ate less, with a greater emphasis on bread and less on animal protein. Under this regime it seems likely that only single people, childless couples or couples with only one child could have escaped some kind of undernourishment, which could have become serious if the chief wage earner was out of work for some time. The implications of this will be one of the questions discussed in the next chapter.

Chapter 3

The effects of unemployment on health

The question of whether unemployment has an effect on the health of individuals and communities was the subject of a lively contemporary debate, and is still a contentious issue today. It is an extremely complicated subject, and two basic underlying difficulties cause most of the complications involved. The first is the fact that it is not easy to show an objective standard of good or poor health; health is a relative state and one which is open to individual interpretation. The second is that deciding what contribution unemployment made to standards of health involves assessing the importance of unemployment as against many other factors which will influence health. Environmental conditions, public health services, education, and many other conditions are likely to have a powerful effect, and it is far from easy to isolate any one of these and assess its relative impact.

These two problems can be seen in both the contemporary and present-day debate on the subject. Throughout the inter-war years the officials of the Ministry of Health were adamant that unemployment did not have an adverse affect on health.[1] They pointed out that those areas with high unemployment rates were also ones with a long tradition of poor standards of health, and they claimed that it was this tradition which was responsible for low standards of health in these areas: a theory which must have been at least in part true. As to the possibility that the unemployed were suffering from bad nutrition caused by inadequate relief scales, Ministry advisors believed that any malnutrition amongst the unemployed was more likely to have been caused by ignorance rather than lack of money. This view was challenged by various individuals and pressure groups, who were called by J. Macnicol the 'family poverty lobby'.[2] This lobby believed that unemployment caused poverty which resulted in poor nutrition and ill-health.

experiments to verify this theory. Lady Rhys
nents in the Rhondda valley which suggested a
tion and maternal mortality.[3] Dr Kathleen
that women with slightly malformed pelvises
tion in youth) were most at risk in childbirth.[4]
the arguments of their opponents were difficult
one another because, in Macnicol's words 'the
r child poverty in the inter-war years was clouded
all sides to define accurately just what constituted

es which also threw up the problem of the need for
standard of health centred around different clinical
observations. Dr McGonigle, the Medical Officer of Health for
Stockton during most of the 1930s persistently advertised his view
that unemployment had adverse effects on health, in his Annual
Reports, correspondence to newspapers and in representations to
the Ministry of Health.[6] Even more insistent on this point was Dr
Walker, MOH for Sunderland, who wrote a letter to the *The Times*
in 1934 about standards of health in the town, which initiated
fierce debate in that newspaper's letter page, and even instigated a
government inquiry into health in County Durham.[7]

The present-day debate on the question of unemployment and
health which has attracted considerable press coverage, suffers
from similar problems.[8] The most prominent figure in this debate is
Dr Harvey Brenner, who claims to have found a statistical
association between rises in unemployment and rises in the death
rate. This is apparent on a very large sample (usually a whole
country) and shows a time lag between the rise in unemployment
and fall in standards of health, because of the time taken for the
impact of unemployment to have an effect on health.[9] Unfortunately Brenner's work does not take into account the inter-related
causes of health; he looks only for a simple relationship between
unemployment and health rates, without taking any other factors
into account. This means that even if it is valid on a macro level
(and it would be far more convincing if based on a more
complicated model) it is of little help in trying to understand the
impact of unemployment on the health of three particular
communities, each with their own local conditions and problems.[10]

Apart from the conceptual problems involved in isolating
unemployment as a cause of ill-health, there are some practical

difficulties in dealing with the limitations of the health statistics. The most frequently used are the death rate, infant mortality rate, and maternal mortality rate. Also useful are lists of the incidence of infectious diseases. These provide a basic guide to the standards of health in an area, and are commonly used as such by health officials, but provide only a crude reflection of the complete situation. They conceal a great deal of ill-health, for minor ailments will not be accurately reflected in them. The death rate is only really useful if it is 'corrected' or adjusted according to the age structure of the population. A town with a high proportion of elderly people will normally have a higher death rate than one with a higher proportion of children, even though the former may be exceptionally salubrious. The crude death rate is only really useful to show trends in health in a particular town. In the case of the three towns under study, the population had a higher number of young people than the country as a whole, and so whenever the crude death rate of these towns is compared with that for England and Wales it must be remembered that the adjusted rate for the Teesside towns would be higher than the crude rate. The actual adjusted rate is almost never given in the health reports of the three towns. The infant mortality and maternal mortality rates are more susceptible to environmental conditions, or inadequate health services than the overall death rate, and could thus be regarded as more sensitive indicators, but the reasons for a rise in these rates many not be easy to find.

Health on Teesside during the inter-war years: the background

The inter-war years saw an overall improvement in conditions of health all over England and Wales, and the three towns under study were no exception to this pattern. This is reflected in the improvements in the crude death rate (Table 23).

Table 23   *Crude death rate per 1,000 population, 1919 and 1939*

Year	Middlesbrough	Stockton	Darlington
1919	18·39	16·5	15·7
1939	13·30	12·87	12·5

Source: Reports of Medical Offices of Health in Middlesbrough, Stockton and Darlington

More significantly infant mortality was also much reduced in
each town, (see Tables 24, 25 and 26) and there was a continual fall
in the reported incidence of infectious diseases. It is against this
background that the health of these towns must be studied: the
chief question being whether the effects of unemployment in any
way retarded the general improvement. This question will be

Table 24 *Crude death rate, and infant mortality rate per 1,000 live births
in Middlesbrough, 1919–39*

Year	Death rate (Middlesbrough)	Death rate (England & Wales)	Infant mortality rate (Middlesbrough)	Infant mortality rate (England & Wales)
1919	18·39	14·0	139	89
1920	15·32	12·4	135	80
1921	14·41	12·1	118	83
1922	14·50	12·8	111	77
1923	13·30	11·6	86	69
1924	16·75	12·2	135	75
1925	15·56	12·2	97	75
1926	13·16	11·6	99	70
1927	14·20	12·3	87	70
1928	14·26	11·7	88	65
1929	17·11	13·4	100	74
1930	14·13	11·4	79	60
1931	14·07	12·3	100	66
1932	12·96	12·0	84	65
1933	13·35	12·3	91	65
1934	13·17	11·8	79	59
1935	13·22	11·7	86	57
1936	12·23	12·1	73	59
1937	13·80	12·4	91	58
1938	12·31	11·6	73	53
1939	13·30	12·1		

Source: Compiled from Middlesbrough MOH reports.

Table 25 *Housebuilding in Middlesbrough, 1921 and 1930*

Year	Estimated population	Inhabited houses
1921	131,070	25,541
1930	133,100	29,800

Source: Compiled from 1921 and 1931 census.

Table 26 *Chief causes of death in Middlesbrough, 1916–39: rate per 1,000 population*

Year	Influenza	Heart disease	Diarr' enteᵣ	Cancer	Bronchitis	Pnuemonia	TB
1916	0·11	1·04	0·99	0·68	1·31	3·16	1·76
1919	1·17	0·94	0·85	0·87	1·43	3·26	1·34
1922	0·19	0·10	0·90	0·84	1·24	2·21	1·21
1925	0·38	1·30	0·29	0·95	1·23	2·44	1·31
1931	0·35	2·33	0·17	1·21	0·58	2·02	1·64
1935	0·32	2·44	0·13	1·42	0·40	1·34	1·07
1939	0·13	2·33	0·16	1·33	0·39	1·11	1·22

Source: Compiled from Middlesbrough MOH reports, 1919–39

considered in a case study of each town's health record, health services and general environmental conditions for the inter-war years.

Middlesbrough
Middlesbrough had a tradition of poor standards of health from the time that the town first grew so precipitately and uncontrollably in the mid-nineteenth century.[11] The inter-war years were the first time when a determined effort was made by the town's authorities to combat this unenviable legacy, something which is surprising given the fact that in 1919 the Medical Officer of Health was making his twenty-first annual report.

Most of the improvements instigated by the local health department were designed to improve the poor environmental conditions which adversely affected health. In the 1920s most of the responsibility for these improvements rested with the sanitary department of the town. This department was obliged by law to watch over cases of notifiable disease in the town, to collect statistics on the incidence of disease, as well as to inspect Borough drainage and sewage, refuse collection and disposal, and make any necessary recommendations. It had to watch over slaughter houses, and the premises of 'offensive trades' as well as dairies, cowsheds and milkshops. The department also inspected ordinary dwelling houses, with reference to the various housing acts, and offices and factories to administer the factory and workshop act and the smoke abatement act. Also, and very importantly, numerous tests were done on samples of food and drink, checking for purity, adulteration and possible infection.

This work was the standard requirement of any sanitary department, something which had developed over the years since the nineteenth century environmentalists had discovered the close connection between poor health and poor environmental conditions.[12] In Middlesbrough, though, it was especially badly needed, for many of the conditions deplored by the early environmentalists still applied in this town.

The reports of the sanitary inspector of the town show that his department was kept busy, and often needed to take action to enforce an improvement. In 1920 there was 7,015 notices served on the owners of houses to 'abate nuisance'. In the same year the staff of the sanitary department cleared 5,875 yards of main drains at the back of houses as part of a scheme which continued for several years. There was considerable concern about the purity of the milk supply to the Borough, because infected milk was known to be a common carrier of TB. In 1919 the report of the sanitary inspector expresses concern that the bulk of the milk supply to the Borough came from long distances away, even as far as Scotland. This problem became worse, for while in 1919 there were 17 cowsheds and 133 cows within the Borough, by 1920 the figures had dropped to 9 cowsheds and 80 cows. The sanitary inspector was worried that the fact that cows' milk was not always fresh would encourage people to use dried or condensed milk instead, which could harm small babies.[13] The concern of the sanitary inspectors seems to have found some practical outlet, because in 1924 an optimistic report stated that recent findings showed how easy it was to ensure the production of clean milk, and that great care was being given to the production of clean milk on nearby farms.

The scale of infected meat was also a source of concern to the sanitary department. The report of 1919 said that there was 'great difficulty in tracing any impure meat to its source' and there was 'frequent evidence of contamination' especially with TB. Inspections of a large number of carcases were made each year, and although in the first years of the period these inspections seem to have had little effect, by 1927 the sanitary inspector reported that of 33,498 animals slaughtered, 98·47 per cent were sound, 1,074 were affected by TB, and 0·46 by other diseases.

There is evidence that, as a result of supervision, working

conditions began to improve in some trades. The early reports mention frequent cases of unsatisfactory conditions of work: in 1920 forty-eight workshops and two bakehouses were struck off the official list. In 1924, though, the sanitary inspector's report stated that 'on the whole, workshops, retail bakehouses etc. were found to be in a satisfactory condition. No legal proceedings were instituted.' This state of affairs continued, with only occasional verbal warnings being given.

The main improvements in the environmental conditions of the town were made in the 1920s, and consolidated in the 1930s. In the thirties the health department turned to new ways of improving the health of the town. One of these was an attack on the housing shortage. Since the end of the First World War there had been concern expressed by the Medical Officer of Health about overcrowding, because during the war housebuilding had stopped and an ever-growing population had to live in the same number of houses. Housebuilding did start again in the twenties (see Tables 25).

However these new houses were insufficient to remedy the housing shortage, and were in any case mostly aimed at the owner-occupier.[14] From the beginning of the thirties comments of the Medical Officer of health reflected the national concern about the problem of slum housing. In all the large industrial areas of Britain there were districts where people lived in overcrowded conditions, in back-to-back houses which were often damp, dark, without adequate ventilation, and sometimes without water supply. Middlesbrough's working class housing was not so old as that in most other industrial areas (including Stockton and Darlington) but it had been built hastily when the town grew, and so was not necessarily of good quality. In 1930 the Medical Officer of Health made a report on housing conditions in the Borough. There were many houses in a poor state of repair. Three hundred and eight were deemed by the housing department to be 'unfit for human habitation' and a further 11,629 were in the elusive category of 'not in all respects fit for human habitation'. (By 1932 this number had risen to 12,638.) In the poorest part of town there were also 'unlicensed hutments, so-called caravans' where families lived in cramped conditions without water or sanitation. People moved into the caravans because of lack of suitable houses to rent, and the rent charged for them was often the same as for small houses nearby.

The health department decided to co-operate with the housing committee of the town council in a programme of slum clearance. In the 1920s the council had begun a policy of building new houses on the outskirts of the town, and 2,756 such houses were built by 1930.[15] Commendable as these efforts were, they were of little help to the poor, because the rents charged (about 9s) were out of the reach of any except those earning an above average wage. The first scheme directed at the 'insanitary areas' began in 1930, when new houses were built for the inhabitants of one street. In the 1930s, local authority subsidies were given for slum clearance, and the 1935 Housing Act gave local councils a legal duty to provide houses to prevent overcrowding. In 1934 there was a new plan to abolish 485 houses and re-house, 2,294 people. Work began quickly; 238 houses being replaced in 1935. The MOH report of 1937 reported, with some satisfaction, that whereas in 1934 there had been 2,100 families overcrowded, in 1937 there were only 900.[16] Of course 900 families still amounted to a large number of people affected, and the official definition of overcrowding – more than two persons to a room – was not a stringent one. In many cases a family which was not overcrowded according to the official definition might have to use one room for eating, cooking, washing and as a bedroom for one or more of its members.

The health reports do not mention the contemporary discussion about the problems of slum clearance. Some contemporary observers believed that simply providing better environmental conditions would not help standards of health, either because the people who lived in them were insufficiently educated or simply had too little money. (Stockton's Medical Officer of Health had strong views on this, as will be seen later.) Others pointed out that the new houses were built only to provide dormitories, without shops and pubs and often a long distance from the works. Altogether, the value of the new houses in improving standards of health is difficult to assess, and this will be referred to again.

Another new emphasis for the health department in the thirties was increasing its maternity and child welfare services. This reflected the national trend of concern about the health of mothers and babies, something especially needed in Middlesbrough.[17] The town had always had a high infant mortality rate: in 1919 it was 139 per thousand live births, which was doubtless caused by the environmental conditions of the town, the prevalence of infectious diseases (to which young children were especially vulnerable) as well as poor health care, inadequate feeding, and lack of education. It was the last three which the new services sought to correct. A maternity and child welfare service was set up, which operated from six centres for mothers and children and through the health visitors it appointed. The centres were partly funded by private, charitable sources. Of these six Maternity and Child Welfare Centres, five had a weekly session for mothers and children, and one had a twice weekly session, and they all had an ante-natal clinic once a month. Table 27 (taken from the MOH report of 1930) gives an idea of their popularity.

Table 27 *Average monthly attendance at Middlesbrough maternity and child welfare centres, 1930*

	Infant welfare	Ante-natal clinics
Elizabeth Purvis Centre	128	19
Grove Hill Centre	99	14·7
Cannon Centre	188	30
American Red Cross Centre	82	20·6
Settlement Centre	99	25·5
North Ormesky Centre	104	21·8
Total	700	131·6

Source: Middlesbrough MOH Report, 1930.

An average attendance of 700 mothers each month in a town of 126,000 people suggests that only a small proportion of mothers attended these clinics.[18] The ante-natal clinics were better attended. In 1937 the MOH report claimed that in the case of thirty-six per cent of births the mother had had contact with a municipal clinic. This left a large number of mothers who had, presumably, no ante-natal care. Such care would be available from private doctors but in a town like Middlesbrough, most people only went to see a doctor if they were badly ill.[19]

It is difficult to gauge the importance attached to these centres by the Middlesbrough Health Committee. The reports of the Maternity and Child Welfare Committees make no comment on them, and give no descriptions of their work, and nor do any of the MOH reports. It is probable, though, that they followed the common practice of using these clinics as somewhere to give advice and, if necessary, treatment to children and prospective mothers.[20]

The minutes of the maternity and child welfare committee give lists of quantities of free milk and vitamins given at these clinics.

One aspect of maternity and child welfare which was a matter of clear concern to the health department was the practice of employing 'handy women' or unqualified midwives at a birth instead of trained midwives. The MOH reports frequently note with satisfaction the fact that an increasing number of births were attended by qualified midwives. In 1927 the MOH included a table showing the decline in the activity of handy women (Table 28).

Table 28 *Numbers of 'handy women' found to have acted in place of a midwife, 1924–7*

Year	No.
1924	109
1925	85
1926	73
1927	40

Source: Middlesbrough MOH Report, 1927.

A municipal midwife service was begun in the year 1937, and in that year, out of a total of 2,898 births, 2,513 were notified by midwives. The MOH reports also suggest that health visitors helped an increasing number of people during the 1920s, and in 1931 the MOH reported with evident satisfaction that in that year a health visitor paid at least one visit to ninety-six per cent of babies which were notified as being born that year. The fact that this work was being extended was obviously an encouraging sign, but of course there was no guarantee of the efficacy of their work. In many cases the health visitors were dealing with families who had little money, poor housing conditions, little education, and precious little time, and who might well not have been in a position to heed good advice.

The education committee took a responsibility for the health of schoolchildren in the 1930s, by providing free milk to some children, and in a few cases also school meals, as well as arranging for inspections of schoolchildren.[21] This was a modest contribution in the national movement to provide free milk and school meals to children, as a way of ensuring good nutritional standards through-out the country. In 1932 this committee ruled that free milk should be provided to children of any family where the income after rent was less than 6s per head per week.

The sum of these measures, environmental and social, must have contributed to the improvements in health shown in Table 24. The effect of the environmental improvements is indicated by the fact that those diseases which showed a marked decline in the twenties where those which are frequently associated with environmental conditions: scarlet fever, diphtheria, whooping cough, diarrhoea and enteritis. The last two were especially responsible for the heavy infant mortality, and their decline was almost certainly a factor in its improvement.[22] While it is more difficult to make positive associations between improved health and better social services, it seems reasonable to suppose that they were a contributory cause. The question which remains is whether the effects of unemployment retarded this improvement. Some clues, which go someway towards suggesting an answer, can be found in the reports of Middlesbrough's two Medical Officers of Health in the inter-war period, and in the reports of some of their subordinates.

The early assessments of health in Middlesbrough are strongly influenced by an optimism which resulted from the dramatic improvements which took place after the First World War. In 1920, Charles Dingle, MOH for Middlesbrough, writing his twenty-second annual report wrote 'the year 1920 was noticeably favourable from the health point of view, with a great improvement in birth and death rates . . . the principal infectious diseases showed a large decrease'. His assessment of 1921 and 1922 was 'during the two years under review the health of the town has been exceptionally good, and this is the more satisfactory when the conditions of unemployment and the housing shortage are taken into consideration'. In comparison with the average for England and Wales, Middlesbrough's health was by no means 'exceptionally good' but Dr Dingle, who had seen the appalling conditions of health in Middlesbrough in the late nineteenth century concentrated only on the improvements he saw. In the 1920s there were few attempts made by officials to consider the question of whether unemployment retarded the health improvements of which they were justifiably proud. Dr Dingle did recognise the possible effects of trade depression on health, and from time to time made general observations to the effect that the health of the town had been good 'in spite of' unemployment, but he does not make clear whether he thought that unemployment retarded the improvements, or whether better conditions counteracted any effects that unemployment might have had. Often his reports made reference to the fact that Middlesbrough had always known 'a considerable amount of poverty'.[23] Poverty was an accepted feature of the town, and the members of the health department felt no need to regard it as anything but an unfortunate, everpresent difficulty, as would be a poor geographical setting.

Dingle did point out various reasons why he believed that trade depression was actually beneficial to health. In his annual report of 1923 he suggested that the lessened atmospheric pollution caused by the depression might be a reason for improved health, and that a lower infant mortality was due, in part, to the fact that mothers could not afford to drink so much alcohol. Some people, though, began to feel that the ill-effects of unemployment counteracted any such beneficial ones. In October 1928 the local MP, Ellen Wilkinson, wrote a letter to the *North Eastern Daily Gazette*, claiming that there were a large number of ill-nourished children in the town. Her information came from a woman doctor of her acquaintance who compared the prevalence of rickets in Middlesbrough to that in Vienna after the war, and attributed this to the industrial depression. Ellen Wilkinson felt that school meals were the answer to this problem. In her letter she said that she had spoken to Dr Dingle who agreed that some diseases may be caused by malnutrition, but didn't feel that school meals were necessary. Dr Dingle replied to this letter saying that there was 'much poverty in our midst' but that it was not true that a large proportion of the town were suffering from underfeeding. He claimed that Ellen Wilkinson's assertions would alarm parents who went to great lengths to see that their children were well fed.[24] The question of whether children suffered from malnutrition continued to be a controversial one. In some towns this question was considered at length in school medical reports, but no such records exist for Middlesbrough. However the education committee did consider the question on several occasions. In 1932 this committee called for a special report on the subject by a Dr Weaver, and it commented on his report thus: 'The Board are glad that, in spite of prolonged industrial depression in the area, Dr Weaver found no evidence in the schools which he visited of any widespread under-nourishment of children.' This again illustrated the fact that health is a relative concept; different doctors could look at the same conditions and reach completely different conclusions.

The person to express concern about the effect of unemployment on health in the 1920s was the TB officer. By the mid-twenties he was seriously worried about the high rates of death from respiratory diseases in Middlesbrough. He pointed out that in the years 1921–5 Middlesbrough had the highest death rate from pneumonia of all northeastern towns, and the second highest rate for all respiratory diseases.[25] At this time he was not entirely clear of the reason for this, and his reports discuss possible answers. It had long been thought that working conditions were an important factor, but he pointed out that similar working conditions could be found in some Midlands towns, which did not have the same high TB rates. Various surveys done by the Health Department showed some correlation between overcrowding and the incidence of TB. One, done in 1928, showed that people who moved into the better housing conditions on the new estates suffered less from TB. The TB rate in the new housing estates was the lowest in the town, and the death rate from TB, the lowest but two of all wards. In 1926 another survey showed that in the case of 769 houses with a tubercular patient only 157 were able to provide a separate bedroom for the patient, and only 396 a separate bed. However it is probably also significant that in general the people who moved to the new estates (especially in the 1920s) were those who could afford higher rents. It is likely, though, that T.B. could not be stemmed or cured while people were living in overcrowded conditions.

The TB officer came to the conclusion that it was the depression which caused most of his problems. In 1924 he pointed out that the Middlesbrough death rate from TB was the highest since 1918. He stated quite unequivocally: 'the causes of this increase are not far to seek. The cummulative effect of almost four years of unemployment and the consequent poverty amongst the working classes are unquestionably the immediate cause of increased mortality.' He continued 'until a revival of trade recurs I do not look for any material improvement in the incidence of and mortality from pulmonary tuberculosis'. Modern research on TB confirms that it is often linked with malnutrition.[26] In fact, the TB death rates in Middlesbrough did not improve until 1934, when there was an easing of the depression, although this could in part have been due to the increase of new houses in Middlesbrough, with a resultant lessening of overcrowding.

The pessimism shown by the TB officer in the 1920s begins to be reflected more generally by other health officials in Middlesbrough in the 1930s. This was not because mortality rates ceased to improve, because they did. There appears amongst the more cheerful utterances characteristic of the previous decade some sort of dissatisfaction that the improvements were not as great as they could, or should be. The gains of the twenties were great, but after they had taken place the two Medical Officers of Health in the thirties cease to compare health conditions in Middlesbrough with those of the previous century, and started to look to other parts of the country for a standard. In 1930 the TB officer said that although the death rate from the TB was improving in Middlesbrough, the improvement did not correspond with the even greater amelioration in the country at large. In 1932 Dr Dingle qualified an otherwise optimistically phrased report by pointing out that the infantile mortality rate was still 'higher than it should be'. This wording heavily implies that the causes of infant mortality were remediable, and that the remedy was within the power of the community.

In 1936 Middlesbrough had a new Medical Officer of Health, a Dr Metcalf-Brown. His first report mentions the improved health in the previous few years, but expressed his concern about the high

Table 29 *Ward death rates per 1,000 population in Middlesbrough, 1921–39*

Ward	1921	1925	1931	1935	1939
Ayresome	10·53	8·98	10·92	9·83	11·66
Acklam	12·20	10·72	12·04	10·13	12·09
Cannon	14·87	18·60	17·97	16·57	16·22
Cleveland	15·68	16·55	12·92	17·01	15·57
Exchange	12·23	13·36	11·92	15·80	17·93
Grove Hill	9·19	10·87	11·52	10·07	9·74
Linthorpe	11·55	10·68	11·90	9·33	9·24
Newport	16·46	19·96	17·11	15·97	20·41
Ormesby	13·96	13·32	12·35	13·59	12·27
St Hilda's	26·00	22·29	21·68	25·20	22·88
Vulcan	13·96	14·81	14·03	15·35	13·30

Source: Middlesbrough MOH report, 1930.

infant mortality rate. The next year he said that the overall death
rate in Middlesbrough was high. The corrected death rate for the
town allowed for the fact that it had a larger proportion of young
people than most parts of the country, and so ideally it should have
a death rate lower than the national average. The adjusted death
rate for Middlesbrough was 16·3 per 1,000 as opposed to 12·4 for
England and Wales; a very significant discrepancy. In re-examining
Middlesbrough's health record, to find the cause of her still
unfavourable rates, Dr Metcalf-Brown became concerned at the
ward death rate in the town. These (see Table 29) showed that
although some parts of the town were reasonably salubrious, there
were others with crude death rates far above the average for
England and Wales. The worst, St Hilda's ward, had a crude death
rate around ten points above the national average for most of the
1930s, and its adjusted death rate would have shown an even
greater discrepancy. It is not easy to judge the reason for these
continually bad conditions of health. The wards with a high death
rate had seen an improvement in the inter-war years; in fact they
account for much of the general improvement in the average death
rate for the town. They were areas with traditionally poor
environmental conditions; the map of Middlesbrough (Figure 8)
shows that they were the parts of the town which were densely
populated and situated near to the works. Fragmentary oral
evidence suggests that those people who lived 'north of the railway'
(St Hilda's Ward) were considered to be less careful with their
housekeeping and general care of themselves than the other
inhabitants of Middlesbrough. It is not easy to link the bad rates in
these wards with unemployment, because there is not real statistical
evidence to consult, but in view of previous indications that
unemployment did have an adverse effect on the health of
individuals it seems possible that the unemployment which affected
these areas did help to retard the improvements within them. The
evidence of the ward death rates shows that although there were
noticeable improvements in the health of those areas of Middlesbrough with a tradition of poor health, they were not great enough
to prevent disquiet amongst the health officials of the town.

Stockton-on-Tees

It is useful to compare changes in standards of health in Stockton
with those in Middlesbrough, because there were a number of

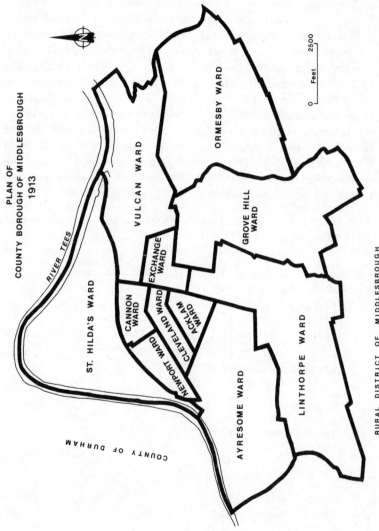

PLAN OF
COUNTY BOROUGH OF MIDDLESBROUGH
1913

RIVER TEES

COUNTY OF DURHAM

ST. HILDA'S WARD

VULCAN WARD

ORMESBY WARD

CANNON WARD

EXCHANGE WARD

NEWPORT WARD

CLEVELAND WARD

ACKLAM WARD

GROVE HILL WARD

AYRESOME WARD

LINTHORPE WARD

RURAL DISTRICT OF MIDDLESBROUGH

0   Feet   2500

broad similarities between the towns in matters which were likely to have an important effect on health standards. Both were towns where most men worked in heavy industry, with all the resulting disadvantages to health. In both towns living conditions had been harsh, and in spite of the high wages which could be earned before the war the large pool of casual labour together with the exigences of the trade cycle meant that poverty was by no means unknown. As was the case in Middlesbrough, in 1919 Stockton had a high death rate and infant mortality rate, with respiratory diseases and enteritis taking a heavy toll of life. (See Table 30.) The difference between them was that living conditions in Stockton were not as bad as those in Middlesbrough. Stockton had developed more slowly, it did not have the massive environmental disadvantages that Middlesbrough did, something which probably accounts for the fact that the Stockton death rate, of 16·5 per 1,000 in 1919, was more than two percentage points below that of Middlesbrough. However, in the

Table 30 *Crude death rate, infant mortality rate per 1,000 live births in Stockton-on-Tees, 1919–39*

Year	Death rate	Infant mortality rate
1919	16·5	105
1920	15·59	109
1921	12·9	92·2
1922	15·4	102
1923	11·96	75
1924	14·52	111
1925	14·38	92
1926	13·34	90
1927	13·55	91
1928	12·85	69·7
1929	15·26	109
1930	12·49	65
1931	12·51	79
1932	12·76	77
1933	12·72	96
1934	12·15	62
1935	12·23	56
1936	11·26	47
1937	12·50	71
1938	11·53	52
1939	12·87	68

Source: Compiled from Stockton MOH reports, 1919–39.

inter-war years Stockton had the problem of an even higher unemployment rate than Middlesbrough. It is against this background that the progress of Stockton's health must be seen.

The environmental problems suffered by Stockton were tackled in much the same way as those of Middlesbrough, and improvements achieved roughly contemporaneously with those of that town. As in Middlesbrough, the work of the sanitary department was especially important in the 1920s. Its first tasks were tightening up the inspection of food and drink which was brought into the town, and inspecting workshops, sewers and houses. In the early twenties the inspection of meat was described by the Medical Officer of Health as 'haphazard' but the work was conducted in an increasingly systematic way. Great care was taken to ensure that no infected milk was sold, and any unclean milk was traced to its source. Also, by 1926 the town was converted to a water carriage system of sanitation. By the 1930s the work of this department became one of regular inspection than major reform.

As in Middlesbrough, the reduced incidence of diseases normally connected with poor environmental conditions accounted for much of the improvement in health. The mortality rates of the two towns showed a similar improvement (relative to their original rates) in the 1920s, and in both cases began to close the gap between their rates and those for the country as a whole. In Middlesbrough in 1919 there were 4·39 per thousand points difference between the crude death rate of that town and the national average; by 1928 the gap was 2·66 points. Stockton's position was slightly better: in 1919 there were 2·5 per thousand points difference between Stockton's rate and the national average, and by 1928 there were 1·15 points between them, before they had been adjusted.

The thirties saw more improvements in both towns, but the amelioration in Stockton was greater, in relative terms, than that of Middlesbrough. Both towns still had rates above the national average, which were more acute than appears from a calculation of the crude death rate because both towns had larger than average proportion of young people. Even so, the improvements in Stockton are interesting, especially in view of the fact that during the thirties it saw one of the highest unemployment rates in the country. In the 1920s both Middlesbrough and Stockton had high infant mortality rates, and those of Middlesbrough remained high, but the rate in Stockton fell below that for England and Wales as a whole. As the infant mortality rate is especially susceptible to economic influences this is particularly significant. The history of standard of health in Stockton in the thirties is clearly a moderate, and in some cases more than moderate, success story which might seem surprising, in view of its high unemployment rate.

Housing was a matter of major concern to the Medical Officer of Health. As in many other towns, the cessation of housebuilding during the war had caused overcrowding; and the MOH gave repeated warnings about the dangers to health from this. In response to these warnings the housing committee of the council drew up plans in 1920 to build 1,750 houses. After an initial delay this programme began, and by 1929 1,138 houses had been built. This programme must have helped to some extent to relieve the burden of overcrowding, but it was criticised by Dr McGonigle, MOH since 1924, as being quite insufficient. The number 1,750 was the estimated need of houses in 1920, and by 1929 it was long out of date. Also, the rents of Corporation houses tended to be high, and therefore they could not be afforded by those who were most in need of new homes.[27]

As was the case in Middlesbrough, the work of 'slum clearance' (as opposed to simply building more houses) did not begin on a large scale until the 1930s. Four clearance areas were scheduled, and 639 houses were replaced by 741 houses, displacing 3,039 people. This scheme was completed in 1933. Two improvement areas were designated, in which 300 houses were demolished and replaced; this scheme affected 1,500 people, and in addition 89 houses in different parts of the town were planned for demolition. Most of the slum clearance schemes were completed by 1937.

These schemes were more extensive than those of Middlesbrough and the new housing they provided may have helped towards improving health, but some evidence collected by the MOH suggest that the new houses were very much a mixed blessing. A study done of 141 families in council houses showed that the high rents charged for council houses meant that these families had significantly less money to spend on food, and that the death rate amongst unemployed living in council houses was higher than amongst those in privately rented homes. From this evidence it seems that the beneficial effects of the housebuilding in Stockton were limited to easing the demand for privately rented houses, and thereby lessening overcrowding.

One aspect of health in Stockton in the late twenties and thirties which distinguished it from Middlesbrough, and indeed from most other towns in England, was the exceptionally good health services which were developed there. While the officials of Middlesbrough achieved improvements along tried and tested lines, by environmental amelioration, and then extended the health services in accordance with the law; Stockton became a model example of the application of then new methods of health care. This was a time when the local health authority had a considerable potential influence on the town; as J. Hadfield put it 'in the 1930s, after the implementation of the great 1929 local government act, but before the second world war and the National Health Service, was the high-watermark of local authority responsibility and activity in the sphere of public health'.[28]

The influence of the health department was largely brought about by the MOH from 1924–38, Dr McGonigle. His first, and abiding concern was with infant welfare. In his first report he asserted that infant mortality in Stockton was higher than 'it ought to be' (words which were used in Middlesbrough in the later years of the thirties) and said that this was a matter for particular concern because healthy mothers and children were the 'keystone of a healthy society'. To back up this point he commented that 'much preventable sickness and disability arises during the pre-school period'.

Much of the work of child welfare was instigated by child welfare and ante-natal clinics. McGonigle attached great importance to the work of these clinics, and great efforts were made to publicise them, and to make them acceptable to the mothers of the town.[29] McGonigle realised that the first problem to be solved was to win the confidence of the people who went to them, and at times his health reports comment with satisfaction that their work was appreciated by the mothers who attended them. Table 31 shows the increase in popularity of these centres in their early years.

The average monthly attendance in 1925 was 644 people. In Middlesbrough, a town with about twice the population of Stockton, the average attendance at clinics in 1930 was 700; which clearly suggests that these clinics were more popular in Stockton.[30]

Much of the work of the maternity and child welfare centres was educative; McGonigle himself denied the common allegation that mothers only attended them to obtain free milk by pointing out that

Table 31 *Total attendance at child welfare centres in Stockton-on-Tees, 1921–5*

1921	2,981
1922	2,976
1923	2,789
1924	4,172
1925	7,733

Source: Stockton MOH report, 1925.

the centres in the poorest areas of Stockton (which were well attended) gave out the smallest amounts of food. As it was believed that incorrect feeding was the commonest cause of infant death, particular stress was placed on advising mothers on diet for babies and small children. Milk and vitamins were also issued in some cases, and any ill child could be treated by the clinic. In 1928 the infant mortality rate fell to 67·9 per 1,000 births, from 105 per 1,000 in 1919. By the mid-thirties the infant mortality rates in Stockton were actually lower than those for England and Wales, a remarkable achievement for a town with so many environmental and economic disadvantages. It is especially interesting in view of the fact that the nutritional analysis of the unemployed budget in Chapter 2 suggested that mothers and small children were likely to suffer poor nutrition if the family breadwinner was out of work.

Maternal mortality continued to remain high all across the country and was a vexed question for medical specialists in the inter-war years.[31] Here again, Stockton had a better record than the rest of the country. This was almost certainly because of the emphasis laid on ante-natal care, because similar good results were achieved by Merthyr, in Wales, another town with exceptionally high unemployment but a good ante-natal care service.[32] In most towns ante-natal care took second place to child welfare, but in Stockton some pioneer work was done in this field. Again, special attention was paid to nutrition, and new theories about the importance of certain vitamins in the diet of expectant and nursing mothers were tested. Expectant mothers who came to the centre were given supplements of vitamins A, D and E. It was believed that vitamin E might prevent a woman from miscarrying, and it was administered to some women who appeared to be in danger of miscarrying, most of whom produced healthy babies.[33]

The exceptionally good results achieved from this kind of work in Stockton, and similar experiments such as those done by Lady Rhys Williams in the Rhondda Valley, indicate that good health services which had the confidence of the town could make for high standards of health even in a town experiencing high unemployment. Of course the work of the health services in Stockton were exceptionally energetic, and it might be reasonable to suppose that if a similar campaign had been made in a town with little unemployment and low wages, then the results might have been even more striking.

The Stockton MOH reports, like those of Middlesbrough, contain some comments about the possible effects of trade depression on the health of the town. Many of these come from Dr McGonigle, who had a clear standpoint on this issue. He was one of the medical men, described earlier in the chapter, who firmly believed that unemployment and low wages were the cause of ill-health. It is important to bear this in mind when assessing his statements on the subject.

Table 32 *Principal causes and numbers of deaths in Stockton-on-Tees, 1921–5*

	1921	1922	1923	1924	1925
Pneumonia	93	154	87	157	136
Heart disease	73	98	82	91	118
Tuberculosis (all forms)	90	90	79	87	83
Bronchitis	71	89	38	89	69
Cancer	54	77	61	69	66
Congenital debility	71	63	51	42	58
Cerebral haemorrhage	54	52	42	47	50
Influenza	8	64	16	65	64
Diarrhoea (under 2 years of age)	35	24	16	22	20
Violence	34	20	20	22	32
Measles	24	0	56	4	37
Arterio-sclerosis	13	11	27	28	20
Whooping cough	4	37	6	48	2
Totals	624	779	581	771	755

Some of the remarks made about connections between unemployment and health are reminiscent of those in Middlesbrough which suggested that in some ways the health of the town could benefit from unemployment. In 1921 the MOH report related that the general consensus of doctors working in the town was that 'unemployment is thought to have reduced serious illnesses by lessening exposure to fatigue and weather changes, but on the other hand to have increased slight illnesses and invalidity, especially among women'. It must be remembered that workers in heavy industry were subject to danger and great physical stress, and so the immediate impact of unemployment might well be better health. The comment about women suffering is reminiscent of many other observers in the inter-war period who found that when the family budget was limited the mother often cut down on her own food, in order to feed her children and husband.[34]

The new MOH, though, asserted that unemployment was a cause of ill-health. His second report, in 1925, expresses this view implicitly, saying that there had been a steady decrease in the death rates in Stockton during the last five years, but 'it is reasonable to suppose that had conditions (of trade) been better the improvement would have been even more pronounced'.

McGonigle believed that a partial solution to the ill-effects of unemployment could be found in public services, and in 1930 he exprssed this view in his annual report:

The standard of health remains high, and the standard of living has not fallen noticeably. The receipt of unemployment benefit by unemployed men and women, the increased social services, the higher standard of education, and the better housing conditions all help to maintain the standard of living, although the depressing effect of continued unemployment may later react on the general health, and undermine the desire to maintain or improve those conditions.

This statement is interesting also because it is one of the few hints about the possible psychological effects of unemployment that the MOH reports of the three towns give.

By the 1930s McGonigle had become convinced that unemployment caused ill-health, because it resulted in inadequate spending power and poor nutrition. In his report of 1935 he puts this unequivocally:

The root of the matter is inadequate purchasing power. The public conscience should not be salved by vague statements that inadequate nutrition is caused by the ignorance of the housewives. Such statements are unfair to a large body of women which by hard work and bitter experience has attained a large measure of domestic efficiency.

In stating this McGonigle was not concerned with the problem of relative improvements in health, as he had been in the statement of 1930 given previously, but with his own belief that the budget of many families was not sufficient to provide them with adequate food. The question of whether standards of health were worse because of unemployment, than they had been before the war, did not concern him; he was only interested in the fact that standards were less good than in his view they should have been.

In order to prove such a belief McGonigle faced the difficulties which were common to all those in the 'family poverty lobby', and indeed their opponents (see page 71). He acknowledged these difficulties, saying that many conflicting reports had appeared about the nutritional state of the unemployed and their children, because this type of assessment was so much 'a matter of personal opinion', but this did not alter his own opinion, that 'poverty is a potent cause of ill-health'.

McGonigle did make some attempts to prove his own opinions by scientific demonstration. In 1935 the maternity and child welfare clinics acted on evidence from experiments done by Dr Kathleen Vaughn, which showed that inadequate nutrition in childhood caused abnormal pelvises in women, which later caused them to be at risk in childbirth.[35] A survey of expectant mothers in the Stockton clinics, according to Dr Vaughn's standards, found that only fifty-nine per cent had a perfectly normal construction of the pelvis.[36] Assuming that the average age of the women was between twenty and thirty, this would suggest that nutritional standards in Stockton between the Edwardian era and the early twenties had been poor. Other surveys were done to assess current nutritional standards. Also in 1935 mothers were checked for a variety of disorders (see Table 33).

A number of these conditions – dental decay, bone conditions, anaemia, and to a lesser extent diarrhoea and bronchitis – are often associated with inadequate nutrition. The chief problem with this, as with similar surveys done in Stockton and elsewhere, is that the assessments made are not according to a fixed standard, and other doctors doing a similar survey with the same people might have found quite different results.

This problem also affects the findings of the school inspections in Stockton, which also provided important evidence to support McGonigle's theories. Surveys were done by a school inspector into

Table 33 *Incidence of various disorders amongst women attending Stockton-on-Tees maternity clinics, 1935 (%)*

Condition	Incidence
Bone condition	43
Pharyngeal conditions	17
Dental decay	27
Squint	3·8
Anaemia	31·2
Diarrhoea	39·2
Bronchitis	36·7

Source: Stockton MOH report, 1935.

the health of schoolchildren, which found high levels of inadequate nutrition amongst the children.[37] In 1934 53·8 per cent of children inspected were found to be suffering from bad nutrition, and 22·8 per cent of children from subnormal nutrition. These standards improved, but remained high enough to be a cause for concern. Surveys done across the country showed that the standards adopted by different doctors were vastly different, and the fact that the results in Stockton were exceptionally bad is more likely to be due to the high standards of the investigators than the fact that conditions in Stockton were much worse than in other severely depressed towns.[38] In the light of these discrepancies it is difficult to assess the extent and severity of poor feeding among schoolchildren. The Stockton figure shows that a doctor who presumably applied high standards to the assessment of nutrition and health found a majority of children suffering from inadequate nutrition. In view of the fact that John Boyd Orr in his nationwide survey of nutrition using strict (and by modern standards over-high) standards found that only a third of the nation was adequately fed on all counts, the Stockton result might not seem surprising. However, the numbers listed as suffering from 'bad' instead of 'subnormal' nutrition were such as to indicate that even if the figures were exaggerated the situation was bad.

The other survey which attempted to prove scientifically the extent of undernourishment amongst the poor of Stockton was the study by McGonigle and Kirby of the unemployed who moved to new housing estates.[39] This was not a representative sample, but it showed clearly that these people, who had to pay high rents, were likely to be under-fed if the breadwinner was unemployed. One important thing which the study showed was how crucial to the level of nutrition and health was a few shillings a week, which could easily make the difference between a healthy and unhealthy family. This reinforces the fact that factors such as family size, and good money management were of paramount importance to the health of an individual family.

Darlington

In matters of health, as in others, Darlington makes an interesting contrast to Middlesbrough and Stockton. A typical comment from its Medical Officer of Health was that 'the town prides itself for its reputation for cleanliness, well-paved streets and highly skilled artisan population. The health statistics have characteristics usually associated with the residential south rather than the industrial north.' In 1919 Darlington already had many of the environmental advantages which Middlesbrough and Stockton had to create in the twenties. It was a wealthier town, and its population included more of the better paid, better educated members of the working class, whose standards of living, mode of living, standards and expectations were quite different from the poorly paid or casual worker. One thing which distinguished Darlington from the residential south in the inter-war years was its unemployment rates, which although they were far below those of the other two towns, were still characteristic of somewhere suffering from the depression.

For the purposes of this study there are two chief problems to be considered about the health of Darlington in the inter-war years. The first is to compare the standard of health in this town, as compared with that in Middlesbrough and Stockton, and to judge whether any differences are due to: – environmental and social differences; or because of the different workings of the local health services; or because of the different economic standards of their populations. The other is to consider the health of the unemployed of Darlington, and see whether their health suffered.

The Darlington health statistics show the fairly steady ameliora- tion of health throughout the period, as was the case in the other two towns, and the country as a whole. For most of the period the Darlington death rates were similar to the average for England and Wales, and the fact that its death rate crept above the average at the

end of the period was because of the increasingly high proportion
of elderly people in the population.[40] The infant mortality rates in
Darlington were high in the twenties, but fell below the average for
England and Wales in the 1930s (see Table 34).

Table 34 *Crude death rate, and infant mortality rates per 1,000 live
births in Darlington, 1919–39*

Year	Death rate (%)	Infant mortality rate (per % live births)
1919	15·7	138
1920	12·4	91
1921	12·3	97·7
1922	14·1	98
1923	11·9	67
1924	12·7	94
1925	12·7	106
1926	11·9	91
1927	11·6	67
1928	10·4	59
1929	13·1	81
1930	11·5	76
1931	12·5	73
1933	11·2	67
1934	12·0	67
1935	10·8	59
1936	12·2	59
1937	12·7	58
1938	12·9	58
1939	12·5	56

Note: No figures are available for 1932.
Source: Compiled from Darlington MOH reports.

The great environmental improvements instigated by the health
department which characterised the story of health in Middlesbrough and Stockton in the twenties were not evident in Darlington. While the MOH reports of Darlington give familiar warnings
about the dangers of unhealthy abattoirs, the poor sewage system,
and the unhealthy sanitary arrangements in some parts of the town
these exhortations made little impact on the local council.
Occasional suggestions by the MOH that saving money on health is
a false economy suggests that the council was reluctant to spend
money on these projects. It was not until 1933 that the town was

converted to the water carriage system of sanitation, and only in the
early thirties that the sewage system was overhauled.

The results of this lack of change can be seen in the fact that
certain diseases which are closely associated with poor environment
and sanitation persisted in Darlington after they had virtually
disappeared in Stockton and Middlesbrough. Enteritis, in particular, was far more prevalent in Darlington until the 1930s. However,
these deficiencies in public health care did not mean that the health
figures in Darlington were worse than those of the other towns, for
they were not. The most reasonable explanation of this was that
what was not done by official bodies was done by individuals.
Evidence on housing suggests that many people in Darlington were
able to afford better living conditions.

In the early 1920s there was overcrowding in Darlington caused

Table 35 *Housebuilding in Darlington, 1918–38*

	Private enterprise		By Corporation		
Year	Without subsidy	With subsidy	Without subsidy	With subsidy	Total
1918	2				2
1919	6				6
1920	17				17
1921	9			86	95
1922	187			152	339
1923	264	1		35	300
1924	103	208		18	329
1925	96	399		15	510
1926	81	256		56	393
1927	56	334			390
1928	58	274			332
1929	63	419			482
1930	264				264
1931	200	2			202
1932	311		6	8	325
1933	770		29	132	931
1934	1,013			40	1,053
1935	735			34	769
1936	551				
1937	455		5	104	564
1938	426		51	62	539

Source: Compiled from Darlington MOH reports, 1918–38.

by the cessation of housebuilding during the First World War. An estimated ten per cent of families were overcrowded in 1923.[41] By 1931, though, this problem had eased considerably, and the 1931 census showed that there was an average of 0·91 people to a room in the town, as opposed to 1·07 people in 1921. These figures compared favourably with other North East towns where the averages ranged from 1 to 1·23 persons per room. These changes took place because of housebuilding by the private sector in the town (see Table 35). The fact that houses in Darlington tended to be larger than average, and families smaller, also helped to produce these favourable rates. The reason why so many houses were built by private contractors must have been that sufficient people could afford to buy or rent them, and thereby improve the environment by individual instead of collective effort. Presumably these people were also able to afford a reasonable diet and good living conditions, which would have contributed to the general well-being of the town. However, Darlington did have its slums, and the reports of the Medical Officer of Health during the 1930s showed that he regarded them as a matter of paramount concern. A special report on housing in 1930 said that while, in general, housing conditions were improving 'this has not to any great extent altered the conditions in back to back property. The general work of sanitary inspectors reveals that increasing numbers of houses are becoming sub-let and sub-divided, so that the conditions of the poorer classes are on the whole unimproved.'

Darlington's Medical Officer believed that the health hazards of the insanitary back to back houses were much greater than those of overcrowding. In the same report he wrote: 'Pieremont Ward, though equally like Central Ward – the most crowded in population per acre – has no back-to-back houses, boasts the lowest death rate during the past five years, and therefore provides a simple basis for comparison with the other seven wards, all of which are "infected" in varying degrees by old insanitary property and the usual unpleasant associated features.' He continued to say that areas with insanitary houses had a greater incidence of scarlet fever, diphtheria, measles, pulmonary and non-pulmonary TB, and pneumonia, all diseases connected with poor environmental conditions, and 'the danger seems to overflow and infect the "contact" good property'.[42] Some slum clearance was done, (see Table 35), but Darlington town council clearly did not see it as a priority as it was in the other two towns. All through the 1930s the MOH reported that work of building new houses for the poor was slow. In 1934 he wrote, 'The increase of unemployment has caused many to seek accommodation that is inadequate to their needs. There is a great need for houses built on different lines to the semi or detached houses, as these are beyond the income of the small wage earner, or those who are unemployed for long periods.' In a town where a good proportion of the population could care for themselves, the needs of the poor were felt to be less pressing by the authorities.

Further information about the different characteristics of Darlington can be found in the operation of her health services. These were active and well-promoted, but followed a different pattern from either of the towns studied so far. The work of the maternity and child welfare centres was most like that of the other two towns. MOH reports from the early twenties place great stress on the importance of their work, and continually report that attendance was increasing. The fall in the infant mortality rate, which by the thirties was lower than the national average, was attributed by the MOH to the work of these clinics. No figures of attendance or detailed information about their work is given, so it is difficult to compare their work with that done in Middlesbrough and Stockton, but it does seem that they exerted an important influence over the town.

One feature of the Darlington health service which does not appear to any great extent in either of the other two towns was a great emphasis on health propaganda. Every year there was a 'Baby Day' to which mothers were invited to bring their children, which publicised the work of the maternity and child welfare centres. This event was invariably attended by a number of local dignitaries (usually the mayor and his wife were there) and a picture of the proceedings normally appeared in the local press. In a similar vein there was a 'Health Week' each year, when posters and pamphlets would be distributed, and films on health matters were shown in local cinemas. This kind of propaganda appears to have been well received. In 1932 the MOH report commented on 'the extraordinary interest taken in every aspect of our health work during the year by our general population'. All manner of organisations, such as the Trades Council, the Rotary Club, and women's clubs asked for talks by health officers. All this activity reinforces the image of Darlington as a place which fostered activity by the individual, and one where many of the individuals were sufficiently well-off and well-educated to be able to take advantage of this.

One area in which the local health services believed themselves to be failing during the inter-war years was maternal mortality. The MOH reports continually refer to the fact that the maternal mortality rates were above the national average, and indeed the concern about this problem was nationwide. The MOH reports contended that the problem was insufficient ante-natal care, and exhorted the local council to provide more money for these services, but it seems that again they were reluctant to increase their costs.

Other information from the MOH reports suggests that conditions for the Darlington poor were at least as bad as in the other two towns. During the 1920s the Darlington MOH repeatedly expressed concern about the housing conditions of the town's poorer inhabitants. Most of the new houses built in the 1920s were too expensive for people living on low incomes. In 1926 the MOH wrote: 'In pre-war days there was a surplus of sufficient size to keep rents from advancing out of proportion of the capacity of people to pay and to permit the free movement of the population by stepping i.e. advancing from a poorer to a better class of housing. This is no longer the case.'

In 1930 the sanitary inspector reported that overcrowding was a common feature of life amongst the poor, and that housing conditions of the poor had not improved; indeed he said 'the general work of the sanitary inspectors reveals that increasing numbers of houses are becoming sub-let and sub-divided'. Statistical evidence, collected from a special survey of people in back-to-back houses showed that there was a high incidence of scarlet fever, diphtheria, and TB in these houses even if they were not overcrowded. The MOH frequently urged the council to build houses to be let cheaply, to house those who could not afford the 8s or 9s which most corporation and many privately owned houses cost to rent. In 1934 he urged: 'There is a great need for houses built on different lines from the semi-detached or detached houses as these are beyond the small wage earner, and those who have been unemployed for long periods.' From this kind of evidence it appears that while the standards of living of the employed improved in Darlington, those of the poor and the unemployed fell. In this respect the unemployed of Darlington were probably worse off relatively, and perhaps also absolutely, than those of Stockton and Middlesbrough, where the depression caused a general levelling of standards, and health services counteracted some of the problems of poverty.

Other than the connection between unemployment and poor housing, the Darlington health reports make few direct links between unemployment and health. There is again a tacit assumption that unemployment might lower health standards, because from time to time they state that improvements have taken place 'in spite of unemployment'. As in Stockton, though, the reports of school inspectors do suggest that some children in the town were inadequately fed.

In 1928 the school examinations revealed only twenty-six cases of children out of 3,783 who were classified as mal-nourished, but the eye specialist reported, 'during the past year an unusual number of children have been brought to the clinic suffering from night blindness due to a deficiency of vitamin A. These children invariably belong to families whose parents are earning poor wages or, are out of work.' In the same year it was also reported that there had been no provision of school meals that year (apparently they had been given before) and the school inspector's report commented 'This is a matter for regret particularly during the period of distress and unemployment in the town.' He asserted that most parents could afford to feed their children but some could not. The report of 1929 stated that thirty-six children were found to be suffering from malnutrition, but added 'the Medical Officers have been struck by the large number of children who were found on examination to be of subnormal nutrition, either due to improper feeding or poor environmental conditions'. Thirteen per cent of the children they examined were classified as suffering from subnormal nutrition. No indications from the Darlington health reports can be found to suggest whether these conditions were new, or just newly found, but it does seem from various pieces of evidence that the unemployed of Darlington did not enjoy the improvements of health which their employed fellows did.

The psychological impact of unemployment

Hardly anywhere in the health records of the three towns is there anything said of the psychological impact of unemployment. The only, indirect, reference to mental health is in the Darlington reports which listed the number of suicides recorded each year. It is difficult to say how accurate these figures are, and because they are from such a small sample they give little helpful evidence (see Table 36).

Table 36 *Number of suicides recorded in Darlington, 1920–39*

Year	Number of suicides
1920	2
1921	?
1922	9
1923	9
1924	17
1925	6
1926	7
1927	21
1928	8
1929	5
1930	9
1931	7
1932	8
1933	11
1934	11
1935	10
1936	11
1937	11
1938	5
1939	8

Source: Compiled from Darlington MOH reports, 1920–39.

Various national studies, though, had found a definite connection between unemployment and psychologically induced illnesses. The Pilgrim Trust found many people suffering from strain, and quoted the findings of a Dr Halliday who found that many unemployed people, in a survey he made, were suffering from some kind of psychosomatic illness.[43] A study done by another doctor, quoted by Beales and Lambert, had very similar findings.[44] These results were not disputed by the authorities; in 1932 the Chief Medical Officer in Britain said that people who had been out of work for long periods often suffered from depressive illnesses.[45] In spite of strong evidence on a national level, information for Teesside on this question is rather sketchy. Occasionally a local newspaper reported the suicide of a man who had been out of work for a long time and was very depressed. One informant described how his father had attempted suicide after his dole money had been disallowed.[46] Many more interviewees back up the impression given by the contemporary investigators, by referring to unemployed men who became unhappy and listless. Of course these people were not qualified to describe whether these common feelings of unhappiness led to actual illness, but in view of the evidence previously quoted it seems likely to have done in some cases. One interviewee sums up the feelings of many:

'That's the queer part of unemployment. I didn't want to do anything. I used to have to go down to the Labour Exchange every morning, and after that, well perhaps I used to take a walk or come home and read . . . but the fact of being unemployed seemed to take away any desire to do sort of unpaid jobs out of my mind.'[47]

Conclusions

The evidence of all three towns shows that even very high and prolonged levels of unemployment in the inter-war years did not reverse the trend towards better health. The chances of an individual on Teesside being healthier and living longer were better in 1930 than in 1910, and better in 1939 than in 1930, even if he or she were unemployed. There is though, a body of evidence which suggests that high and prolonged unemployment had the effect of retarding the improvements of those years. This is seen in the concerns of health officials in each of the three towns, and to some extent in the relative mortality rates of Stockton and Middlesbrough as against those of England and Wales. However, it is difficult to say exactly what part unemployment played in this retardation because the interrelationships between causes of good or bad health are so complex that it is impossible to isolate one. There is slight but strong evidence, though, that the mental health of some of the unemployed in the three towns suffered. To some extent, therefore, unemployment had a negative effect on standards of health.

Chapter 4

Unemployment and crime

Introduction

The effects that the depression might have had on the levels of crime was another serious contemporary concern. Two of the social investigations of unemployment found cases of unemployed people who turned to crime.[1] Many officials who dealt with offenders believed that unemployment was responsible for many people breaking the law.[2] This concern was taken up by the press, who presumably reflected and instigated anxiety in the population at large.[3] However, Mannheim, in the most comprehensive and careful study of crime in the inter-war years, found that while in some parts of the country there was a correlation between unemployment and crime figures, in others even very high unemployment rates did not cause an increased tendency for people to break the law.[4]

The question of how the depression affected crime is an extremely complicated one on two counts. One is that the very nature of crime, and of criminal behaviour is a controversial question amongst criminologists. For example some criminologists would question the value of using criminal statistics to study crime. Others question the value of social explanations for criminal behaviour, and would also claim that only individual characteristics will explain a person's tendency to break the law.[5] It has been assumed that the crime statistics do give some impression of criminal behaviour, as defined by a particular society, although the limitations of the statistics will be fully considered. Inevitably, this study rests on the basis that social explanations of behaviour (including crime) are valid, but the importance of individual characteristics in determining behaviour will not be forgotten.

The second major problem is that it is not easy to attribute changes in the crime rate to unemployment, because many other factors may have influenced the trend. As with health, deciding exactly what part unemployment played in influencing criminal behaviour is difficult.

Criminal behaviour in this chapter will be considered from two angles. The first will be a study of the crime figures for Teesside, and will seek to discover whether unemployment rates correlated with a tendency to break the law. In this section 'crime' will be seen as breaking the law, and will be referred to as 'lawlessness' not in any pejorative sense but merely to describe that specific type of action. The patterns on Teesside will be shown in their national context.

The second section will be a discussion of what the people of Teesside felt about the extent of crime in the area. This question is important for several reasons. It is a historical commonplace that what people thought was happening is as important as what actually happened, and part of the purpose of this exercise is to discover what people thought was going on, and their reasons for doing so. However, the difference between what people thought happened and what did happen may not be a different perception of the same thing. It is quite possible (and it is often the case) for something to be against the law, but not a crime in the eyes of the local community. Similarly some kinds of anti-social behaviour may not be against the law. Because of the lack of any precise information, it is difficult to know the extent and strength of these community attitudes, but a study of them is very important to understand the whole question of crime and community.

Before embarking on section one, it is important to consider the many problems involved in using the criminal statistics. These are problems which should be borne in mind before any attempt is made to interpret the recorded crime figures.[6] Some of these are quite simply the effects of changes in the law, or of police administration. The most important of these is the fact that in 1932 the method of counting 'indictable offences known to the police' changed. Before 1932 some possible larcenies were counted in a separate list of 'suspected stolen' items. After 1932 this 'suspected stolen' list was abolished, and all possible larcenies had to be categorised as either stolen, or lost property.[7] Naturally, many of them were considered to be larcenies, which accounted for the fact that the number of offences known to the police rose from 159,378 in 1931, to 208,175 in 1932. A similar rise should be expected in the local figures. Also, in 1934 juveniles were counted as everybody up to the age of seventeen, and not sixteen as previously. This misleadingly increased the amount of juvenile crime.

Other incidental influences will affect the crime figures. The inter-war period brought new opportunities for crime. The motor car and bicycle, both often left unattended, could easily be stolen, or have parts of them stolen without much fear of detection on the part of the thief. The number of thefts of bicycles and cars rose tremendously throughout the inter-war period, reflecting the rise in the number of bicycles and cars themselves. These figures naturally swell the crime statistics. There is also the possibility that more professionalism in crime, and greater mobility of criminals boosted the statistics without contributing to any increase in lawlessness in the community at large. If more crimes were being committed by the same people then the crime rate would rise, even though there would be no general increase in lawlessness.

There are other difficulties in understanding the crime statistics which are far more complex. One is the problem of assessing the 'dark number' of unrecorded crime. Various recent studies have shown that certain crimes are frequently unreported, if the victim distrusts the police, has little confidence in their ability to help, or deals with the problem himself.[8] Of course it is impossible to estimate this dark figure, but it is clear that some offences are more readily reported than others. Petty larceny may often go unreported, because the victim sees little point in going to the police, but major thefts and thefts with violence are more likely to be recorded.

Despite these problems criminologists still have to rely on the recorded crime figures. Gatrell and Hadden commented: 'The officially recorded figures are in fact used by modern criminologists on the unproved, though generally uncontested assumption that they do bear a fairly constant relationship to the real incidence of the offence in question.'[9]

A related problem is the one of knowing the mentality behind the collection of the crime figures, because this involves a knowledge of the attitude of the local police. Crime figures are not (as in theory perhaps they should be) a meticulous account of every contravention of the law known to the local police. They reflect decisions made by policemen as to which offences merit their attention, and it is impossible to know certainly on what grounds those decisions were made. There are, though, some influences which commonly affect crime figures, and it is important to bear these in mind. The

Chief Constable of a particular force will have an important effect in determining police policy, and therefore the criminal statistics. Often the number of prosecutions for a particular offence will reflect his concern. This kind of influence is probably greatest in the treatment of such offences so gambling or drunkeness, which some people view more seriously than others, and where it would be almost impossible to note every contravention of the law. In these cases the degree of vigilance encouraged by the Chief Constable would be crucial to the number of prosecutions. If the degree of vigilance encouraged were always constant it might be possible to interpret the figures in the light of any general trend, but this will not necessarily be so. A sudden rise in the number of prosecutions for gambling might just as well be the result of a sudden campaign against gambling, than as the result of an actual rise in the number of offences.

The attitude of the local police force will have a similar effect to that of the Chief Constable. The attitude of the community to a certain offence may well be reflected in that of the local force, who invariably came from that community. For example, oral testimony for Teesside suggests that the local 'Bobby' often dealt with petty crime in an ad hoc and unofficial way. This was particularly common in the case of juveniles, who might be warned, and have the offence reported to their parents. Similarly a respectable man or woman, known to the policeman, could escape with a warning for a minor offence.

This evidence from Teesside is substantiated by Mannheim's study. He found that there was a deep-seated reluctance on the part of the police, the public and various private institutions to bring juveniles before the courts, and came to the conclusion that 'statistics of juvenile delinquency can do little more than indicate the varying degrees of willingness on the part of the police to bring this category of delinquents before the juvenile courts'.[10]

The attitude of the local community will not only be reflected in the behaviour of the police, but in the likelihood of certain crimes being reported to them. Some offences are not regarded as being wrong by a large part of the community, and are therefore rarely reported and often concealed from the police. In inter-war Teesside gambling is just such an offence, and in this case the number of prosecutions could never reflect the full extent of the practice. Besides suppressing some offences, community disapproval may cause an increase in the crime figures for a particular offence. Mannheim found that if a certain crime was given a sudden prominence in the newspapers, the incidence of that offence would often rise soon afterwards, because public awareness of it would encourage people to recognise and report cases.

All these problems will be borne in mind when considering the Teesside crime figures.

Background: crime and unemployment in England and Wales

Before embarking on a local study, it is important to know something of the patterns of criminal behaviour in England and Wales in the inter-war years, and to consider previous discussions on the question of unemployment and crime.

Studies of crime and society began in the nineteenth century, and information available from them provides a useful background to the study of crime in the inter-war years. Gatrell and Hadden concluded that, with certain qualifications, 'the rule that nineteenth-century property crime increased with depression and diminished with prosperity holds true'.[11] In the inter-war years the number of indictable crimes known to the police rose steadily. There were many reasons for this rise, some of which (such as traffic offences) could hardly have any connection with unemployment. Other trends, such as the persistent increase in crimes against property, may have been caused by the depression. S. K. Ruck, writing about the 1920s, felt that these trends (see Table 37) could only be explained in this way.[12]

Mannheim in his full and detailed study of crime in England throughout the whole of the inter-war period also suggested that there might be a connection between the increase of crime and the depression, but he was very cautious about this conclusion.[13] His study showed that it was often the case that fluctuations in criminal statistics did not coincide with fluctuations in numbers of unemployed. The crime rate rose far more just after the First World War than in the depression of the early twenties. In 1921, a year of high unemployment, there was actually a decrease of crimes against property with violence; a category of crime which is often believed to be especially sensitive to economic trends. Also, the number of crimes against property continued to rise even after the depression of the thirties eased, and these trends continued up to the beginning

Table 37 *Indictable offences per 100,000 population reported to the police, 1900–29*

Year	Number
Average 1900–1904	254
Average 1905–1909	289
Average 1910–1914	270
1920	271
1921	272
1922	281
1923	287
1924	291
1925	293
1926	342
1927	320
1928	330
1929	340

Source: S. K. Ruck, The increase in crime in England, *Political Quarterly*, 1932.

of the Second World War. Local studies also show that the connection is by no means fixed. Some areas had a rise in crime which paralleled the rise in unemployment, but others with a high unemployment rate saw little rise in the number of offences. In conclusion Mannheim wrote: 'Unemployment as a causative factor in crime seems to play a widely varying role in different districts. Whilst in some cases there is to be found an almost complete harmony between fluctuations of unemployment and crime, in some others not even the slightest analogy exists.'[14]

There are, of course, many reasons why a connection between unemployment and crime should not show itself in a neat correlation of figures. Other factors might override the effects of depression: the first years after 1919 were very untypical because of the disruption of the aftermath of war, and it is not surprising that easily understandable patterns do not emerge from them. Also, if people had turned to crime during a depression it is possible that they would not return to their former law-abiding ways when prosperity returned, which might partly account for the continued rise in crime figures at the end of the period. The effects of juvenile crime may be linked to more factors than juvenile unemployment, because the effect of having a father out of work could be as great as being unemployed oneself.

Mannheim also included in his study the informed opinion of governors of prisons and heads of remand schools. The evidence from them is less equivocal. 'Hardly anywhere has the overwhelming force of unemployment as a crime producing agency been more clearly recognised than in these documents,' is how he described the light they shed on the subject. These experienced people who worked with convicted criminals usually believed that unemployment was the chief contributory factor towards the swelling of the prison population. Another general conclusion from their reports was that the effect of unemployment was cumulative; that a man was more likely to commit a crime after two years of unemployment than one.

These kinds of assertions were made with even more assurance in the case of juvenile offenders, which backed up the statistical indications of a connection between juvenile unemployment and crime. As a result of this Mannheim wrote of juvenile offenders without his customary caution: 'There are ... many cases on record which show more distinctly that unemployment frequently acts as a direct cause of delinquency.'[15]

All this evidence definitely suggests that of those people convicted of offences in inter-war England some (and we do not know how many) were encouraged to turn to crime by the experience of unemployment. This tendency was more marked in some areas than others; in some places other factors kept the unemployed as law-abiding people. This is very useful information, but as such it is limited. It does not show the relative importance of unemployment and other factors. Nor does it show how likely the average unemployed man was to commit an offence. Section II will consider these questions in a local context.

Section I   Lawlessness on Teesside

Criminal statistics for inter-war Teesside are available from two sources. The first is the Chief Constable's reports for Middlesbrough, and the second the Joint Standing Committee Minutes for County Durham. The figures are presented in six ways. The categories are: 1. Indictable offences reported to the police. These cover all types of offences and no distinction is made between them. 2. The number of prosecutions in different categories of offence, such as offences against the person, offences against property with

and without violence, and so on. 3. Prosecutions for the major
street offences, such as gaming, fighting, begging. 4. Prosecutions
for drunkenness. 5. Lists of offences committed by juveniles. In the
1920s these lists gave only the number of juveniles who appeared
before the courts, but in the 1930s as a result of the general concern
about juvenile crime more detailed lists were kept showing types of
offences committed by juveniles. 6. (In the case of Middlesbrough
only) A list of the numbers of people in receipt of unemployment
benefit or parish relief who were convicted of indictable offences.

The general trend of criminal offences is shown in Tables 38, 39
and 40, which show indictable offences known to the police in
Middlesbrough, and numbers convicted of offences in County
Durham. (Separate figures for Stockton and Darlington are not
available.) These show in both cases an unsteady rise in offences
throughout the whole of the inter-war period. This was quite
typical of the country as a whole, and it is most probable that the

Table 38 *Indictable offences reported to the Middlesbrough police,
1920–38*

Year	Number	% of work-force unemployed
1920	553	n.a.
1921	559	33
1922	640	26
1923	706	n.a.
1924	705	23
1925	591	24
1926	881	40
1927	692	20
1928	604	17
1929	–	14
1930	666	37
1931	812	41
1932	801	45
1933	801	44
1934	832	29
1935	861	22
1936	1061	17
1937	1218	–
1938	1099	22

Source: Compiled from yearly statistics in Middlesbrough Chief Constable's reports.

Table 39 *Numbers convicted of criminal charges in County Durham, 1919–29 (adults only) (February)*

Year	Numbers	Year	Numbers
1919	1,602	1930	2,789
1920	3,223	1931	2,586
1921	n.a.	1932	2,598
1922	2,090	1933	3,116
1923	2,200	1934	n.a.
1924	2,746	1935	3,116
1925	2,298	1936	2,690
1926	2,310	1937	2,837
1927	2,862	1938	2,759
1928	2,773	1939	2,233
1929	2,753		

Numbers convicted of civil offences in County Durham, 1919–28 (adults only) (February)

Year	Numbers	Year	Numbers
1919	1,014	1929	n.a.
1920	1,397	1930	3,656
1921	1,975	1931	2,088
1922	2,029	1932	n.a.
1923	3,936	1933/34	n.a.
1924	5,887	1935	1,827
1925	3,936	1936	2,328
1926	4,196	1937	1,499
1927	6,406	1938	2,456
1928	5,342	1939	2,565

Source: Compiled from annual statistics in Durham Joint Standing Committee Minutes.

rise was caused by much the same things as caused the national trend: increase in population, new types of crime, more professionalism in crime, and in police activity. However, certain patterns within the general trend may be significant. In the case of Middlesbrough there was a sharp increase in the number of offences in 1926, the year of the General Strike, and it seems likely that the unrest and disorder of that year, as well as the poverty suffered by some, caused an increase in offences. The number of criminal prosecutions in County Durham do show a possible connection with unemployment, in that the two years which

Table 40 *Crimes known to the police in different categories of offence in Middlesbrough, 1920–9*

	1920	1921	1922	1923	1924	1925	1926	1927	1928	1929
Offences against the person	38	50	37	36	16	26	31	31	23	45
Offences against property with violence	57	58	56	32	61	74	65	89	94	105
Offences against property without violence	445	451	528	618	560	475	695	540	463	472
Malicious injuries to property	1	8	0	4	3	0	1	1	0	1
Forgery and offences against the currency		15	5	0	47	1	7	22	12	3
Miscellaneous	12	13	14	14	18	15	12	9	12	14

	1930	1931	1932	1933	1934	1935	1936	1937	1938	1939
Offences against the person	48	34	26	25	27	36	11	28	41	
Offences against property with violence	94	73	168	214	122	102	126	132	197	
Offences against property without violence	501	683	590	536	637	709	911	1043	839	
Malicious injuries to property	2	3	2	5	1	2	1	3	12	
Forgery and offences against the currency	8	11	6	15	25	3	4	0	1	
Miscellaneous	13	8	9	8	20	12	8	2	9	

Source: Compiled from annual statistics, Middlesbrough Chief Constables' Reports.

showed a sharp increase in prosecutions, 1920 and 1933 were ones
of heavy unemployment, but the pattern is not repeated in other
years of high unemployment (1922, 1931 and 1932) and so the
connection seems to be tenuous. The general trend of offences in
Middlesbrough showed no clear correlation with unemployment
figures.

The variations in certain different categories of crime, shown for
Middlesbrough on Table 40, give a more detailed picture of the rise
in offences. The most noticeable feature of these is the fact that
during the period there was a substantial rise in crimes against
property without violence, and a smaller but quite distinct rise in
crimes against property with violence. These are statistics which
present least in the way of problems of interpretation. Although the
influence of the attitude of police and community will still have an
effect on these figures, it will not be so marked in these cases as
others. More importantly, these attitudes are far more likely to be
consistent, and in consequence any trend will be more clearly
discernible.

Some of the rise in crimes against property without violence may
be accounted for by the theft of cars and bicycles, but only part of the
increase can be explained away by this. The rise does not show any
direct correlation with unemployment trends, which indicates that
unemployment was not the sole cause of the rise, but in the absence
of other sufficient explanations, it seems reasonable to suggest that
the long-term effects of the depression helped towards the increase.
This seems especially likely as these offences are most sensitive to
economic influences. Of course these figures provide no solid proof,
but they indicate that the possibility of a connection is there.

This possibility was taken seriously by Middlesbrough's Chief
Constable. Between 1924 and 1938 the numbers of adults in receipt
of unemployment benefit or relief who were convicted of indictable
offences were kept (see Table 41). Unfortunately it is not possible to
know how many of those convicted were likely to have committed
an offence even if they were in work and so it is not possible to see
any direct link between lawlessness and unemployment from this
table. However, the numbers are not particularly high; in 1931
there were 116 such cases, out of a total of 812 indictable offences
reported to the police. As we do not know the total number of
offenders, it is not possible to say what proportion of them were
unemployed, but the figures suggest that far fewer than half of

Table 41 *Numbers of people in Middlesbrough in receipt of Unemployment Benefit or Parish Relief convicted of indictable offences, 1924–39*

Year	No.	Year	No.
1924	103	1932	49
1925	148	1933	166
1926	122	1934	111
1927	51	1935	151
1928	30	1936	93
1929	?	1937	129
1930	108	1938	113
1931	116	1939	

Source: Compiled from Middlesbrough Chief Constable's reports, 1924–39.

indictable crimes were committed by unemployed people at a time when unemployment was fifty per cent of the working population of the town. Also, the police reports note that most of the unemployed people had been convicted of drunkenness; an offence which they were unlikely to commit as a result of their unemployment (see Table 42). Indeed it seems that the Chief Constables of Middlesbrough (there were two in the inter-war period) were little concerned about the connection of unemployment with adult crime. In 1922 Chief Constable Henry Riches wrote:

The unemployed . . . speaking quite generally – have conducted themselves exceedingly well, and although great distress still prevails in many homes the town has been singularly free from all forms of petty theft, which reflects to the greatest credit of those who have been so severely punished through no fault of their own . . . I should record that the leaders of the unemployed have always counselled moderation, and that spirit has been faithfully adopted by their followers.[16]

He reiterated this sentiment in subsequent reports, and commented that unemployment relief had gone a long way towards alleviating distress.

It seems that if unemployment was a cause of people turning to crime, as the rise in certain offences sensitive to economic influences might suggest, it was only the case in a minority of people, who may have become professional criminals.

The figures for juvenile crime in Middlesbrough, as was the case nationwide, show a much stronger connection with unemployment (see Table 43). Juvenile offences rose quite dramatically in

Table 42 *Prosecutions for drunkenness in Middlesbrough, Stockton-on-Tees and Darlington, 1911–38*

Year	Middlesbrough	Stockton	Darlington
1911	1,299		
1912	1,316		
1913	1,236		
1914	1,577		
1915	1,469		
1916	938		
1917	518		
1918	201		
1919	555	333	49
1920	1,561	652	104
1921	1,189	349	115
1922	1,314	243	77
1923	1,137	213	71
1924	1,022	216	84
1925	1,034	232	86
1926	889	139	88
1927	1,235	216	97
1928	1,006	242	115
1929	842	221	91
1930	630	218	71
1931	423	212	68
1932	236	71	33
1933	224		
1934	277		
1935	289		
1936	377	149	33
1937	376	103	39
1938	317	123	59

Source: Compiled from Statistics in Middlesbrough Chief Constable's Reports.

Middlesbrough during the inter-war period. In the early twenties between two and three hundred juveniles appeared before the courts, and by the late thirties each year there were between six and eight hundred. Some of this rise is accountable for by the change of 1934, when juveniles were counted as anyone under seventeen, instead of sixteen as previously, but this could by no means account for the total increase. It might also be the case that the increase in the statistics represented an increase in concern about the number of young offenders. The reports of two successive Chief Constables

Table 43 *Young people appearing before
the Middlesbrough Juvenile Courts,
1921–38*

Year	No.
1921	240
1922	415
1923	342
1924	309
1925	296
1926	407
1927	315
1928	278
1929	110
1930	365
1931	407
1932	473
1933	409
1934	654[a]
1935	621
1936	836
1937	688
1938	646

Note: (a) In 1934 young people up to the
age of seventeen were counted as juveniles,
and not sixteen, as previously.
Source: Compiled from figures in Middlesbrough Chief Constable's Reports,
1921–38.

testify to an increasing concern about the extent of juvenile crime in
Middlesbrough, which was also felt nationwide. However, this can
only explain some of the increased interest in juvenile crime which
was almost certainly the product of a real problem, for the statistical
increase was too great to be accounted for by newly-awakened police
vigilance, and all the available evidence of the state of juvenile crime
in England shows that the increase was genuine enough.

The pattern of the juvenile offences shows a probable connection
with the depression. Large numbers were prosecuted in 1922, when
unemployment was high, there was a falling off and a second
increase in 1926, and then another fall until the depression of the
thirties. As was the case nationally the rise continued in the late
thirties after the depression began to ease.

Comments from Chief Constables' reports stress this connection. Of Middlesbrough's two Chief Constables of the period, the first, Henry Riches, was most concerned. In 1923 he wrote a special report on 'Juvenile Depravity and Unemployment'. In this report he said that 'there is in the town a volume of misery and moral deterioration brought about by unemployment' and that 'employment is the only way of stopping this serious deterioration of character'.[17] He reported that unemployed youths were far more likely to break the law than unemployed men. Riches made this kind of comment repeatedly during this term of office, and showed a particular concern at the increase of shopbreaking by young offenders. This problem was further investigated by Riches' successor, Donald Head, who took over in 1933. In 1936 he reported that of sixty-six persons apprehended for shopbreaking fifty-nine were juveniles. He also commented that juvenile gangs were becoming more professional in approach. He was, though, less convinced of the connection of unemployment. In 1933 he wrote 'I am of the opinion that one of the main factors (in juvenile crime) is the absence of rigid discipline in the home.'[18] This could, of course, have been a by-product of unemployment among parents, and the apathy and demoralisation it seemed to engender.

This divergence of opinion between two men equally well-qualified to pass judgement highlights the whole problem of assessing the connections between unemployment and crime. As there are normally many reasons which might make an individual commit an offence, it is difficult to isolate one and assess its importance, and the assessment may depend a great deal upon personal opinion.

The weight of contemporary opinion, though, went with Riches. The reports of prison governors and heads of remand centres who came to know offenders personally, (which most Chief Constables did not) testify to the effects of the unemployment on young offenders, and their conclusions were much in accord from all parts of the country. Donald Head's assertions about a weakening of home discipline run counter to the oral testimony of ordinary Teessiders and three teachers who related that in many homes discipline was strict, but that the phenomenon of some children being little cared for by their parents was by no means a new feature of Teesside life in the inter-war period. Mannheim found

Table 44 *Middlesbrough juvenile crime – numbers of persons charged with the most frequent offences, 1930–8*

Offences	1930	1931	1932	1933
Housebreaking	–	5	2	5
Breaking into shops, etc.	3	7	18	19
Larceny from the Person	2	6	7	1
Larceny by a servant	1	2	4	2
Larceny (simple)	86	126	143	111
Assault (common)	1	1	1	16
Footballing	42	74	69	68
Offences concerned with bicycles	69	44	29	32
Offences concerned with motor cars	3	2	17	16
Malicious damage	17	10	30	53
Discharging missiles	22	23	23	38
Gaming	11	10	9	17
Begging	2	2	3	–

Offences	1934	1935	1936	1937	1938
Housebreaking	5	12	13	13	14
Entering shops, warehouses, etc.	20	13	46	32	28
Larceny of pedal cycles	4	21	11	21	14
Larceny of unattended vehicles	11	–	4	17	9
Larceny from shops and stalls	80	39	97	119	62
Larceny from automatic machines and meters	5	13	7	18	5
Other simple larcenies	95	97	112	121	104
Malicious damage	36	60	58	38	45
Discharging missiles	22	28	35	8	15
Footballing	102	70	96	35	44
Gaming	39	50	27	32	37

Source: Compiled from figures in Middlesbrough Chief Constable's Reports, 1930–8.

that a young man who was unemployed, and who came from an unstable family was more likely to commit an offence than one who was simply unemployed, but as the unstable background normally preceded the youth's unemployment it seems reasonable to suppose that the latter was the final cause of him breaking the law.[19]

It seems, therefore, that there was a definite link between juvenile unemployment and crime, but only a weak and tentative link between crime and unemployment amongst adults. This could easily be explained by the fact that while people who lost their job after some years of work had already established their own moral standards, young people who had never had a job entered the adult world with little prospect of any satisfaction or reward except from crime, and their attitudes changed as a result. However, some evidence suggests that again it was a minority of juveniles who turned to crime. The Chief Constables' reports for Middlesbrough frequently refer to the fact that gangs of youths were becoming more professional in their approach to crime, and that certain gangs were committing a large number of offences. This suggests that some of the increase of juvenile crime could be accounted for by a large number of offences committed by a relatively small number of people. The 'gang' explanation was popular in the inter-war years, but there was little hard evidence for it. One contributor, however, describes the activities of a 'prigging' gang. (See p. 126 post.)

Not all offences increased in the inter-war period. In each of the three towns under study convictions for drunkenness decreased, and in the case of Middlesbrough and Stockton drunkenness offences fell each time unemployment rose. There seems to be a clear economic correlation here with fewer people being able to afford to drink to excess as the numbers of unemployed grew. This change was commented upon by the *North Eastern Daily Gazette*, who welcomed it as one of the few beneficial effects of unemployment.[20]

Table 45 shows the number of street offences – gambling, begging, fighting – which show no discernible pattern throughout the period. The figures for these offences are the most sensitive to the effects of police activity and attitude, which would account for this, but also the lack of distinct pattern indicates that the community as a whole became noticeably neither more disorderly nor well-behaved during the years of the depression.

This confirms the general impression of all the figures except those for juvenile crime. Many unemployed people continued to be as law-abiding as they had been before, in the face of poverty and a disruption in their lives which could easily have made them bitter and turn to crime. A minority, though, often people with other difficulties besides unemployment, probably did start to break the law; and a larger minority of juveniles did so also. The general impression, however, of Teesside in the depression is of a place with a continued stability in the community, despite the strains and

Table 45 Principal street offences in Middlesbrough, 1918–32

Offences	1918	1919	1920	1921	1922	1923	1924	1925	1926	1927	1928	1929	1930	1931	1932
Abusive words and obscene language	50	66	126	132	102	70	95	101	90	105	77	25	17	73	–
Assaults on constables	24	39	102	75	57	60	60	51	55	46	56	33	27	23	7
Betting and bookmaking	–	25	34	12	63	38	18	19	46	7	33	26	13	–	–
Begging	5	4	11	14	21	19	12	13	11	13	12	10	14	9	9
Brawling	3	10	–	–	–	6	–	1	1	8	–	–	9	–	53
Children trading in streets	4	52	12	8	3	2	–	–	–	1	–	–	–	–	–
Damage to property	35	67	206	57	37	24	35	50	46	50	60	49	24	–	58
Fighting, etc.	2	14	15	27	17	26	24	32	21	31	41	29	37	17	17
Footballing	28	74	187	238	343	271	272	194	207	193	136	130	91	152	–
Gaming	81	75	70	32	36	92	158	65	119	102	59	118	77	134	134
Obstructing footways	6	28	45	30	26	66	56	10	53	19	25	27	53	79	33
Offences to owners of vehicles	10	16	44	57	15	17	18	14	12	11	16	11	16	–	13
Prostitution	11	14	6	5	11	10	8	3	11	3	–	7	7	21	5
Discharging missiles	13	7	7	5	30	28	20	75	33	31	37	31	28	37	24
Unlicensed ticket porters	–	4	2	–	–	8	3	3	2	–	–	–	–	–	–

Source: Compiled from Stockton and Middlesbrough Chief Constable's reports, 1919–39 (no figures available after 1932).

difficulties of the inter-war years. This will be discussed further in the next section.

Section II   The community attitude to crime

The prepared list of questions for interviewees in this study did not originally include the subject of law and order, but it was a subject on which a number of interviewees talked unprompted, and in later interviews a question was put on this subject. Most people commented on how little crime they remember in inter-war Teesside, and even those who looked back on the twenties and thirties as hard times best over still seemed to feel that the disappearance of law-abiding tendencies of those days was something to be regretted. The purpose of this section is to examine these views, and see what light they shed on the subject of unemployment and crime.

Typical statements on the subject are these: 'There was a very strong regard for law and order in the unemployed thirties. At that time you'd expect the crime rate to rise. It didn't. People respected the law in those days . . . morality in those days was far superior.'[21] Or: 'There was none of this violence there is today. People didn't lock their doors. I don't think half of them had a key.'[22]

The assertion that Teesside was a strongly law-abiding community is a familiar theme throughout interviews, but it is clear from the crime statistics that this was not true. Several respondents suggested that there was no increase in crime in the inter-war years, which again is clearly untrue. The illusion that many people had, though, was based in fact. Further discussion of the question of law and order showed that what many people meant when they said that Teesside was a law-abiding place was not strictly that, but that it was a place where they felt secure. They believed that they were safe from attack, and from theft, and that in some almost indefinable way the community in which they lived was under control. This kind of feeling or the reverse belief, can also be an illusion. Increased public awareness of a crime such as mugging may heighten concern and increase many people's feeling that they are at risk from this crime even if the statistics show that the likelihood of them being mugged is very low. Various examples, and individual stories suggest that there was a solid basis for this feeling of security.

The reason for this was that on Teesside there was a definite moral code within most communities, to which the majority of people kept, and which was enforced by the community itself. Sometimes things which were illegal were acceptable within this code, but the presence of what was in fact lawlessness did not worry the interviewees provided that everything was done within it. One man, who had agreed when his wife said 'There was none of this violence there is today' backed up her point by saying 'If two men were fighting, the crowd would see they kept to the rules. If one man went to kick another man the crowd would stop him.'[23]

Street fighting, of course, was against the law, but several interviewees mention fighting on a Saturday night, which they dismiss as a harmless enough activity. The fact that it was against the law and violent did not suggest to these interviewees that they were living in a lawless or violent place, because this activity was controlled by the community.

Another example of this attitude comes in the story of an interviewee who had been an unemployed youth in the early thirties. He readily admitted to having done a number of illegal things. One was taking bicycles, from a bicycle hire firm, using them for a day, and then returning them to the same place in the evening, but without paying for them. He also played snooker for money even though he could not afford to pay his debts if he lost; in which case he would fight his creditor, which seemingly was an honourable way of settling the debt, but he insisted that he and his fellows did not behave irresponsibly: 'We won't do what they do today. We wouldn't break windows. If you broke a window in the street you all had to put a copper a piece and mend it. They break a window today and they're off.'[24] Again the themes of a set code – 'borrowing' bicycles being different from stealing them, and being prepared to fight over a debt, and of a self-policing community – emerge. While being prepared to break the law this interviewee and his friends were conscious that they should not do anything to harm their neighbours or their property, and that if they did they would be expected to make due recompense.

Other ways of breaking the law were quite acceptable to many people on Teesside. It was quite common to gather waste coal from blastfurnaces or railway lines, and although this was stealing in the eyes of the law, few Teesside people thought of it that way. Gambling was a widespread and accepted activity. Several people described the gangs of men who used to play pitch and toss and similar games, and who had well-orchestrated schemes to avoid being caught. In most cases small boys were posted to be on the look out for the police, and would give the alarm when necessary. One interviewee described a complicated escape system for gamblers which used to be used in Stockton:

Now in the side streets there was an elaborate system, different every day, in which two or three front doors were open and two or three back doors, about three streets deep, so that when the police did raid (they used to come raiding probably once a month) there was an organised system of retreat. The bookie would disappear into one house and you were never sure which street he would disappear in, and of course the police were barred, they couldn't go into the house.[25]

What is significant about most of the interviewees who described or took part in such schemes was that they did not in general feel that there was any lack of respect for the police, and often they praised the good job done by their local 'Bobby'.

Oral testimony from three teachers and one man who became a policeman on Teesside confirms the general impression given by other interviewees of a society which was at times unruly but by no means ungovernable. One schoolmaster who taught boys up to the age of fourteen in central Middlesbrough said that 'mild hooliganism' was not uncommon, but there were rarely serious incidents and that the boys never resented being caught by the police, or other people in authority.[26] He said that these boys looked on certain kinds of mis-behaviour as a game they would play with the police, but if the police caught them they were beaten. Former teachers and pupils alike described co-operation between parents, police and teachers to discipline children. Any child caught doing something wrong by a policeman would risk having its behaviour reported home to its parents, and children who were punished at school risked extra chastisement at home if their parents found out.

What emerges from the comments of many of the interviewees is not a picture of an impeccably law-abiding society, and one which by many people's standards was rather harsh, but one in which most people felt secure, because they believed that they were not threatened by any illegal behaviour. The experience of one interviewee, a Mr McGee from Middlesbrough, is a good illustration of the tough but disciplined world in which many Teessiders lived.

McGee was a member of a large family, who was a teenager and young man during the thirties. He had a stepfather who was not prepared to keep him, and so he had to leave home at fourteen and live off his wits, with a little help from siblings but no prospect of permanent work on Teesside. We always had to be looking for ways of earning money or food, and if this meant temporarily joining the Salvation Army (he was a Catholic) or visiting the wake of a stranger for a cup of tea or a bowl of soup he was not above either of these. 'I'd join anything for a bowl of soup, me.' McGee relied on charm, persuasion or persistence to get a number of the short-term jobs such as singing in pubs, but he insisted that 'I never cadged, really, I earned it.' Like other teenage boys he had no compunction about 'borrowing' bicycles, and on one occasion when he and a friend had managed to get to London to look for work he was prepared to lie to the landlady by saying that they were in work, and then to leave at the end of the week without paying any rent. If he was cheated, he took the law into his own hands. On one occasion he worked for a week for a window cleaner who refused to pay him his due of 5s, 'And I took the ladder from underneath him and all the family came out fighting me . . . I was getting me five bob's worth.'

McGee, though, made it clear that he believed that at least most of his actions were responsible. It was he who described boys paying for broken windows (see page 123). Most of the time he kept within a code of behaviour which he felt to be important.

The reason why the Teesside code held up reasonably well during the depression was probably because it was designed by, and for, a poor community where life could be both hard and harsh. In particular it held that the property of neighbours was not to be touched, (as was quoted before, most people did not lock their doors) and that people within a small community should ensure that its members behaved. Fighting seems to have been the solution to a number of problems and disputes, but it was monitored by the community as well. In general there was a respect for authority, although this did not mean that every aspect of the law was strictly adhered to.

Oral testimony suggests that many young men broke the law in some way. Sometimes it was in the ways already described, which were not greatly frowned upon by the community, but sometimes in other ways too. The taking of bicycles, which was not regarded very seriously by many Teessiders, increased considerably during the inter-war years; because there were more bicycles and possibly because young men who had no job found this practice an increasing source of diversion. In this way the crime rate would rise without there being any difference in the depravity of the offenders. Sometimes this undoubtedly lead to a clash between the values of the community and the law. One interviewee was caused considerable distress in his youth because what began as a piece of devilment on his part ended with him being caught and fined 10s, a sum which neither he nor his family could pay.[27] (The exact nature of the offence was not given.) Also, some young men drifted into more systematic lawlessness, as the statistics indicate. One interviewee from Stockton describes this:

I joined a prigging gang, six or eight in number; main activities thefts from market stalls, at night time. Some would prig sweet stalls, others fruit, the rest pies etc., which were always shared out and eaten in the back streets off the High Street. Ma found out – good hiding and kept in. 'Fortunately' the gang was picked up and sent to reform school.[28]

Another interviewee, who had been a teenage girl in Middlesbrough in the thirties, said in answer to the question whether people turned to crime in the depression: 'Of course they did. Of course they stole and this is the most tragic thing when you come from a family where your motto is to show every kindness to everybody . . . that you could see you and your brothers stealing.'[29]

If the oral testimony does to a small extent back up the statistical and other evidence that juvenile crime was linked with unemployment, it also goes some way to explain why there was not in the inter-war years a strong link between unemployment and crime. The answer seems to lie in the fact that there was a strong sense of community, and strictly enforced community rules; which in any case were geared to a fairly harsh world with occasional hard times. Only the young were prone to abandon these rules, because they grew up into a world which allowed them no vested interest.

Chapter 5

Politics on Teesside

Introduction

Unemployment was one of the major problems which faced the governments of the inter-war years. Two main questions presented themselves: how to deal with the problem of supporting large numbers of unemployed people, and how to tackle the problem of unemployment itself. Inevitably there were party differences on aspects of both these questions, and some of these became electoral issues. However, in the general elections of the inter-war years the wider question of the performance of the economy as a whole was more important than the specific problem of unemployment. Although at least one government broke up chiefly on the performance of the economy, none came to power or fell from it predominantly on the issue of unemployment.[1] In this chapter the importance of unemployment as a party and electoral issue on Teesside will be considered.

Before considering the importance of unemployment as a local election issue, it is necessary to know how it was seen by the different parties on a national level, as this will have influenced the behaviour of local parties and local electors.

The immediate practical problem facing all governments was that of benefit for the unemployed. All governments relied on the insurance principle, which had been established in the 1911 Unemployment Insurance Act, and was confirmed by the Act of 1920.[2] Although the insurance principle was most dear to the Liberals, who had established it, it was subsequently accepted by all parties; although the actual system of benefit was constantly changed and modified.[3] The chief ideological objection to this principle came from within the Labour movement; a minority of Labour supporters advocated 'work or maintenance' or that a standard non-contributory benefit should be paid to every unemployed person as of right, but this idea, which was chiefly held by members of the ILP, never seriously challenged the insurance principle.

There were other problems concerned with the administration of unemployment relief which caused inter-party strife, and national concern. Some of these were caused by the fact that the system of relief was never completely adequate to cope with the size and extent of the unemployment problem, and various temporary measures were taken to attempt to cope with it. During the early twenties it became clear that the insurance scheme was quite insufficient to cover those many people who had worked in insurable occupations, but remained out of work for some time. The system was baled out by a scheme of 'extended benefit' which was given to people whose insurance contributions had run out, but only after a gap of five weeks, when they had to seek help from the Poor Law Guardians. The large numbers of people who then had periodic recourse to the Guardians in depressed or necessitous areas meant a great strain on local rates, and in these areas there was a strong movement to get the gap system abolished.[4] This movement was supported by the Labour Party, which abolished the gap in 1924.

Another contentious issue in the 1920s was the 'Not Genuinely Seeking Work Clause'. Under this clause any unemployed person who could not prove that he had been looking for work was liable to have his benefit stopped. Many left-wing people considered this clause to be unfair, on the grounds that the offender was presumed guilty and had to prove his innocence. However, in spite of objections from the left-wing of the party the First Labour Government did not abolish this clause. The second Labour Government did so in 1929.

The next part of the relief system to cause protest and disagreement was the Means Test which was introduced in 1931 by the National Government. Feelings in the country ran high against the Means Test, and it was the cause of a parliamentary disagreement. The responsibility for the Means Test was laid at the door of the National Government, and some Labour and Liberal MPs attacked the Government on this issue. It was not, though, a specifically Conservative principle, the Labour Government of 1929 had approved the idea of a Means Test but had not stayed in power long enough to put it into operation.

In these various contentious issues the Labour Party always took a sympathetic stance in favour of the unemployed, but their actions were not always much different from those of other parties. The leadership of the Party was reluctant to appear too soft in their attitude, and it tempered the abolition of the Not Genuinely Seeking Work Clause in 1929 with an Anomalies Act, which deprived married women and some other classes of unemployed persons of benefit. This bill was fiercely attacked by the ILP and their idiosyncratic critic, Oswald Mosley, but accepted by the bulk of the Party. The Labour Party did genuinely desire to raise the level of benefits, but this wish was completely at variance with its determination to keep to the orthodox principle of a self supporting Unemployment Fund. On the other hand it was the Conservative-dominated National Government which finally legislated for the unemployed of all categories to be cared for under a central system of relief, funded by National Government, by the Act of 1934, which was described as the act by which 'a Conservative Government Consolidated the Welfare State'.[5]

The problem of how to tackle the problem of unemployment was a serious and difficult one. In the eyes of most politicians unemployment was not a problem to be tackled on its own, but only within the context of correct economic management. If the economy recovered, then unemployment would disappear. Only towards the end of the inter-war period did a few young politicians, notably Harold Macmillan, and Robert Boothby, formulate the idea of a regional policy which would make a direct attack on the special difficulties of depressed areas.

Throughout the whole of the period the bulk of the Conservative Party held the belief that the best response to economic depression was retrenchment and wage reduction. It was believed that when wages fell, prices would fall and industry would revive. Taxation was seen as a way of attracting money away from industry, and therefore in times of depression as little should be raised from taxation as possible. In accordance with this principle, the Party had little faith in the beneficial effects of any government schemes to provide work for the unemployed. Such schemes, it was believed, would use government money just at the time when it could lease be spared, and would hamper further the initiative of private investment when it was most needed. Employment schemes might have a social value, but no economic benefit.

This view was one which, at least until the mid-thirties, was shared by the majority of informed opinion, and by many of the Conservative's political opponents. The policy which most clearly distinguished the Conservatives in economic matters was their belief in tariffs as a way of protecting export industries. The Conservatives argued that the days of free trade were over, and that the export industries, which were particularly weak during the inter-war years, needed a protective tariff. Although, this was the most distinctively Conservative solution to Britain's economic problems, it is likely that it was not the strongest appeal to the electorate.[6] The Conservative Party was identified with the orthodox economic policies, even though they were not their only advocate, and it was on this issue that many people were likely to vote.

In practice, at least, the bulk of the Parliamentary Labour Party agreed with the orthodox diagnosis of how best to cure economic depression. Certainly both Ramsay MacDonald and his Chancellor of the Exchequer, Philip Snowden adhered very rigidly to this view of the economy.[7] There was, though, a fundamental ideological difference between Labour and Conservative parties on economic matters. The Labour Governments of the inter-war years were committed to the idea that the only permanent cure for economic ills was a completely socialist economy. Unemployment, therefore, was seen as being the inevitable result of the workings of the capitalist system. Paradoxically, this belief in the need for totally radical changes in society resulted in a policy of fatalistic inaction on the part of some Labour Ministers, who believed that there was no point in trying to cure unemployment under a capitalist system that they were not ready to change.[8] Not all Labour supporters were so Utopian in attitude, and many were in any case prepared to embark on contra-cyclical relief works on humanitarian grounds. The Labour Government of 1929 spent almost £77 million on unemployment relief works, a scheme which the National Government wound up almost completely.[9]

The Liberal Party, under the aegis of Lloyd George, rejected orthodox methods of dealing with economic depression, and put forward a plan to counteract unemployment by public spending. In doing this it adopted the ideas of radical economists, who by the end of the 1920s were beginning to formulate the idea that public spending might give a boost to a depressed economy. These economists, the best known of whom was John Maynard Keynes, argued that if a depression was sufficiently severe then it might not in fact correct itself, as classical economics decreed. This would have to be done, they argued, by an artificial boost to the economy such as massive government spending. Once the initial boost to the economy had been made, it would recover under its own momentum, and in this way providing work for the unemployed could actually cure unemployment. The increased incomes people would get would lead to increased spending power, which would generate more trade and thus 'the forces of prosperity . . . work with cummulative effect'.[10] In support of these ideas the Liberal Party consistently advocated heavy government spending. In the election of 1929 the Liberal Party manifesto was heavily based on a bold scheme on these lines, from the Liberal Pamphlet 'We can conquer unemployment' which advocated spending £250m on public works schemes, which would be financed by government loans.

The influence of Keynesian ideas was also seen in policies put forward by MPs of other parties. In the Labour ranks a prominent Keynesian rebel was Oswald Mosley. He was a member of the Labour Unemployment Committee in 1929–30, and put to his party a radical scheme to counter unemployment with large scale public works, as in the Liberal plan, but also state credit for industrial expansion, early retirement pensions, banking reforms and import controls. This plan, which was a mixture of Keynesian ideas and Mosley's own socialist ideas was firmly rejected by the Labour Party, and after its rejection Mosley left to form his own party, with little support from his former Labour colleagues.[11] During the 1930s some of the younger backbench Conservative MPs demonstrated an interest in Keynesian ideas, and one historian has suggested that the economic divisions of the inter-war years were not between parties but between economic conservatives and economic radicals.[12] However, the majority of the Conservative Party rejected radical ideas because of the need for government borrowing, as well as a serious distrust of their feasibility, and the majority of the Labour Party rejected them either on similar grounds or because they saw them as mere tinkering with a defunct system.

The result of attitudes to the problem of unemployment in different parties was not a great practical difference of policy, but there were still distinct choices before the electorate on the issue of unemployment. The Labour Party had an avowed sympathy with the

plight of the unemployed, and were committed to the idea of raising
benefits (something which they only once felt able to do) and to
providing work schemes for the unemployed. The Conservative
Party was closely identified with economic orthodoxy, and
although Labour also followed sound orthodox strategies they
could never be their champion in the same way as the Conservatives. The Conservatives were also firm advocates of protection,
whilst the Liberal and Labour Parties were in favour of Free Trade.

There were also two radical alternatives put to the electorate.
One was the proposition that only socialism could cure the
country's economic ills, which included unemployment, and
however disappointed they may have been by the actions of two
Labour Governments, people who believed this would naturally
vote for the Labour Party. The Liberal Party also consistently put
forward Keynesian ideas after 1929, and from this time these were
an option open to British voters.

It is difficult to tell how the British electorate reacted to these
specific choices, and thus to judge how unemployment affected
voting patterns, because the politics of the era were not even fights
between different political approaches; they were dominated by the
decline of the Liberal Party, the rise of Labour and the consequent
major strength of the Conservative Party, in the face of a weak and
divided opposition. However, Chris Cook has demonstrated that
support for the Labour Party held up well in the depressed areas
right through the period, and even at times when Labour's national
support faltered.[13] The Conservative Party was in any case in a very
strong position, but the weight of support for the National
Government in the 1930s was in part due to the fact that the
majority of the nation trusted to orthodox economic strategies to
guide Britain through depression. Conversely the Keynesian ideas
of the Liberal Party made little impact on the British voter. In view
of the Liberal Party's weakness in 1929 it would indeed have been
surprising if Lloyd George's manifesto had rallied much support,
but the ideas suggested were too new and too radical to be
considered by the average British voter.

The political response on Teesside

Each of the towns under study was of a different political
complexion, which makes them interesting case studies of political

behaviour during the inter-war years. Middlesbrough was a traditional Liberal stronghold, and Middlesbrough West was almost unique in that it remained a Liberal seat during the whole inter-war period.[14] Stockton was a traditional Liberal seat which followed the more usual inter-war pattern of a weakening of Liberal support, which resulted in its becoming a marginal Labour/Conservative seat. Darlington was a traditional Conservative constituency, which was once, in 1929, captured by Labour.

The task of considering how politics on Teesside were influenced by the experience of unemployment was difficult: in many cases the evidence available was frustratingly sparse, and that which presented itself was in many cases contradictory. Much of the evidence came from local newspapers, which are not, of course, necessarily a reliable guide to the majority of local feeling. It was possible to track down a fairly good set of election addresses of the candidates in general elections, which do give a superficial picture of the prominent issues in each election, but no detailed analysis of local politics could be made from these. Most of the minutes of local parties were lost, with the exception of some for the Conservative Party in Middlesbrough. It was the same story for Trade Union records and those of the Trades and Labour Council. In particular, oral testimony provided less than might have been hoped for, and the reactions received were often contradictory.

The study of the political response on Teesside will be considered from two angles. The first will be the response of the politicians: how important unemployment was as an electoral issue in their appeals to the electorate. This will take the form of a case study of each town. The second will be the electorate's response, and much of the evidence for this will be taken from oral testimony.

Middlesbrough
The political complexion of the two Middlesbrough seats appears, from the patterns shown in Table 46, to be decidedly unusual, with one ward remaining Liberal and the other won at some point by each of the three main parties, but it can be explained to a certain extent in terms of local political trends. The continued Liberal dominance in Middlesbrough West was due in part to a strong Liberal tradition and equally importantly to a local weakness in the Conservative Party. Middlesbrough's Liberal character had been enforced by a large Free Trade Lobby, and non-conformist support

Table 46   *General election results in Middlesbrough, 1922–35*

1922				
Middlesbrough East			*Middlesbrough West*	
J. W. Brown (C)	885		T. Thompson (Lib.)	16,811
M. Conolly (Lab.)	7,607		P. N. Levik (NL)	7,422
P. Willams (Lib.)	6,295			9,389
Conservative gain	1,278			

1923				
East			*West*	
P. Williams (Lib.)	9,241		T. Thompson (Lib.)	16,837
M. Conolly (Lab.)	7,714		D. White (Lab.)	7,413
J. Reid (C)	5,390			

1924				
East			*West*	
E. Wilkinson (Lab.)	9,574		F. K. Griffith (Lib.)	10,717
Warde-Allan (C)	8,647		A. R. Ellis (Lab.)	10,628
P. Williams (Lib.)	6,668		Sadler (C)	8,213

1929				
East			*West*	
E. Wilkinson (Lab.)	12,215		F. K. Griffith (Lib.)	14,674
E. J. Young (Lib.)	9,016		A. R. Ellis (Lab.)	13,328
J. Wesley Brown (C)	8,275		A. E. Bauder (C)	8,813

1931				
East			*West*	
E. J. Young (NL)	18,409		F. K. Griffith (NL)	26,011
E. Wilkinson (Lab.)	12,080		H. Keige (Lab.)	13,040

1935				
East			*West*	
A. Edwards (Lab.)	12,699		F. K. Griffith (Lib.)	13,689
Chetwynd Talbot (C)	12,632		H. Keige (Lab.)	12,764
E. J. Young (Lib.)	3,555		Spofforth (NL)	11,387

Source: Compiled from reports in the *North Eastern Daily Gazette*.

for the party, which continued during the whole of the period. However, a co-incidental weakness in the administration and organisation of the Conservative Party made an equal contribution to the Liberal strength. In most British constituencies at this time the Conservative Party won a considerable number of votes from the declining Liberals, but the Middlesbrough party was not in a position to do this.[15] This is evident from the fact that in 1922 and 1923 the Conservatives did not put forward a candidate in Middlesbrough West; and the records of the Local Conservative Association which survive for the 1930s confirm that the local party was hardly strong. In the 1930s the Association was persistantly in financial trouble: in 1932 it had an overdraft of £1,769, and the overdraft was not cleared until 1934. It is not possible from the evidence available to say exactly why there was this local weakness, which was especially apparent in the West Ward, but there were complaints which crept into the Association's minutes about organisational inefficiency. The most serious of these came from Mr Chetwynd Talbot, the defeated candidate of 1935 who strongly criticised the local electioneering organisation, and refused to stand as candidate again until the party 'put its house in order'.[16]

The Conservative weakness in Middlesbrough West did not by any means leave the Liberals in an unassailable position, for during the period the Labour Party made considerable inroads into its strength. The number of votes polled for the Labour Party in this Ward increased fairly steadily throughout the period; and in 1924, a year when Labour achieved a national success, the Labour candidate came within eighty-nine votes of winning the seat. In years when the party achieved less national success this was to a degree reflected in Middlesbrough West, but the Labour vote still held up very well. It seems that if the Conservative Party had been stronger, and had taken more votes from the Liberals, Middlesbrough West would have followed the pattern of many other similar industrial constituencies, and become a marginal Liberal/Labour or Labour/Conservative seat, with the Labour Party gaining control at some point during the inter-war period.

This pattern did in fact happen in Middlesbrough East. As East Middlesbrough contained more of the poorer districts of the town it might seem that the Labour Party was more likely to be successful there, but in fact the Labour share of the vote in East Middlesbrough was little greater than in the West. In the East Ward there were conditions in favour of all three parties: the Liberals had a tradition of strength and support which did not finally wane until 1935, the Conservatives were able to capitalise on the incipient weakness of the local Liberals, and the Labour Party grew in strength throughout the period. Each party might at any time benefit from the divided opposition, and indeed each party was in control of the seat at some point. Labour won the seat on the occasions when the party also took office – in 1924 and 1929. In 1931 the Labour vote held up well but faced only one opponent, a National Liberal, and so lost the election. When in the next election there was again a three cornered fight Labour won again. By the end of the period the Liberals were a minor force in the Ward, and the seat had become a marginal Labour/Conservative one.

The question of how important the issue of unemployment was in Middlesbrough's own electoral battles is difficult to determine in the same way as it is difficult to isolate the issue in national trends. The growing strength of the Labour Party in both Wards, though, provides a strong indication that it was an important factor. Chris Cook demonstrated that the Labour vote held well in the depressed areas, even in times when the party's total electoral fortunes were low. This was exactly the pattern in Middlesbrough. Table 47 shows Middlesbrough's similarity with other depressed areas.

The issues on which the Middlesbrough elections were fought also provides an insight into the relative importance of unemploy-

Table 47   *Areas of highest unemployment, 1932*

Borough	% unemployed	1931 Labour vote as % of 1929
Sunderland	36·6	93·4
South Shields	35·9	108·3
Merthyr Tydfil	35·8	108·5
West Hartlepool	34·7	130·8
Middlesbrough East	27·7	98·9
Middlesbrough West	27·7	97·8
Newcastle East	26·9	83·8
Newcastle West	26·9	80·2
Rhondda East	25·9	116·2
Rhondda West	25·9	99·1

Source: J. Stevenson and C. Cook, *The Slump*, London, 1979, p. 107.

ment as an electoral issue. The problem of unemployment was continually raised by candidates of all parties, in speeches and election addresses, and each one was keen to demonstrate that he or she had the best, or only solution to the problem. On this issue the Conservatives usually stressed the need for industrial revival through a policy of retrenchment, the Liberals advocated a policy of public spending, and the Labour candidates more frequently expressed concern about the level of benefit. Probably the last approach had most effect on unemployed voters, because it responded to an immediate problem. Candidates of all parties frequently expressed the opinion that unemployment was the most important political issue of the day. The Means Test came under considerable attack after 1931 from both Liberal and Labour spokesmen, and in 1931 the Liberal candidates were at pains to point out that the previous Labour Government had agreed to a Means Test, and to limit Unemployment Benefit to 26 weeks.

Unemployment, then, was a rallying cry of all three parties which masked their different policies, but these different policies were still important in political campaigns. There were other rallying cries which were again used by each party; one was social reform and the other was the housing question. These, and especially the former, were mentioned in speeches and addresses at least as frequently as unemployment, and again each party claimed to have the best approach. For example, in the 1923 campaign the final brief message to electors put in the *North Eastern Daily Gazette* mentioned social reform.[17] Trevelyan Thomas said that the Liberal Party was for 'progress and free trade', the Labour candidate stresses the importance of reforming legislation, and the Conservative candidate summed up his campaign by saying that the Conservative Party was for social reform and the leadership of Baldwin. It is possible that the keen interest shown in reform by all candidates reflected the fact that Middlesbrough was a depressed town with many social problems, but the issue of social reform also hinged on another question – the clash of political philosophies which was strongly brought out by the rise of a new party and the decline of an old one.

This ideological battle was waged with considerable vigour in most of the elections of the period, particularly between the Middlesbrough Liberal and Labour parties. The Middlesbrough Liberals clearly felt that they were always in danger of losing support to the Labour Party, and the Liberal candidates similarly believed that in order to win votes they had to present a convincing alternative to the Labour reforms. The two Liberal candidates of the twenties made the Liberal alternative to Labour the focus of most of their speeches. They both stressed that the Liberals were a progressive party, but one which believed in individual freedom (which they claimed the Labour Party did not) and did not foster class war. After the Labour Party achieved office, the Liberal candidates were persistently critical of their achievements in the field of social reform. Perry Williams's election address in 1924 claimed that the Labour Government dissolving when it did had 'destroyed the progressive majority in the House of Commons' and went on to point out that 'after eight months of Labour rule the housing problem is as acute as ever' and concluded by saying, 'Liberals as much as Socialists deplore existing conditions; they believe that these can be remedied by reforming the existing system, and not by attempting social and industrial revolution which has never yet met with success.' Both Conservatives and Liberals in Middlesbrough made much of the Labour Party's interest in trade and other links with Russia, and the spectre of communism was always kept in the voters' minds.

The response of the Middlesbrough Labour candidates to this type of ideological offensive was somewhat mixed. In the early twenties Labour candidates were mild in approach. James Dundas, in his final message to the electorate in 1923, was content to point out, 'The Labour Party has been instrumental in achieving some of the best legislation of the times.'[18] Ellen Wilkinson, candidate in 1924, 1929 and 1931, was always quite clear in her speeches that she believed in a socialist system, but her election addresses tended to stress the reformist nature of the Labour Party.[19] Martin Conolly and A. Ellis, both Labour candidates for West Middlesbrough, also emphasised the reforming zeal of the Labour Party, rather than advocating fundamentally socialist beliefs, but Alfred Edwards, candidate in 1935 and MP thereafter, was more decidedly left-wing.[20]

It is clear that unemployment was always a background issue in Middlesbrough elections, either as a topic in its own right or as one affected by concerns with the economy. At least as important, though, was the rise of the Labour Party, which while it was helped in this case by being in a depressed area was a movement which took place regardless of unemployment. The direct attacks which non-Labour candidates of both parties made on the political philosophy of the Labour Party were a response to what these candidates realised was a serious threat. They realised that Labour had an appeal to the working class, and were keen to correct the impression that the Labour Party was most likely to instigate social reform.

Stockton-on-Tees

Although the electoral pattern was somewhat different from that in Middlesbrough East, the underlying trends seem to be much the same. Like Middlesbrough, Stockton was a traditionally Liberal seat, but the political trend in this town more closely reflected the national one, and a Liberal decline left the seat to be contested by the Labour Party and Conservatives. Whereas in 1923 the Conservatives lost to the Liberals by seventy votes, a year later the Liberals were at the bottom of the poll, which was their position at every election they contested thereafter. Where Stockton was untypical of the nation as a whole, but similar to Middlesbrough and other depressed areas, was that the Labour vote was always strong, even when the Labour Party lost badly, as in the case of the 1931 election. Stockton became as Middlesbrough East did, and Middlesbrough West would have been but for exceptional Conservative weakness, a marginal Conservative/Labour seat.

The prominent issues in Stockton elections were much the same as those in Middlesbrough. Social reform, unemployment, the debate between Free Trade and Protectionism, and between socialist and non-socialist ideologies were the recurrent themes. In Stockton, though, the question of social reform was most frequently and fully discussed. This was probably because both of the candidates from 1922 to 1931, Frank Riley (Labour) and Harold Macmillan (Conservative) had a very strong personal interest in this question. In his election addresses Riley consistently emphasised more help for the unemployed, for the aged, and for improvements in education. Macmillan also took an interest in the problem of the unemployed, and in the housing question – he wrote many articles in the local papers on the matter.[21] While they were both interested in unemployment, they looked to different solutions. Riley, in common with other Labour candidates, constantly pressed for higher rates of benefit, and during the 1930s he spoke out against the Means Test. Macmillan expressed concern about low rates of benefit, but his main line of interest was a growing belief in the desirability of public works to cure unemployment, and of a regional policy to counteract the specific problems of the depressed areas.[22]

The political battles in Stockton show again that whilst many national interests were of crucial importance in elections, two concerns which were particularly appropriate to the depressed areas, social reform and unemployment, were held as important by

Table 48 *General election results in Stockton-on-Tees, 1922–35*

1922			
	J. Watson	(NL)	12,396
	F. Riley	(Lab.)	11,185
	R. Stewart	(Lib.)	9,041
1923			
	R. Stewart	(Lib.)	11,734
	F. H. Macmillan	(C)	11,661
	F. Riley	(Lab.)	10,619
1924			
	F. H. Macmillan	(C)	15,163
	F. Riley	(Lab.)	11,946
	R. S. Stewart	(Lib.)	8,971
1929			
	F. Riley	(Lab.)	18,961
	F. H. Macmillan	(C)	16,571
	Hayes	(Lib.)	10,407
1931			
	F. H. Macmillan	(C)	24,416
	F. Riley	(Lab.)	18,168
1935			
	F. H. Macmillan	(C)	23,225
	S. Lawrence	(Lab.)	19,217
	G. L. Tosfel	(Lib.)	5,158

Source: Compiled from reports in the *North Eastern Daily Gazette*.

many candidates of all parties, and these subjects were well aired in election campaigns. It seems that the view of a particular candidate on unemployment could not bring him or her victory in the face of a national trend in favour of the opposite party; but a professed interest in the problems of the unemployed was almost a prerequisite of a successful candidate.

Darlington

Politics in Darlington were different from those of Middlesbrough and Stockton in a number of ways. Darlington was a traditionally safe Conservative seat, which was strengthened by the fact that one local family, the Peases, had dominated local politics for many years and there was a strong tradition of loyalty to them. Throughout the inter-war years Darlington remained a fairly safe Conservative seat, but once, in 1929, the Labour candidate was elected. This was chiefly because in 1929 (unlike 1924 and 1931) there was a Liberal candidate who split the non-Labour vote, but it is also indicative of the growing support for Labour which was evident in Darlington as in the other two towns.

The nature of electoral campaigns in Darlington was also slightly different from those of Stockton and Middlesbrough. The same familiar issues were raised, but there was a difference of emphasis, and a considerable difference in tone. Conservative's election campaigns were fought on a strong anti-socialist basis, and they argued that a Labour Government would completely transform the country, undermine all its familiar institutions and customs. H. P. Pease's election address of 1922, aimed at the new women voters, was entitled, 'What Socialism means to Women' and said that in Russia all property was taken away, people had no personal possessions, young children were set to work, marriage and the family was discredited, conscription was enforced and religion abolished. The clear implication was that all those things would happen in Britain should a Labour Government take office. These very extravagant claims were not repeated after the existence of the first Labour Government, but the argument that socialism was alien and dangerous was often repeated. In contrast, the Labour candidate from 1924 was a committed socialist. Whilst many of the other Labour candidates on Teesside were decidedly less left-wing, and preferred to stress the reformist temper of the Labour Party, Arthur Shepherd advocated a completely socialist state. He called for nationalisation of industry and land, and redistribution of wealth, as a permanent way to solve the nation's problems.

This was an ideological battle, which was not directly concerned with the problem of unemployment, but although it was one of the most important issues it was not the only point in Darlington politics. As in the case of the other two towns, social reform was frequently referred to. Candidates of both parties usually spoke of the need for social reforms; housing and pensions were the most frequently mentioned. Unemployment as a separate issue was less prominent in Darlington, but was often mentioned by the three-times Labour candidate Arthur Shepherd. He had an especial

Table 49 *General Election results in Darlington, 1922–35*

1922			
	H. P. Pease	(C)	13,266
	W. Sherwood	(Lab.)	9,045
	T. Crooks	(Lib.)	4,425
1923			
	W. E. Pease	(C)	11,635
	W. Sherwood	(Lab.)	9,284
	R. A. Wright	(Lib.)	6,697
1924			
	W. E. Pease	(C)	15,174
	A. Shepherd	(Lab.)	13,008
1929			
	A. Shepherd	(Lab.)	17,061
	Castlereagh	(C)	15,596
	Richardson	(Lib.)	6,149
1931			
	C. V. Peat	(C)	24,416
	A. Shepherd	(Lab.)	15,798
1935			
	C. V. Peat	(C)	23,310
	A. Shepherd	(Lab.)	18,106

Source: Compiled from reports in the *North Eastern Daily Gazette.*

concern about the plight of those unemployed men who took to the road to look for work, and sought shelter in the casual wards of workhouses on their journeys, and he wrote many newspaper articles on the subject of their treatment in the workhouses.

Conclusions

The issue of unemployment emerges as a perennial and important issue in Teesside politics. The need to solve the problem of unemployment, and to provide for the unemployed was constantly put before the electorate by candidates as an important task to be tackled by their party when in power. Some of the other questions which were given great importance in election campaigns also had a bearing on unemployment. The question of free trade or protection was partly a domestic issue over the cost of living, but also involved a divergence of opinion as how best to manage the economy in times of depression. Some of the Labour candidates believed that socialism was the only ultimate way of curing unemployment, and so socialism was presented to the electorate as the solution.

However, not all important local issues were directly or even indirectly connected with unemployment. The opposition of socialist and non-socialist ideas was quite independent of the depression, although it was perhaps hard fought on Teesside because the depressed areas had a decided tendency to turn Labour. Social reform was a similar case, being an issue independent of the Depression but interest in it was probably heightened by the depression. It is interesting to note that most of the MPs who represented Teesside in the inter-war years had a special interest in social reform. A number were also advocates of new or radical ideas: Harold Macmillan, Ellen Wilkinson, Arthur Shepherd and Arthur Edwards were all prepared to take a radical approach to social problems.[23] It seems that these Teesside constituencies attracted or developed such people.

The response of the electorate to the ideas put forward was difficult to determine exactly. It is fairly clear from the increased support for Labour that many people in depressed areas did feel that this party was the most likely to find a solution to their problems; although whether it was the Labour Party's interest in unemployment, or in social reform that appealed is not so clear, nor is it really possible to say why the Labour Party's programme came

over as more convincing to the electorate. It is possible that this
party's emphasis on higher unemployment benefits seemed a more
immediate attack on their problems than plans to re-organise the
economy. Certainly some issues were of great importance to
individual candidates, but appear to have made little impact on the
electorate. The electorate of Middlesbrough, for example, were just
as happy to vote for the firmly left-wing Ellen Wilkinson as they
were with her more moderate successor. Even the wide distinctions
of political philosophy within the Labour Party seem to have held
little interest for the Middlesbrough electorate. It seems that
although Teesside produced a handful of radical MPs the electorate
was not similarly advanced.

Table 50 *Percentage turn-out in General Elections in Stockton-on-Tees,
Middlesbrough and Darlington, 1918–35*

	Middlesbrough East	Middlesbrough West	Stockton-on-Tees	Darlington	UK
1918	48·4	50·5	unopposed	67·8	55·7
1922	78·8	68·4	85·9	88	73
1923	77·3	68·6	89·5	86·8	71
1924	83·7	83·2	90·2	86·1	77
1929	80·8	82·2	87·1	89·6	76·3
1931	84·5	85	88·4	89·5	76·4
1935	81·1	79·4	86·3	84·8	71·1

Source: F. W. S. Craig, *British Parliamentary Election Statistics 1918–70*,
London, 1968, and *British Parliamentary Election Results 1918–49*,
London, 1969.

To what extent the electorate were politically interested at all is
again a vexed question. Table 50 shows that in all three towns the
electoral turn-out in the inter-war years was higher than in the
nation as a whole; and indeed the general level of turn-out was
sufficiently high to suggest a keen popular interest in politics. All
people interviewed were questioned about whether unemployed
people took an interest in politics, and the answers fell into two
distinct camps. The majority seemed to feel that many unemployed
people felt fairly cynical about politicians. A typical reaction came
from the Middlesbrough man who said, 'Well, I don't think they
were much interested in politics. It never cropped up much except
when it came for the council to be in. But as regards MPs and that

they weren't much interested.'[24] Another man said, 'Well you didn't think much of politicians.'[25]

These reactions are reminiscent of the findings of the Carnegie Trust in South Wales, who interviewed many young men:

The overwhelming majority of men had no political convictions whatsoever. When asked why they invariably replied, 'What does it matter!' . . . It was not so much 'A plague on all your parties' as 'A plague on all your politics'. It has, perhaps, been assumed that because men are unemployed their natural state of want and discontent must express itself in some revolutionary attitude. It cannot be re-iterated too often that unemployment is not an active state; its keynote is boredom − a continuous sense of boredom.[26]

Other informants felt that the people they knew did take strong interest in politics. They spoke of election time being one when feelings ran high. One informant described a time when Harold Macmillan and his wife were pelted with tomatoes and eggs by Labour supporters in Stockton.[27] Others suggested that in some cases the experience of unemployment did alter people's political views. A Middlesbrough schoolmaster said, 'Yes, I think there probably was a connection between politics and unemployment, because when people are . . . people tend to rebel to a certain extent and their rebellion may take them . . . to a political meeting.'[28] A daughter of an unemployed man said, 'I think with a lot of people it was a very bitter experience and it did change their views considerably.'[29]

Some of the people interviewed had taken an active interest in politics, and the individual stories of these people seem to be very pertinent to an understanding of Teesside politics. Most of these people had been deeply influenced by one of the two world wars, and the depression was only a background to their beliefs. The 'Grand Old Men' of Teesside politics had all lived through the First World War, and many of the younger political figures approached (most of whom were not subsequently interviewed) said that their own interest in politics had begun during the Second World War, even if they had not been quite old enough to be politically active during the thirties.

A good example of the former type was Jack Singleton, who throughout the inter-war period worked for his Union, the Trades Council, the Labour Party and then the Communist Party:

And I came into contact with it (politics) in the army. The experiences in the army, and particularly through being a prisoner of war in Germany and all this. I had a pretty wide experience. I must have been a bit attentive to things because they registered you know, and what I saw was in that period, during the formative years of the Labour Party, a very real and honest desire of ordinary people to understand. It could be seen reflected everywhere on Teesside, and as I did myself, anyhow, get on a coal cart in North Ormesby market place and talk to the crowd. The crowd would gather, several hundred people listening to what you had to say . . . And in winter they would take the town hall in Middlesbrough often for this purpose . . . To me it was the most exciting time . . . 'cause I was involved in it up to here.

Singleton went on to describe the fact that the Labour Party in North Ormesby had a hall which was used for all kinds of social events (which proved very popular) and for the work of the Workers' Educational Associations – WEA – which in his view contributed to the rise of the Labour movement by providing stimulating education for eager young people. He concluded, 'I am convinced of that, that the period at the end of the First World War, and particularly at the end of the War, a political consciousness was created.'

Although Singleton went on to describe some of the work which was done by the Labour Party for the unemployed, it was clear from what he said that his own political awakening was not directly connected with the depression; in fact he went on to describe the disillusionment of many hopeful young left-wing men and women of the twenties. His own response to that disillusionment was to join the Communist Party in the thirties.

Another interviewee, much younger than Jack Singleton, explained how his political views had been partly influenced by living through the thirties, but had not actually formulated until he had been away in the Second World War: 'Well, it changed my views to this extent, I became a rabid socialist. When I first was made unemployed I used to read a library book a day . . . So I did a lot of reading, and when I was demobbed from the army I was a rabid socialist.'[30]

This man went on to explain that when he came back from the army he felt that everybody should have life's basic comforts; food and a good home assured, and he felt that the Labour Party would assure this. Another man voiced a similar view. 'I think politically it was obvious that they must have changed . . . and I think it was only through seeing the poverty before the war and the war changed people's attitude.'[31]

A few other interviewees of different political persuasions felt that the experience of the depression affected, directly or indirectly, their political views. One such was Ted Leesson, who was chairman of the Young Liberals in Middlesbrough East from the late twenties. Ted Leesson had worked in the chemical industry during the early twenties, before becoming unemployed. He was brought up in a political household, but was converted to Liberalism by his brother, and was particularly committed to the Liberal approach to unemployment. He said that the Liberal 'Little Yellow Book' was his Bible in 1929. These views, he claimed, were shared by many of the Middlesbrough Young Liberals he knew. In view of the fact that the Liberal Party's policy on unemployment did not impress the electorate as a whole it seems that Leesson's enthusiasm was probably a little unusual, and was fostered by the fact that he was living in a town with a strong Liberal presence, as well as being by nature a politically minded person.

Another interviewee, Councillor Ellenor, a Conservative, expressed the view that it was growing up during the thirties which had formed his Conservative views. The system of self-help, which sustained his own family, and other people of his acquaintance had been very important, and shaped his political consciousness. He too, though, was an example of someone who did not become politically active until after the Second World War.

Two people whose political views had, by contrast, grown during the inter-war years and resulted in them becoming politically active during that time were a couple (interviewed separately) who had both turned to socialism and communism. They were Mr and Mrs Chilvers; they both grew up in the depression and both felt that, in Mrs Chilvers' words 'something was wrong' when they saw crowds of unemployed men. They both looked to the Labour Party and Communist Party for a solution.

Mrs Chilvers was 'brought up in a political household' where her father and older brothers held left-wing views. This background, and her feelings for the plight of her unemployed father and neighbours were what formed her political ideas. She joined the Communist League of Youth and later on the Labour Party. She was certainly unusual in that she was from an early age a person with a strong interest in politics, and a desire to be involved in them, which was fostered by the attitude of her family. Mrs Chilvers was one of the few sources of information the author had about the Communist Party on Teesside. She described it as small, but very active, and said that it did a good deal of work to help

individual unemployed people. Many of its members, she said, were
middle class or educated people, and she clearly found being one of
them an intellectually exciting experience.

Mrs Chilvers was also the only informant to mention the British
Union of Fascists. She believed that they had a strong hold in
Middlesbrough just before the Second World War, and mentioned
that Oswald Mosley had visited Middlesbrough in an attempt to
rally support for his party.

Mr Chilvers was an unemployed youth and then a merchant
seaman in the thirties, usually in work but sometimes unable to get
a job for a few months at a time. He said that the depression
fundamentally affected his political views, which changed 'slowly
and painfully'. However, other things besides the depression
affected him: his self education, his experience of antagonism to the
police in strikes, and his enthusiasm for the Spanish Civil War. He
joined the Labour League of Youth, but became disillusioned with
the Labour Party and later joined the Communist Party. It is
interesting that many of the Teesside people interviewed who
embraced left-wing views were influenced by a number of recurrent
factors: the First World War; the education which was encouraged
for those who joined left-wing groups; and the opportunity which it
provided to meet and become friendly with well-educated and
intellectually stimulating people; the experience of strikes; and the
conditions of the poor and unemployed. Whilst these people were
always interested in the problems of the unemployed it was rarely
this factor alone which persuaded them to political activity. It
seems that it needed more than the depressing experience of
unemployment to make left wing political converts, or indeed any
kind of political converts. People who had undergone the shock and
disruption of one of the World Wars, who had had their
imagination caught by a new education, or by the enthusiasm of a
major strike seemed to be more likely to join a political party;
although when they did their experience of the depression always
influenced their views.

Minority political groups

During the inter-war years there were various groups, diverse in
character and aims, which took an interest either in the problems of
the unemployed, or in unemployment as a political or economic

question. Some were minority political parties, some pressure groups, and one at least a forum for discussion on political and economic questions. Some of these groups also provided social functions for unemployed people, but this will be discussed elsewhere.

Studies of the national political importance of these kinds of groups have shown them to be largely ineffective in changing national policy. Chris Cook in his extensive study of the effects of these groups concluded that despite them, 'Britain emerged from the depression with remarkably little change in the nature of her political institutions and the tenor of her public life.'[32] Contemporary political agitators acknowledged this in their accounts of events; Wal Hannington concluded that a spirit of political listlessness had spelt the failure of the National Unemployed Workers Movement.[33] Allen Hutt explained that even the most politically militant areas of Britain were affected by this lack of interest in politics.[34] In view of what has been said before about the lack of interest shown by many unemployed in conventional political parties, the fact that few of them seemed interested in more specialised or militant groups is hardly surprising.

In general terms the example of Teesside is no different from the national experience. Teesside was not noticeably more revolutionary than other parts of the country, nor did the minority political groups concerned with unemployment drastically affect local issues. However, the particular example of Teesside acts as a reminder that these groups cannot be dismissed out of hand; that at times they could muster considerable support.

The information on these groups is fragmentary, taken from cursory reports in the local press, or from unrevealing comments in official minutes. Some groups are recorded in local newspapers, with their names, but it is quite possible that there were others whose records (if they ever had any) are lost, and they failed to receive lasting publicity. Often Guardians or council minutes refer to 'a deputation from the unemployed' without giving any clue as to where the deputation came from. The Darlington Council Minutes are of a very scanty nature, they never record the process of any decision taken, and indeed sometimes not the decision itself; and so it is quite possible that groups made representations to this body which were not recorded. Most of the records of the Trades and Labour Council, a powerful pressure group on behalf of the unemployed, are lost in the case of each of the three towns. Because of these kinds of difficulties there is a good deal of important information about these groups missing, but there is still some interesting indications of their importance.

The minority political groups fell roughly into two kinds: those which worked continually for the interest of the unemployed during the whole of the period, and those which grew up for a few years and then waned in strength and eventually disappeared. While it might seem that the latter were of less importance, they often were, for a few years, remarkably well supported. These kinds of groups were most active in the early twenties and early thirties; in these years there are various reports of them in local newspapers, and in Guardians and Council minutes. They held mass meetings, outside or in a hall, often the town hall. In the early twenties the chief rallying cry was higher benefits, and in the early thirties protest against the Means Test. Although they were always minority groups, they did attract quite considerable support. This is not easy to measure for the twenties, because no lists of membership are reported, but the fact that meetings were large enough to warrant hiring the town hall suggested that they may have had sizeable support. Local newspapers sometimes give an estimate of membership of the later groups. The Darlington Unemployed Association was reported as having 800 members in 1931, all of whom paid 1d per week.[35] There were a number of similar organisations in Middlesbrough, one, the Middlesbrough Unemployed Association was reported to have 500 members, and another 100 members.[36] Even assuming that 1931 was the year of peak membership for the Darlington Association (which is likely in view of the fact that this was the year of the introduction of the Means Test) the fourteen per cent of the unemployed population which 800 people represents is quite a substantial membership; enough to make it a very important pressure group.

These groups lost membership and impetus quickly, and if they survived it was usually to provide a social function rather than a political one.[37] Ted Leesson, who worked for the Middlesbrough Liberal Party, noted this phenomenon of political interest, especially in left-wing groups waxing and waning. He said that the Depression of the twenties 'brought out the Trotskyists' and that normally moderate Labour People turned more left wing in the early thirties, but that after a year or two people became 'politically listless'.

In view of this information it seems that although these minority groups were to achieve little, the concern of contemporaries that they were a powerful force was justified. Harold Macmillan felt that after 1931 Britain was in a potentially revolutionary state.[38] The same belief was held by Stafford Cripps, John Strachey and Oswald Mosley.[39] They were all wrong, but in the light of the Teesside experience it seems that they could be forgiven for being so.

The various unemployed associations protested on national issues, but they also sent deputations on local issues to the Boards of Guardians, and to the town councils. This role was also adopted by the NUWM, the Trades Council, and a joint committee on unemployment of the Labour Party and the ILP. These bodies carried less spectacular strength, but they had an established reputation, and consistently advocated changes in the treatment of the unemployed, and their strength lay in their endurance and good organisation rather than size of membership. The NUWM, for example, was a small group with an enthusiastic membership. Mrs Chilvers described it thus: 'the NUWM . . . was a great movement, one of the best I think that ever came out of the unemployed, and it gave the men an incentive, they knew they were doing something about it . . . I remember it starting off in a very small way in Middlesbrough, about six men.' She did recognise, though, that the movement did not achieve widespread support, and said that a lot of unemployed men were not interested in it because it was discredited by the press, which always played on its communist connections.

The chief successes of these various groups came from their pressure on local institutions; these were limited, but some changes were achieved this way. Most information about the response of local institutions to this kind of pressure comes from the records of the Middlesbrough Board of Guardians, and the Middlesbrough Town Council.

The Middlesbrough Guardians received deputations from all the groups mentioned. Their demands were always mixed in character, often calling for relief works to be organised by the Guardians and paid at a Trade Union rate of wages, and for rises in the rate of outdoor relief to the unemployed. Generally these representations were met with a mixture of sympathy and reserve. The Guardians usually expressed their deep concern for the problems of the unemployed, but were only prepared to act on a certain range of issues. Demands for more work were always met with encouraging replies, for it was the policy of the Middlesbrough Guardians to provide relief work whenever possible, but they persistently refused to pay the standard Trade Union rate which would have involved defying national government. Demands for higher rates of relief were generally met with sympathetically worded refusals, on the grounds of their own insolvency.

A typical demand was the one put forward by the Middlesbrough Labour Party and Trades Council in March 1926. The requests were:

1. To consider the large number of men disallowed extended benefit, and to work on their behalf.
2. To consider the difficulty of men receiving out relief and living in lodging houses and living on 10s per week. They should receive 12s 6d per week.
3. Camp beds should be used in the casual wards.
4. That the town Council and Unemployment Committee should be urged to provide more work for the unemployed at the Trade Union rate of wages.
5. That the Guardians oppose any measure which may be brought forward by the Government with a view to the disenfranchisment of persons in receipt of out relief.
6. That the Guardians discontinue the practice of deducting 1s per week from the amount of relief in the case of persons who have received a pair of boots from the Guardians.
7. That a conference be convened by the Guardians of all local authorities, Trade Unions and other bodies to discuss matters relating to the whole problem of unemployment.

The Guardians response to each item was:

1. To be left in the hands of the clerk, who was to appear before the local committee or court of referees.
2. Deferred to a meeting at which lodging houses keepers to attend.[40]
3. Left to the Chairman to arrange.
4. Everything possible is being done in this matter.
5. Not within their jurisdiction.
6. This practice should cease forthwith.
7. Agreed.

As will be seen from the response to the deputations' demands, small or practical requests (such as 1, 3 and 6) were usually agreed to, but ones which would involve a complete change of policy, or a clash with central government were not so well received.

This same pattern can be seen in the representations or response from the town council. The pressures on this body ranged from requests to provide a warm room for the unemployed in winter months, to demands for extra relief, more feeding of schoolchildren, bigger work schemes, and 'a sufficient number of full-time Medical Officers of Health to cope with the sick poor'.[41] Again requests such as the first one, which asked only for a small amount of practical help, were invariably complied with, but complete policy changes – never.

Records of one other political group interested in unemployment survive. This was the Stockton Unionist Labour Advisory Committee, which was a group of Conservative working men who met for discussions and lectures, which were always on the subject of unemployment and the economy. It is not clear from the minutes whether the members were all unemployed themselves, but some undoubtedly were because the Committee sometimes acted in their interest. The Advisory Committee appears to have had a threefold function. One was to discuss the economic question of unemployment and their own attitude to it; another to act as a pressure group on the question of unemployment; and the third to help any of their own members who were unemployed, and had trouble receiving benefits.

There is no surviving list of members of this group, but the numbers attending each meeting were listed, and the best attended meeting had fifty members present. It was a serious-minded and well-informed body, the members discussed each unemployment bill as it was presented to parliament and its practice seems to have been to go through any proposed legislation clause by clause. As the result of their discussions they might send a resolution to the Government, or to the MP for Stockton, suggesting an alteration in Government policy. On the 2 February 1926 the Committee sent to parliament the following suggestions on the conditions of extended benefit:

1. Special consideration should be given to necessitous areas.
2. The conditions for disallowance should be more definitely laid down by the State.
3. Claimants should produce written evidence of their efforts to find work.
4. The Chairman should be an official of the Ministry of Labour.
5. Ex-servicemen's pensions should not be taken into account.
6. Part-time workers' earnings should be taken into consideration when applying for extended benefit.

The members of this group were, as might be imagined, normally in favour of the status quo; they were not putting forward any radical changes in the system of help for the unemployed, but they watched all legislation concerning unemployment with a careful and critical eye. In a meeting in 1931 it was reported that there had been a 'long discussion regarding the Means Test and how it was being administered locally.'[42] The Labour Advisory Committee was not against the Means Test in principle, but it is clear that they had some reservations about it because on 14 April 1932 it was recorded that the secretary was instructed to write a letter of thanks to the local MP for his plea in parliament for the alteration of the Means Test.

In pursuit of its other aims the Association wrote from time to time on behalf of one of its members who for some reason had had their claim for Unemployment Benefit disallowed.

In the light of the fact that this organisation was so well-informed it is especially unfortunate that the records of other organisations are lost. However, the information available about them does suggest that they were, as a whole, a lively and determined force in Teesside society. Although they were never more than minority groups they did attract considerable support at times, and they were certainly capable of influencing local councils, Boards of Guardians, and local MPs.

Conclusions

The evidence from Teesside suggests that most local MPs or candidates for election felt that unemployment was an important issue, or was likely to be an important issue to the electorate. Much of the oral evidence rather goes against this, for it suggests that many Teesside people felt that unemployment was not susceptible to a political solution, although the experience of the depression may have affected them when they formed political views later on. However, there clearly was some political feeling amongst the Teesside unemployed, and this is shown in the short-lived but quite strong movements of protest against specific government actions, such as the Means Test. While it seems to have been difficult to sustain this feeling at a high level, it was there to be mobilised from time to time.

Chapter 6

The administrative reaction to unemployment

Although central government was the controlling influence in the care of the unemployed in the inter-war years, it was all carried out by local institutions, which could have an important effect on the lives of those unemployed people for whom they were responsible. In this chapter the influence and effects of local institutions will be considered, and it will be looked at from two angles. The first is the ways in which local institutions affected the unemployed themselves, and the second is to examine the relationship between these bodies and central government. These two aspects provide an interesting contrast of behaviour.

Section 1

The local organisations which had the greatest responsibility for the unemployed were the Board of Guardians, the Public Assistance Committee, and the local councils. Of these three, two had a specific responsibility for the unemployed: the Guardians before 1930 and after 1930 the PAC. Both these bodies gave relief to the uninsured unemployed. In the case of the Guardians this meant dealing only with a substantial minority of the unemployed because most of the Teesside workforce were from insured occupations; but the PAC was responsible for far more people as after 1930 a majority of the Teesside unemployed relied on this committee for benefit, for, with the grinding down of the local economy, those in receipt of Unemployment Benefit became relatively few.[1]

The most important area in which these bodies could make an impact on the lives of the unemployed was in determining relief scales; scales for the uninsured were fixed, within certain bounds, by local bodies and so the generosity or otherwise of these institutions was of great importance.[2] In Middlesbrough the scales

Table 51 *Able-bodied relief scales of Middlesbrough Board of Guardians, 1921–6 (s d)*

Pre 1922		July 1922	
Single persons	10	Single persons	15
Single persons in lodgings	16	Single persons in lodgings	16
Man and wife	20	Single persons living at home	10
Man, wife and 1 child	25	Man and wife	20
Man, wife and 2 children	30	Man, wife and 1 child	25
Man, wife and 3 children	35	Man, wife and 2 children	29
Man, wife and 4 children	40	Man, wife and 3 children	33
Man, wife and 5 children	45	Man, wife and 4 children	36
Man, wife and 6 or more		Man, wife and 5 children	38
children	50	Man, wife and 6 children	40
		Man, wife and 7 children	42

September 1922		
Single persons	12 6	12 6
Single persons in lodgings	16	10
Single persons living at home	10	10
Man and wife	20	20
Man, wife and 1 child	24	25
Man, wife and 2 children	27	29
Man, wife and 3 children	30	33
Man, wife and 4 children	33	36
Man, wife and 5 children	33	38
Man, wife and 6 children	35	40
Man, wife and 7 children	35	42

Scale of 1926	
Single persons	10 12
Man and wife	20
Man, wife and 1 child	24
Man, wife and 2 children	27
Man, wife and 3 children	29
Man, wife and 4 children	31
Man, wife and 5 children	33
Man, wife and 6 children	35
(Half given in money and half in kind.)	

Source: Compiled from Middlesbrough Board of Guardians Minutes.

of Able Bodied Relief (see Table 51) were similar to those of other North Eastern towns, such as Hartlepool and Jarrow, although Newcastle was slightly more generous.[3] They appear to have followed the principle of less eligibility.[4] Nowhere is this specifically stated, but in 1922 the Guardians' Minutes contain a letter from the Ministry of Health which said 'relief given under the poor law should be sufficient for the purposes of relieving distress but that the amount of relief given should of necessity be calculated on a lower scale than the earnings of an independent workman'.[5] As this letter was published without comment, it seems that the Middlesbrough Guardians were prepared to accept this. The less eligibility principle seems also to have been used to ensure that money available to the uninsured unemployed was less than that provided by Unemployment Benefit; during the early twenties poor relief was higher than Unemployment Benefit for an unemployed man with a large family, but this was altered in 1926 so that this was no longer the case.[6]

During the 1920s the able-bodied scale of relief was reduced several times. This was also in accordance with the less eligibility principle, for wages were falling. These cuts affected most families with several children; which seems hard because these were in most need, but of course it was these families who were most likely to receive a greater income from parish relief than from wages. Others affected were single people; this seems to have been done on pragmatic grounds, as the cost of living fell it was believed that they could live on less. There was only one rise in relief, for single people living in lodging houses, but this was something of an exception.[7]

In the donation of relief, therefore, the Middlesbrough Guardians were neither particularly generous or stringent, but there are indications that their sympathy for the plight of the unemployed was greater than might appear from their scales. In 1922 the Guardians received a deputation from 'the unemployed' protesting at the cuts in relief, and in reply the Chairman of the Guardians said that 'all the Guardians felt the greatest sympathy with the unemployed, and had done and would do the utmost on their behalf', but pointed to the serious and critical financial position of the union. In 1922 the Middlesbrough Guardians had an overdraft of £80,000. Two years later, in 1924 the Guardians explored the possibility of adopting the more generous scale of relief given by Newcastle, where there was a higher limit to the total amount given to families. A member of the Middlesbrough Board was sent to Newcastle to consider this, and he reported back that the Newcastle Guardians had come under no pressure from the government to reduce their scales. Nothing, however, was done about the report, and two year's later the Middlesbrough Trades Council asked the Guardians to adjust their scales of relief in line with those of Newcastle, only to be told that the Board 'did not consider the present time opportune'. There may well have been ideological objections to raising relief, such as the belief that levels of relief should be kept below wages but the economic situation made doing so a difficult proposition. In March 1922 the Guardians faced a different kind of deputation, this time from the Middlesbrough and District Property Association, which asked that there should be no increase in the rates, although they were prepared to support an application for increased borrowing.[8] With large numbers of unemployed, and ratepayers, many of whom were themselves poor, shouldering the burden it would have been difficult to have been generous, even if this had been the Guardians' wish. B. J. Elliott, in his study of unemployment in Sheffield, came to the conclusion that the relative generosity of the authorities there was due to the fact that there were sufficient numbers of unemployed to attract attention, but not so many that they were a serious drain on the city's resources.[9]

There was another formidable force against over-spending on local resources, which was central government. In March 1922 an inspection of Middlesbrough Guardians by the Ministry of Health required them to be more 'efficient' with the threat of a withholding of funds held against them.[10] As the Guardians and local authority borrowed heavily from the government, this was a serious threat.

Other actions of the Middlesbrough Guardians confirm this impression of them as a body which was orthodox, but not wholly unsympathetic in its dealings with the unemployed. Their strictest action seems to have been a special revision committee in 1927, which reviewed the cases of able-bodied unemployed who had 'continuously, or practically continuously been in receipt of relief for three years'.[11] In each ward some cases of long-term unemployed were disallowed, usually one or two out of thirty to fifty cases; but in Newport twenty out of fifty-seven cases were discontinued. The Newport Committee reported, 'in a majority of cases under review, the men have been unemployed for four, five, six or seven years, and in a number of cases the men admitted that they had not done a day's work of any kind, apart from test work and relief work provided by the Guardians or Corporation during the time they had been in receipt of relief'.[12]

This seemingly hard-line attitude was not seen elsewhere. The Middlesbrough Guardians were prepared to press for changes in the administration of the Poor Law.[13] In 1922 they declared that they would not take into account a serviceman's disability pension when assessing relief, although by law they should have done.[14] In 1924 they supported a resolution which deplored the regulation they were ignoring.[15] These actions were no doubt prompted by a feeling that men who had fought in the war should be well cared for by the state, something which was reflected in the local press in the early twenties. However, the Guardians were not automatically in favour of preference for ex-servicemen. They were opposed to the continuation of a ruling that fifty per cent of the men employed on relief work should be ex-servicemen on the grounds that many of the men of Teesside had worked in protected industries, and then become unemployed, and that by the end of the twenties some men too young to have fought had become out of work, and that they should have a good chance of relief work.[16]

The Middlesbrough Guardians, like most others, imposed a labour test for men receiving parish relief, and they also gave their support to relief works organised by the local council by providing money and putting forward men for them. It is clear from the minutes that they did not see the labour test – which provided occasional work for the unemployed to establish their genuine availability – as the best way of employing out of work men, because in 1926 they supported a resolution which asked the government for the end of the labour test, and that instead men 'should be engaged on work of national importance'.[17] Test work, unlike relief work, was done not for wages but for relief, but one concession made to Middlesbrough men was that they received all their relief in money (instead of half in money and half in kind) if they were engaged on this work.[18] Relief work, though, was regarded as a very important way of helping the unemployed.

The Guardians were disbanded in 1930, and replaced by a local Public Assistance Committee, which dealt with all claims of those who were not entitled to Unemployment Benefit, which after 1930 was the majority of the Teesside unemployed. The minutes of this committee provide very little detail of their work, or their attitudes to their duties, but they do give their scales of relief. In some parts of the country the local PAC employed the same scale as the Unemployment Assistance Board in 1930, and it appears that Middlesbrough PAC also considered this but did not do so. The minutes record the decision: 'having regard to the cost of living and the general position of industry, this sub-committee is satisfied, after a very careful consideration of the circumstances that the existing scale of relief is adequate'.[19] By 1930 the cost of living in Middlesbrough had indeed fallen so that it was possible to live on the PAC relief, although they could by no means be considered generous.[20] The scales were increased, though, in January 1936, and in 1937 so that in some cases (such as large families) PAC money was the same as Unemployment Benefit.[21] The increase of 1937 came as a response to a request from the Middlesbrough Labour Party that the scales should be increased in accordance with the cost of living, which indicates that the Middlesbrough PAC was at times prepared to listen to requests on behalf of the unemployed.

The Middlesbrough PAC were opposed to the practice of the Means Test, although they were forced to accept it.[22] However, it seems that some relieving officers unofficially ignored it. In 1931 the Borough Accountant complained to the PAC: 'I have had to pull up more than one relieving officer who has put forward a claim for the full scale without going into the application.' In response to this complaint the Committee re-affirmed that 'each case should be considered on its merits'.[23]

While the Guardians and the PAC cared only for the uninsured unemployed, the town council took upon itself some responsibility for the whole community of out-of-work people. There was an unemployment committee of the council whose job it was to hear petitions on behalf of the unemployed, to initiate schemes to help them, and to organise relief schemes. The last was the task which took up most of their time. Each year they put forward a number of relief work schemes to central government, and administered those which were approved and financed.

It was clear from the council minutes that the town council, like the Board of Guardians, attached a great deal of importance to these schemes. Chapter 6 shows that both these bodies were constantly lobbying central government for extensions of relief work. However, the amount of work actually provided was limited.

There is little systematic information available about the numbers of men normally employed on relief works in Middlesbrough, but in June 1930 a statement to the unemployment committee showed that currently 156 men were employed on these schemes, and that the relief work planned for the winter (when most of the schemes operated) would require 679 men for periods of between 7–40 weeks. Whilst these were clearly relatively large scale works, they helped only a small minority of the unemployed. The town council was limited severely by government regulations and by lack of money to initiate relief work schemes; and the fact that more men were not employed on them was due largely to these two factors. The choice of works was limited by the government ruling that the work should be 'of public utility, put in hand out of the ordinary course expressly for the purpose of relieving unemployment, but that also it should not otherwise be undertaken for a considerable period (ordinarily not more than five years) and that the unemployment sought to be relieved is exceptional'. Most relief schemes were building or maintaining roads, although some hospital building was undertaken, and two parks landscaped.

Even if the council had not been hampered by these rules, it is unlikely that it would have been able to afford to do much differently. By the mid-twenties the council was heavily in debt. In 1930 this problem was discussed in a special meeting of the Unemployment Committee, who unanimously passed the following motion to be sent to central government:

That in view of the increasing difficulty experienced in Middlesbrough by large numbers of ratepayers in payment of their rates, and of the impossibility of the Local Authority financing further works for the relief of unemployment on the basis of the financial assistance at present in operation, the council calls upon the government to expedite as a matter of the greatest urgency the appointment of the Department Committee they are setting up to consider ways and means of making increased grants to necessitous areas.[24]

Middlesbrough Council seem to have tried to see that relief work was distributed and organised to provide the maximum benefit for those engaged on it. Preference was given to ex-servicemen (this was required by law) and to men with large families who were likely to suffer most hardship on parish relief. However, the allowed wage for relief work in the early twenties was seventy-five per cent of the normal council rate for unskilled labour, and this would be little more than a man with a large family could expect to receive in relief. A number of protests about this ruling were sent to the council, and it appears that they were heeded because in October 1923 Middlesbrough Council received a letter from the Unemployment Grants Committee saying:

The Committee have given careful consideration to the representations made and in general circumstances agree to leave it to the discretion of your council to pay unskilled men employed upon this particular class of work such a rate as they themselves think fit provided that: 1. These men are employed on work to which they are fully accustomed by reason of long employment in the iron ore industry and are giving 100 per cent output. 2. It is suitable and profitable to employ men of this class on relief works.[25]

This appears to have been a partial concession, allowing the council to pay full wages to certain types of men; but the principle of paying all relief workers the full rate for the job they were doing had not been accepted.

The unemployment committee also organised various small schemes to help unemployed people, usually as a response to a request from a deputation.[26] The most popular scheme was to provide concerts for the unemployed, but with a perpetual concern for economy it was decided that these should not be financed out of the rates but from fund-raising activities organised by the council. This type of semi-official, semi-private effort characterised many of the schemes to help the unemployed. It seems that the main purpose of the concerts was to provide a warm place for the unemployed to go in the winter, for very few were held in the summer. In 1922 after hearing reports that the Borough Library was always full of unemployed men, the committee decided to establish a warm reading room for the unemployed in the town hall crypt. This was not a success, and it was closed down. Perhaps it was uncongenial, perhaps it was insufficiently publicised. However, later another use was found for the town hall crypt to accommodate the long queues of unemployed men waiting to receive their dole.[27] The plight of the men who queued for hours outside in the cold during the winter had been the subject of a number of letters to the local newspapers. The unemployment committee also arranged for the town slipper bath and the swimming bath to be available free to men who could produce an unemployment card, at certain off-peak hours.

In common with other towns hit by unemployment, Middlesbrough had a Mayor's Boot Fund. This was another institution which was a mixture of official help and private charity; the Mayor gave support and publicity to a fund which provided boots for the children of needy families, and the money which was given by private contributions was administered by public institutions, and the boots were distributed through schools. Many thousands of boots were distributed by this fund; in 1921, 929 pairs of boots were given away, and in 1922 over 1,000, and there could be no doubt that its work was extremely valuable.[28] Shoes were an expensive commodity, and many poor parents were unable to afford to keep buying shoes for their children. Many interviewees referred to children who went barefoot; apparently this was especially common in the twenties. The Trades Council and Labour Party asked for Middlesbrough to set up a Town relief fund, but this request was refused on the grounds that private charity was the most suitable way of helping unemployment.[29]

It was not only the unemployment committee of the council which had to face problems directly or indirectly caused by unemployment. Chapter 3 discussed the role played by the health department in the area of unemployment and health. The Education department was also involved, and faced its own special problems. One area in which it could help alleviate distress was the provision of school meals. Although they were empowered to provide school meals during the whole of the period, such a scheme was not introduced until the thirties.[30] However, they were advanced to the extent that the Juvenile Employment Centre set up in Middlesbrough was the first of its kind in the country.[31] At this centre young unemployed men and women could continue their academic studies, and learn skills such as woodwork, metalwork, and domestic science. The head of the Centre liaised with the Labour Exchange, and tried to find suitable work for his pupils. The only other clue as to the general attitude of the Education Committee is from the oral testimony of a Middlesbrough man who taught in a school in the centre of Middlesbrough in the early thirties.[32] He said that if he knew of a pupil with no shoes, inadequate clothing or food he would report this to the local Authority who would usually provide clothing or school meals for the child. It seems that under this system a good deal of responsibility rested with individual teachers to initiate action.

The responses of official bodies in Stockton were very similar in

many ways to those of Middlesbrough. The same generally
sympathetic, but nonetheless generally orthodox attitude to unemployment relief, the same kinds of official help, and the same
ideological belief that private charity was always more suitable a
response to unemployment than official schemes.

Table 52   *Scale of relief of Stockton Guardians, 1921–3*

September 1921	Scale of relief (per week)	October 1922
Single adult	10s	As for May 1922, but
Married couple	20s	single men in lodgings
Each child	5s	to receive 12s 6d
(Maximum allowance of £2 10s but 'discretion' to be used in the case of large families)		

May 1922	Scale of relief (per week)	June 1923	Scale of relief (per week)
Single adult	10s	Man and wife	20s
Married couple	20s	First child	4s
First child	5s	Second to fourth child	3s
Second and third child	4s	Maximum	35s
Additional children	3s		
(A fuel allowance was provided in winter)			

Source: Compiled from Minutes of Stockton Board of Guardians.

The scales of the Stockton Guardians (see Table 52) were similar
to those of Middlesbrough, but tended to be more generous
towards applicants with a number of children. Cuts in relief were
made in the twenties, and although these met with considerable
opposition in the way of public meetings, marches and deputations,
they were not re-instated.[33] They were more generous than
Middlesbrough Guardians to the extent that they were prepared to
give all parish relief in money, instead of half in money and half in
kind as the government directed. A minute of 1921 records: 'A
circular letter from the Ministry of Health was discussed . . . It was
resolved that the practice of giving the bulk of the relief in money
should continue for the meantime.'[34] The reasons for this decision
are not given, but oral testimony for Middlesbrough showed that

the practice of giving relief half in kind was not popular. It was felt that this practice called into question the recipient's good management, and made their plight public in the shops they went to with their tickets.

The Stockton Guardians and local council supported unemployment relief works; in Stockton, as in Middlesbrough, the local bodies felt that relief works were an important way of relieving unemployment, but that they should be financed nationally as unemployment was a national problem. In 1925 Stockton's Mayor was reported to have said that Stockton's unemployment relief works could only touch the fringes of the unemployment problem.[35] This was quite true, but the unemployment committee still felt that they were worth getting into debt for. As was the case in Middlesbrough the council had several times to borrow large sums of money to cover these works.[36]

There were also the semi-official schemes. The Mayor's Boot Fund was again one of the most important, and the Stockton Mayor also began a social service centre where unemployed men could go and play games or learn skills. This was not an official scheme, it is not mentioned anywhere in the Council minutes, but the interviewee who described it suggested that Councillor Allison used his influence as Mayor to benefit the scheme.[37] In the 1930s the town Librarian set aside a 'rest room' for the unemployed, with books, magazines and games. The rest room was part of the municipal library, but the books were privately donated. The room seems to have been popular; in 1936 the Librarian wrote in his report to the council, 'the use made of the room has again exceeded our expectations, and the men have again and again expressed their appreciation of it. Their behaviour has again been exemplary.'[38]

The Minutes of the Stockton Juvenile Employment Committee survive in full and they show that the authorities in Stockton had a special and serious concern for the problems of the young unemployed. This committee watched over a Juvenile Unemployment Bureau, which was set up in 1924, and a Juvenile Unemployment Centre (later called a Junior Instruction Centre) which was opened in 1925. It was the job of the former to try and find work for the insured unemployed youth of Stockton, and any uninsured unemployed who chose to register there could. In times of depression it was impossible to place more than a handful of those registered, although the Unemployment Committee did meet with employers of juvenile labour and try to place as many of those in their charge as possible. The most important work of the Juvenile Employment Bureau came when the depression eased, and they were able to look not just for any job which might be available, but for work which might last for more than just a few months, and especially for apprenticeships.

The Committee attached great importance to the work of the Juvenile Instruction Centre. Attendance was compulsory for all juveniles drawing Unemployment Benefit, but others were also encouraged to attend. The students did some academic studies, and they also had lectures on health, first aid, and 'social and industrial life' as well as learning practical skills such as woodwork or cookery. Great emphasis was laid on team games, and the centre had several football teams and one team which played other centres in the area. The aim of the centre seems to have been less to train the young men and women for a job than to keep up their morale, and to keep them out of mischief. The reports of the centre often mention how the games played there were designed to foster a 'team spirit'. The head wrote enthusiastic reports on the progress of the centre, and in 1927 he wrote that the centre 'has served and is serving a very useful purpose, and it is an asset to the mental, moral and spiritual welfare of the lads of Stockton and Thornaby'. This enthusiasm appears to have been justified in some cases, such as boys who returnd to visit the centre after they had found work; but others appear to have resented being forced to attend what probably seemed like an extension of school. The report for 1932 said that some parents did not send their sons to the centre 'through the misnomer of "dole school" ' and the reports also mention discipline problems with some of the boys.[39]

The response of the authorities in Darlington is more difficult to determine than those of Middlesbrough and Stockton. The minutes of the Board of Guardians and the town council give very little detail, and so information about their work for the unemployed comes largely from piecemeal information in local newspapers. Even the scales of relief from the Darlington Guardians are not available, but there is a minute that in 1930 the newly formed public assistance committee decided to adopt the same scale of relief as Unemployment Benefit, which was the most generous scale they were allowed to do.

Darlington council's commitment to relief work seems to have been less strong, though, than that of Stockton and Middlesbrough.

In 1924 the *Darlington and Stockton Times* reported that the council was running out of ideas for relief works.[40] This is in contrast to the other two towns, who had ideas constantly turned down. However, Darlington too, was prepared to put pressure on central government to change their rulings. In 1921 the *Gazette* reported that a government ruling had prevented Darlington Council from paying the normal Trade Union rate of wages for relief work, and that they were trying to get the decision reversed.[41] In contrast the Guardians tried to give as many men test work as possible, because they 'had agreed, if possible to find work for the unemployed, rather than pay out relief and get nothing in return'.[42] This concern was far more for the good of the town than the unemployed. It seems that Darlington authorities had less coherent ideas about the best way to help the unemployment problem than the other towns – perhaps because there was less unemployment there.

One pattern which appears as clearly in Darlington as either Stockton or Middlesbrough was the way in which the semi-official schemes previously discussed were instigated and supported. In 1931 the Mayor of Darlington decided to give his official support to the many schemes already operating in Darlington to help the unemployed; to help with organisation and provide them with good venues and publicity. Again, the impetus for the schemes ultimately rested on voluntary effort, but the Mayor decided to use his public position to help them along. The organisation was put in the hands of a man from Middlesbrough who had experience in arranging help for the unemployed, and a team of helpers most of whom were themselves unemployed. Schools were used for classes on various subjects, and school playgrounds for football matches and other games.

Darlington Mayor's Boot Fund was also a well-established institution throughout the inter-war years, and a list of local subscribers, which normally included prominent local businessmen, was regularly put in the local paper.

The administrative response to unemployment in the three towns shows local authorities with relatively little power, and limited means trying to cope with a major problem, often with little help from central government. This situation at times led them to a fundamental re-appraisal of the problem, and the idea that large scale relief works administered by local authorities (something which would have given them hitherto unthought-of power and influence) was the only way of coping with unemployment is often voiced. This aspect will be considered further in the next section. However, the traditional idea that private charity was the most suitable way of coping with an unforeseen large-scale human problem was still a strong one; and this is the other major theme of the response of local administration. Although many local authority officials or employers recognised that their position might make schemes to help the unemployed more effective, usually officialdom was providing a supportive role to private initiative.

Section 2

The relationship between the Teesside local institutions and the government shows them in quite a different light from their relationship with the unemployed. The former shows them to be generally orthodox, and usually acting in an *ad hoc* manner. Their other aspect is that they frequently acted as a 'pressure group' on National Government, and at times demanded some far-reaching changes in the system of dealing with the unemployed. Chapter 5 showed that a number of local political groups put pressure on the local authorities, but it was also true that they, in turn, put pressure on National Government.

In the light of this it must be remembered that neither the Guardians nor the Town Councils of Teesside were essentially political bodies. Guardians were not elected on any political ticket, and many councillors were not either. In Middlesbrough there was almost always a majority of independent councillors, and in Darlington and Stockton a split between 'moderates' and Labour, with Labour gaining an increasing representation during the inter-war years. Even so, only a minority of councillors saw their job as furthering a political end, their first aim was to further local interests. It is interesting that the pressures from Stockton and Middlesbrough were very much the same, although the councils were of a different political complexion. Both councils occasionally asked the government for radical changes in its unemployment policy, and this was rarely the result of a desire for radical government, but reflected the heavy burden which the problem of mass unemployment put on them locally.

As has previously been suggested, the attitude of Middlesbrough and Stockton authorities was generally sympathetic to the unemployed, but they refused to take a political stance at their instigation. They refused to defy National Government, for example by granting higher rates of wages to men engaged on test work. They were also persistently reluctant to raise the rate of relief to the uninsured unemployed, partly out of economic pressure, and partly to ensure that no unemployed person could receive more in benefit than by working. In these matters they were far from being unusual, indeed they were following accepted practice, and accepted economic theory, and these two stances could almost be called a-political. It took extreme circumstances for the authorities to adopt a definite political stance in defiance of government.

These extreme circumstances did apply very occasionally. The most notable episode was the decision by Middlesbrough Council that it could not accept responsibility for enforcing the Mean's Test. This move was accepted unanimously by the Unemployment Committee, and was adopted because 'Middlesbrough is in an entirely different category to the rest of the country' and that as a result people would be put 'onto pauper level'.[43] In his speech proposing this move Councillor Briggs said that 'the class of people who were going to be handed over to the PAC were ... the backbone of the nation'.[44] Eventually the government sent its own officials to administer the Means Test, because of the implacable opposition of local politicians.

The other significant rebellion against official policy was the practice of the Stockton Guardians to give all their unemployment relief in money, instead of half in money and half in kind as the government directive ordered. There is no record of why this decision was taken.

Besides occasionally going out on a limb, the authorities persistently sent letters or resolutions or letters to various departments of government asking for changes in unemployment policy. Sometimes these resolutions were instigated by themselves, often they supported those of other authorities.

The most common complaint was that the cost of unemployment relief was too great a charge on the rates in areas of high unemployment, and that the nation should bear the cost. This complaint was put forward by many authorities in depressed areas to governments of the twenties and early thirties. The submission of the depressed areas was that unemployment was a national problem, and the cost should therefore be borne by the nation. In this case, as in many others, the authorities who pressed for this reform were not champions of a strengthened national government, or of state interference in general, but they were being required to use their limited local resources to cope with an overwhelming problem. In each of the three towns the majority of the ratepayers were of very modest means, and the recession made them even less able to pay the high rates needed to provide unemployment relief. For places like Teesside, the only solution was for the nation to take responsibility for the problem.

The other most common complaint was that government grants were not sufficient to enable the local authorities to organise effective schemes of relief works. This was a request for a less fundamental change in government policy, but it actually showed more initiative on the part of the local authorities, because they had no need to initiate relief works in the way that they were obliged to pay relief to the unemployed. A number of suggestions were sent to the Ministry of Health, and other government departments. A typical one from Stockton in September 1923 was:

That the Stockton Borough Council asks the Government to take more effective steps to deal with the problem of unemployment and suggests that there should be a speeding up in the machinery where grants are made to Local Authorities and special grants are made to Local Authorities where unemployment is in excess of the average, and in order to reduce the cost of housebuilding the cost of laying out the land be borne by the national Exchequer (including the purchase price of the land) thus making it possible for each locality to employ all those men now idle who are capable of employment on house-building.[45]

These suggestions represented in effect, a completely fresh approach to unemployment.

Other similar criticisms simply pointed out the inadequacy of current available help. The Unemployment Grants Committee gave grants of seventy-five per cent of the cost of works, but they had to be schemes which would not normally have been undertaken for at least five years otherwise. Each authority did introduce such schemes, but protested that the help given was not sufficient. One or two of the suggestions which were mooted by the authorities were quite surprisingly radical in tone. In 1924 Middlesbrough

Unemployment Committee supported the following suggestions from the British Legion:

1. That a National Employment Committee be set up to investigate and recommend employment schemes of public utility on a scale commensurate with the problem.
2. To finance such schemes a National Loan of at least £200,000,000 be raised.
3. That whenever the uncovenanted benefit is exhausted suitable work under proper conditions, as far as is practicable, shall be provided, and that any physically fit man refusing to accept such work shall forfeit the uncovenanted benefit and any relief from the Poor Law Authorities.
4. That where it is not practicable to provide work ... men shall be encouraged to attend instructional or training centres where suitable education, technical or physical training shall be provided.

This is a proposal which should have provided work or some occupation to most unemployed people, a proposition which would never have been considered by any of the governments of the inter-war years. The basis of these various suggestions seems to have been the interests of the unemployed themselves. This resolution from Oldham, supported both by Middlesbrough and Stockton is again typical:

That it be urged upon the government that instead of continuing to issue unemployment pay to men out of work, or providing money for unproductive purposes, it would be best in the interests not only of the workpeople, but of the nation as a whole, that national funds should be used to keep men employed at the trades to which they are accustomed.[46]

These resolutions call for a national attack on the problem of unemployment rather on the lines of Lloyd George's scheme five years later. Middlesbrough Unemployment Committee pressed again for a similar scheme in 1934, where it resolved unanimously:

1. This Country Borough of Middlesbrough request the Government to take steps forthwith to create the necessary credit for undertaking great schemes of National Reconstruction, ... and that thereby moneys be lent by the Government to Local Authorities for very long periods at very low rates of interest.
2. That such works be flood prevention, cleansing rivers, streams etc., regional drainage and sewage works, building reservoirs, providing gas and electricity supplies, reclamation of land, bridge construction and repair.[47]

Besides calling, in effect, for complete policy changes, the details of rulings on relief works were often criticised, and these are described in the previous section.

The vast difference between the local authorities on Teesside and successive governments on the issue of relief works was that while governments felt that relief works were a drain on the economy, the local authorities saw unemployment as a very serious problem which required the sacrifice of large sums of national money to be spent on it. The sum of political pressure exerted by local officials, asking for relatively minor as well as major changes, shows that in practice, if not in principle, the municipal authorities of Teesside were completely opposed to government policy on unemployment relief. While their first demand, that unemployment should not be a charge on the rates, was at length conceded, demands for large-scale relief works never were.

On this matter there was no possibility of influencing any of the governments of the inter-war years. The reply sent to the North Eastern Committee on unemployment (of which Middlesbrough Unemployment Committee was a member) by MacDonald's private secretary, in 1934, demonstrates the gulf between the necessitous areas' view of the problem and that of the government:

He (MacDonald) receives many communications like yours, suggesting great National loans, and only repeating proposals every one of which has been carefully considered by the Government, and most of which instead of helping to find employment would only make matters worse than they already are . . . While you will be aware, the Government has abandoned the ineffective policy of relief works undertaken solely in order to create employment it has sought to create conditions in which industry can thrive . . . if the Prime Minister thought he would receive any carefully thought out proposals for dealing with the deplorable conditions in some parts of the North East coast, he would be only too glad to receive the suggested delegation.[48]

This letter was 'discussed at some length' in Middlesbrough, and the committee resolved to send further schemes for relief works to the government. If the Teesside authorities were not always effective pressure groups, they were persistent ones.

Chapter 7

The community response to unemployment

This chapter will consider the ways in which communities on Teesside reacted to the experience of unemployment. 'Community' is not used in any strictly defined sense, but means simply people acting together instead of as individuals, or in a way which was typical of most members of a group, so as to include behaviour common to most housewives, or men of a certain age. The most important contemporary study of unemployed communities was that of the Pilgrim Trust, *Men Without Work*, which demonstrated that the reactions and behaviour of unemployed people were very much influenced by the community in which they lived; the numbers of unemployed within it, and also its own traditional cultural values. For example they found that the traditional cohesion and stoicism of the people of Crook, in County Durham, produced unemployed people who continued to maintain their old standards despite years of being out of work, and generally kept up a spirit of optimism and sense of purpose for the future. By contrast, the people from the Rhondda also kept up standards but tended to lose heart more easily, and in Liverpool the tradition of poverty and short-term unemployment made adjustment easy but morale low. Teesside produced a response which is reminiscent of some of the communities described by the Pilgrim Trust, but also peculiar to itself.

The chapter will be divided into two sections; the first deals with the response of employed people to unemployment, and the second with that of the unemployed themselves.

There is a considerable amount of diverse information available which helps towards building up a picture of the community response, but the material is scattered and often fragmentary. Information is drawn from many sources including local newspaper reports which make numerous fleeting references to charities or organisations which helped the unemployed, although without any detailed information about their size, organisation or for how long their work lasted. It is impossible to estimate the extent of private help, because some organisations probably went unreported or unrecorded, and it is very difficult to assess the relative impact of each organisation or movement. Nonetheless it is possible, by looking at all the available information to build up a picture of the reactions of the Teesside community. Oral history is of course very important in Section II.

I Community attitudes to unemployment

When asked whether any help was given to unemployed people, some interviewees mentioned the work of the local authority or the system of relief, but the majority replied something like: 'None at all. I think the only help that was ever given was from charities.' It is clear that voluntary effort made much more of an impact on the Teesside unemployed than official schemes. Each of the three towns had many organisations of many different types which provided food, clothes, employment schemes, shelter or entertainment for the unemployed. Information about them is extremely elusive; often passing reports in the local press give a brief insight into the work of a particular organisation, but no detail about it. Oral testimony, though, tells which organisations were most widely known.

The two voluntary organisations which were most widely mentioned were the Salvation Army, and the Winter Gardens in Middlesbrough. Most people knew of the help which the Salvation Army would give to the destitute; and the Winter Gardens in Albert Park near the centre of Middlesbrough was the best known of the centres which provided shelter and occupations for the unemployed. It was financed and run by several local wealthy people, including Lady Bell and Lady Dorman, the wives of iron manufacturers, Bell and Dorman. Men could go and sit in the warmth, buy cups of tea cheaply, play games such as draughts, read newspapers, or join classes. In the winter of 1922 the Winter Gardens catered for 600–900 persons daily.[1]

A number of interviewees mentioned the work done by various churches to provide food or clothes for poor families. Often this kind of work depended on the inspiration of the individual clergyman. The man who organised the Darlington Mayor's scheme to help the unemployed was a clergyman – the Reverend Arnold West. One interviewee described the Anglican vicar whose parish included Cannon Street, known as one of the poorest parts of Middlesbrough. This man apparently kept open house to his parishioners, and provided soup for the hungry. Whilst some churches ran charities which were intended to help any poor families, others cared for the unemployed within their own congregations; the Baptists and Methodists had a good reputation for caring for their own.[2]

Another voluntary scheme which was mentioned by two interviewees was the Friend's Allotment scheme, in which unemployed men who had allotments were provided with tools and seeds by the Society of Friends.

One of the interviewees told of voluntary schemes from the other side. She was Mrs Natrass, who had given a great deal of time in the early thirties helping an organisation in Stockton which provided clothes for poor families. This organisation, called the Personal Service League, was a committee of women who took over an unused shop in the centre of Stockton, and distributed second hand clothes which had been sent from 'the affluent South'. Individuals applied to the league for clothes, and a volunteer would visit their house to see whether they were genuinely in need. Files of those families helped were meticulously kept, to ensure that no one got more or less than their fair share. All kinds of clothes were welcomed by the people of Stockton, except plus fours, which had to be cut up to make clothes for children. Mrs Natrass said that she didn't think that people felt degraded by accepting these clothes; they were in such need that they were grateful for anything they could get. However, many mothers did offer to help the League, as a contribution towards the clothes, and this help was always accepted. They had sewing circles where volunteers and mothers worked to mend or remake clothes, and a good deal of money could be raised by house-to-house collections. Mrs Natrass said that to most people she knew voluntary effort seemed to be the most natural and useful way of dealing with the problems of the depression: 'There was a job to do and we got on with it,' she said.

Reports in the local press give further information about voluntary agencies which helped the unemployed. Usually they are not more than a couple of lines about a particular project, with no

information about how it was organised, how many people were
involved, or for how long the project continued, but they do build
up a picture of many different kinds of agencies and people who
decided to do their own bit towards helping the unemployed. Some
were old established Teesside charities which extended their work
to cope with the depression. The best known of these was the
Middlesbrough Settlement, which cared for poor children. The
Gazette reported enthusiastically about the work of the Settlement
at various intervals, but in 1931 it reported that its work had been
hampered by the fact that many of the members had themselves
been made unemployed.[3] The children of the unemployed appear
to have received special consideration from charitable agencies,
presumably because public sympathy is easily roused in the case of
suffering children. Various organisations collected clothes for
children, others provided days out, or visits to the cinema. Various
classes were arranged for adults; the *Darlington and Stockton
Times* reported that in Darlington lectures on politics and
economics for the unemployed were 'well-attended'.[4] In Middlesbrough gym classes were held.[5] In the poorer areas soup kitchens
were set up. Oral testimony relates that the ILP and the NUWM
provided an information service to the unemployed about their
legal rights, and sometimes conducted an individual's case before
the authorities. The employed citizens of Teesside reacted to large-
scale unemployment as they might have done to a natural disaster;
unemployment was felt to be inevitable, caused by forces outside
human control, and presenting a large-scale human problem which
needed an instant and instinctive response.

To a large extent the attitudes of the Teesside community to
unemployment are evident from their actions, but it was not only
the active which had views on the subject. Many attitudes to
unemployment, and concerns about the problem were expressed in
the local press, which while by no means providing a comprehensive survey of local feeling, does give some indication of how the
community felt.

   The two newspapers which have been consulted in this study are
the *North Eastern Daily Gazette*, which covered events in the
whole of Teesside, but especially Middlesbrough, and the *Darlington and Stockton Times*, which concentrated on Darlington,
Stockton and North Yorkshire. The *Gazette* was a Liberal paper

until 1931, when it had a new Conservative editor, and the *Darlington and Stockton Times* was always under Conservative control.[6] The *Gazette* displayed a continual interest in the problems of unemployment throughout the period, but the *Darlington and Stockton Times*, which was a newspaper strongly geared to the agricultural interest of North Yorkshire, did not. While the *Gazette* always gave considerable coverage to the question, it is possible to read inter-war editions of the *Darlington and Stockton Times* for a period of several months (it was a weekly paper) without coming across any reference to unemployment.[7] This serves as a reminder that to some people living on or near Teesside unemployment was a marginal concern.

In the first years after the First World War the main concern shown in the *Gazette*, in letters and editorials, was for unemployed ex-servicemen. In the years 1919–20 unemployment was rarely discussed as a problem in itself, the main worry was that former servicemen could not get jobs. The *Gazette* published a number of letters from out of work ex-servicemen who described their plight, and the newspaper mounted appeals to employers to take on former soldiers, especially if they were disabled. Various letters and articles pointed out that many young men who had enlisted had forfeited the high wages which could be earned on Teesside during the war (upwards of £3 per week) for 30s per week, and all the dangers and lack of comfort of service life, and could get no work on their return. There was a strong feeling that those who had served the nation during the war were in some way entitled to jobs. Even those who took a hard-line attitude to the unemployed usually excepted former servicemen. One letter to the *Gazette*, written in 1921, called for an end to all out-of-work donation 'except for ex-servicemen'.[8] Jimmy Finegan, who was an ILP member during the 1920s, said that his sympathy with the unemployed was first aroused when he saw the plight of ex-servicemen in Eston after the First War. The fact that many people who suffered from unemployment after the war were former soldiers and sailors undoubtedly inculcated a feeling of sympathy, and also responsibility from the community, which may have led to similar feelings about the whole community of unemployed later.

In the early twenties several articles in the *Gazette* suggested that there were easy solutions to the problems of unemployment. In December 1920 an article headed '*Unemployment not Inevitable*', argued that the remedy was the 'exercise of self-restraint by Government, employers and employees in their declining to snatch when things are doing well the last penny they can snatch from the business machine'.[9] Other articles suggested that the depression was a purely temporary phenomenon, caused by post-war dislocation – a very common economic view in the early twenties.[10] Soon, though, it became apparent that the depression was not going to go easily or quickly, and that more than individual goodwill was needed to cure it, and the *Gazette* had a number of articles reflecting this change of mood. An editorial in February 1921 put this in quite hyperbolic terms: 'To every open-hearted citizen, the public anxiety of the day which, more persistent than any other, perches on his shoulder, plucks at his sleeve, and when seemingly forgotten still haunts, scarcely perceptible, and yet disturbing his waking and sleeping hours is unemployment.'[11] With this awareness of the problem, the attitude to it had changed: 'In earlier days the misery of industrial arrest, the starvation, the hopelessness, the degenerace, were all borne as an inevitable human ill, alike by those who suffered ... and others.' In the opinion of the author this change of attitude had been brought about from the war, which was almost certainly true, at least in part.

How to tackle the problem of unemployment was also a subject which appeared frequently in the *Gazette* in the early years of the twenties. Editorials did not keep up a consistent attitude to the problem, veering from the orthodox to the surprisingly radical. Evidently, writers of different political persuasions were employed by the newspaper. The orthodox articles relied on the possibility of a natural recovery in the export industries, or a 'revival in trade'. Other advocated large-scale relief works. In November 1921 an article headed '*Work waiting to be done – what might be done to combat unemployment?*', said: 'We have only to think of the great housing shortage, the condition of our roads and permanent ways, the need for reclaiming our foreshores and the unproductive use of thousands of acres of land that could be prepared for cultivation to see many obvious schemes to bring sound employment in the months ahead.'[12] This theme returns on a number of occasions, and one of the oft-repeated slogans in the Liberal *Gazette* of the twenties was 'work not charity'. On the basis of this, relief works were always welcomed, and during the whole of the inter-war period any relief works undertaken by the Middlesbrough or Stockton local authorities were reported.

The *Gazette* also reflected more local concerns. In the early twenties it published a number of letters from people who had seen the long queues waiting outside the Labour Exchange on cold and wet days in winter, and which asked why they were not allowed to wait inside. Particular inefficiencies or anomalies in the system of relief were publicised, such as the case of a man who did a short spell of work only to lose his relief afterwards because he had been working.[13]

Not all the concern shown was sympathetic. People who spent their unemployment benefit on luxuries were condemned. Headlines such as 'Drunk on the Dole', or 'Sacked one day, married the next', reflect the two major resentments expressed by the *Gazette* against unemployed people. It was clearly considered by many people that money that was not actually earned should be spent responsibly; money given in relief, or in Benefit, was not to be spent as the recipient chose.

Other letters concerning unemployment reflected the suspicion and resentment which is often aroused by misfortune. A number of correspondents blamed at least part of the unemployment situation on women who went out to work, and married women who received Unemployment Benefit were thought to artificially inflate the unemployment figures. The *Gazette* occasionally published articles about dole frauds, often with the comment of a magistrate to the effect that fraudulent claims were ruining the finances of the country. Unemployment also brought to the fore local chauvinism. In the early thirties the *Gazette* published a number of prominent articles to the effect that cheap foreign steel was being 'dumped' on Teesside, something that was clearly going to rouse indignation amongst Teesside steelworkers. Sometimes less serious accusations received a good deal of attention. A letter in 1931 which suggested that large numbers of Stockton men were working in Middlesbrough roused a good deal of indignation, many other correspondents writing to say that this should be stopped, and that Middlesbrough jobs should be given only to Middlesbrough men.[14] In view of the very close proximity of the two towns, this indignation is surprising, and it indicates how adversity intensified feelings of local rivalry.

By contrast, the *Darlington and Stockton Times* had few articles on unemployment, especially in the 1920s. This was doubtless in part because they reflected the agricultural, rather than the urban interest of the area, but is also possibly a reflection of the attitude of one section of Teesside society. One interviewee, a middle class woman from Stockton, who grew up in the twenties and was a young married woman in the thirties, said that she hardly knew that there was a problem of unemployment in Stockton. One major pre-occupation of the *Darlington and Stockton Times*, though, was dole frauds; something which was felt all over the country, and influenced some legislation, such as the Labour Government's Anomalies Act.[15] Stories of employed men drawing dole, of married women spending dole money on chocolates and visits to the cinema, and of unemployed men who did not bother to look for work appeared more frequently than any other story on the subject, during the 1920s. By the thirties the question of unemployment appeared a little more frequently, and more things than dole frauds were discussed. It reported relief works, local charitable organisations (lists of subscribers to the Mayor's Boot Fund were regularly published) and the attitude of the unemployment committees of local councils. This paper contained a number of articles on juvenile unemployment, one on 21 March 1925 declared it to be 'an evil' which was 'vastly depressing'.

The attitude of these two local papers displays the ambivalence of feeling of the employed for the unemployed. The mixture of sympathy, concern, suspicion and resentment is common to both. Again, the problem of the cost which the unemployed imposed on the country was to the fore in many articles on the subject.

The central themes running through all the responses of the employed to the problem of unemployment are a solid belief in individualism, and the value of individual rather than corporate help for the problem, and a strong ambivalence to attitude to unemployment and the unemployed. At once the unemployed were seen as unfortunates, potential troublemakers, a justifiable case for help, and a drain on local resources: These two attitudes were responsible for the almost completely *ad hoc* response to the problem.

II The response of the unemployed

This section will discuss what different groups or communities of unemployed people did to combat the problems of unemployment:

the attitudes of the unemployed to the problems they faced; what help they turned to, and what help they provided for themselves; how the life of different communities changed and how they stayed the same.

Some of the interviewees gave the other side of the story of official and charitable help. Few people seem to have been aware of official schemes to help unemployed people. Local authorities were badly regarded by many because of their connection with the Guardians in the twenties, and the Means Test in the thirties. In Middlesbrough, as in most parts of Britain, to receive relief from the parish carried with it a stigma; the local name for parish relief was 'the pancrack' which was associated with near-degradation. As the number of people turning to the Guardians increased, money was given to the able-bodied in the form of a loan.[16] This was greatly resented. So was the fact that parish relief in Middlesbrough (though not in Stockton) was given half in money and half in kind, which took away from the recipient some responsibility over his own affairs.[17] Later, the local authority was by many completely identified with the Means Test; in fact the 'Means Test' was the local term for PAC money. A fuller discussion of the attitudes to the Means Test will be made later on.

A few interviewees did mention official schemes. One man referred to 'road relief works; under this scheme a man might get six weeks on road relief works, and during this period he might be able to get a new pair of boots, or an extra pint of milk a day'.[18] A couple of people mentioned what they called lumber camps; these were government work schemes where men were usually sent away on a particular project. While there was some criticism of the conditions of work in these camps, they did provide some work and a change of routine:

And the manager of the Labour Exchange said 'I'm sorry but the only thing I have is this lumber camp', and I said 'Well, you'll be keeping me won't you?' 'Oh yes, you'll get your keep like.' So I went down, and we lived in Norfolk . . . and what we used to do was to clean the banks and clean the silt out of the bottom of these dykes, and you used to get four bob a week.[19]

The Mayor's Boot Fund was one official attempt at help which was mentioned by more than one interviewee. Boots from this fund were regarded as a mixed blessing, because although they were a much needed and expensive article of clothing, they had a distinctive piece of steel outside the heel, which was to stop them

being pawned by the children's parents. While people understood
the reason for this precaution, the disadvantage in having a pair of
these boots was that they were easily recognisable as a charitable
gift. However, one appreciative recipient described what it had
been like to have a pair of these boots:

One day somebody came into the classroom and asked how many of us
had fathers who had been out of work for two years, and I put my hand up
and so did some of the other children in the class, and we were taken into a
shop and all given a pair of boots, which seemed wonderful to us, and I
remember the way they clomped all the way home.[20]

Most interviewees had a softer attitude to the charitable help
they remembered than to the official help, but even so there were
some people who were prepared to accept it and some who were
not. One former unemployed youth from a tough area of
Middlesbrough said:

Well the Salvation Army used to give cups of tea or a bit of soup or
something like that. You had to go round to them. If the band was playing
round the streets when I was young I always used to follow it and get a
basin of soup when I went into Cannon Street; their place used to be in
Cannon Street. I'd join anything for a bit to eat, I'll tell you that.[21]

Other children who came from more 'respectable' homes were
still allowed to go to the Lantern Shows which the Salvation Army
held in Stockton. Again, the food which was provided was a strong
incentive:

We were Catholics and at the time we weren't supposed to go into other
Churches . . . but we used to go to the Salvation Army on a Sunday evening
simply because at the end of the lantern show they used to give you peas on
a saucer. . . . Of course they wouldn't give the peas until you'd seen the
Christian lantern show, if they'd given the peas first everyone would have
eaten the peas first and then dispersed. So they sat through the lantern
show which was very enjoyable, and then you had a saucer of peas.[22]

Other interviewees felt that the Salvation Army was beneath their
dignity. Mrs Chilvers remarked:

If we were desperate, my father used to threaten me that instead of going to
the Primitive church, I would have to join the Salvation Army because I
would get a pair of shoes, and although they were only sand shoes, or what
people used to call Spanish rope slippers, which cost 1s a pair, people
couldn't even afford a shilling to buy those. I think that the Salvation Army
did supply people but you had to be very poor to go.

Another interviewee was a regular churchgoer at a church which had a scheme to provide clothes for the poor, but the vicar's wife said to her mother, 'you know we couldn't possibly offend you by sending you any help, you are so respectable'.[23]

Of all the responses described to schemes for the unemployed, the most enthusiastic was a young man who went to PT classes: 'I used to go there (a church hall) and spend an hour a day on physical exercise. You were issued with a gym kit, shoes and that, for the duration of the course . . . and I got to like it that much I used to go there four hours a day . . . I thoroughly enjoyed it.'[24]

The Pilgrim Trust, in their survey of unemployed clubs found that many men appreciated exercise classes; for they gave them a new feeling of vitality.[25]

Of course these kinds of help touched only the fringes of the unemployment problem. One interviewee said of the unemployed, 'they were not cushioned at all, they were completely on their own'.[26] While of course this was not completely true, it did describe the fact that to a large extent, the unemployed communities of the depressed areas were thrown back on their own resources, something which was a cause of financial and psychological strain. Many of the contemporary investigators were concerned about what would happen in these towns, and the people within them; how would they react to the problems of mass unemployment? Generally, the investigators found a remarkable cohesion in heavily depressed towns, provided that they had behind them a strong tradition of close-knit interdependence. The Pilgrim Trust found that areas like Crook and the Rhondda, with unemployment as high as that in Stockton, managed to keep their values and cultural identity well intact. Stephen Constantine in his survey of these contemporary investigations writes, 'The remarkable feature of the depressed areas seems to have been their resilience.'[27] This can be seen, too, in inter-war Teesside.

As far as the vast majority of unemployed men were concerned, the biggest problem they faced was how to occupy their time. For many of them, an obvious way of doing this was to look for work. As the Pilgrim Trust found, to some men looking for work became almost a full-time occupation.[28] Often these were men who had only recently lost their jobs, and still had hope of finding another, but some who refused to give up hope even when the odds were stacked heavily against them, 'old men who have not a remote chance of working again but still make it a practice to stand every morning at six o'clock at the work's gates in the hope that perhaps they may catch the foreman's eyes'.[29] Looking for casual work could indeed take up a good deal of time, as one Middlesbrough man described:

And we used to have to . . . set out from home at five o'clock in the morning and go in what they called the market in the foundries, and wait for the six o'clock shift (six till two) and stand there in the cold weather waiting for the foreman to come, and the foreman used to come round at about a quarter past seven, and he'd see us all stood there, and he'd just put his finger to one or two and he'd say 'I'll have you and you and you and you' and they'd have a job for the day . . . Then you'd try and get a job by going on the next shift, at one o'clock for the two o'clock shift, and do the same routine again. You were doing that all the time.[30]

Rumours of work quickly spread. One man described 'hundreds of men queuing up for a little whisper of a job'.[31] Some men walked or cycled miles to neighbouring towns to try and find work.

After a while, many men gave up looking for work and settled to find alternative occupations for at least part of their time. One of the most popular activities amongst young and old seems to have been participation in some kind of sport. Sports had always been a popular leisure activity, and it became for some almost a full-time one.

There was a lot more sport, organised sport. You played more games, I learned to swim in that river. In summer you'd be down at that river every day. You'd be playing football in the winter, and boxing and wrestling. All physical sport. They used to say that you need only blow a whistle and get the best team in the world.[32]

Football appears to have been most popular, because of the fact that it was easy to play in any available open space, and because many men enjoyed belonging to a team that they could identify with. It was also a way of possibly achieving great status and wealth; one man pointed out that almost the one hope of great achievement to a young unemployed man was to become a professional footballer.[33] Boxing had a similar appeal; anyone could try his luck in the ring, and get money if he won. One North-Eastern boxing champion of the thirties described how poor boys aspired to become boxers; he called them 'hungry fighters'.[34] For those who did not want to play, there was always the opportunity to watch. Attendance at non-professional fights was free, but the custom was that money was thrown into the ring if one man acquitted himself well.

Handball was another game which was often used to pass the time; this was a game similar to Fives played against the end of a row of terraced houses. Young men cycled long-distances, sometimes sleeping out in the summer. Older men played quoits, bowls and card games. Walking was very common amongst all age groups, for it was a way of passing the time, keeping warm, and going to interesting places. Middlesbrough and Stockton are near the coast, and many people walked to the sea for a day. In a rather unusual version of this common pastime, one interviewee described how his father used to follow the local hunt:

The other thing my father did, which seems totally out of period now, was that they were very keen followers of the South Durham Hunt, and they were well known, too, to the Master of Hounds, they were known by name, and he was to them . . . Now if the South Durham Hunt was meeting on a day when they signed on, they would be queuing up at nine o'clock to sign on, dash back home, get their sandwiches made up (and their sandwiches would be bread and marg., sometimes a bit of cheese, occasionally jam) and set off. They knew all the covets and warrens and goodness knows what else, and they would spend a tremendous day in the country, and sometimes they'd walk out Sedgefield way, and this of course took them out and made them very happy and fit.[35]

Another popular pastime was gambling. This had been a popular recreation of the working classes since the nineteenth century, and many contemporary observers believed that it increased in the inter-war years, especially amongst the unemployed. This is disputed in a recent article by R. McKibbin, who suggested that its incidence did not increase noticeably.[36] However, it was another of the traditional leisure activities of Teesside people which filled the time of a great many of the unemployed. Normally the stakes were very small, and probably few people won or lost a good deal of money.[37] The promise of a great gain, though, was one of the reasons why it was so popular a sport. One woman explained why so many people tried their luck:

Hoping 'tomorrow I can bring in sixpence where I can only bring in a penny today'. I remember a neighbour of ours, she used to like her bet, and she used to say to my mother, 'Well Meg, whether it's going to be dripping tomorrow or whether it's going to be meat pie', you see, hoping that she would put that penny or 2d on a bet and she was going to be able to make a meat pie.[38]

Gambling was illegal, but very well organised. A Stockton man described the gangs of men who spent part of each day in this pursuit: 'There were ranks playing crown and anchor along the quayside with organised scouts and lookouts, and I don't think the police dare interfere down there.'[39]

Pitch and toss was another favourite form of street gambling, and there were many others.

Another form of traditional entertainment and companionship for men was the pub or club. The interviewees in this study contained what was almost certainly an unrepresentative number of people who drank very little; and a couple of men said that drink was one thing they cut out when they were out of work. But others mentioned the pub as a normal place of entertainment, and several described the ritual of drinking on a Saturday night. One man described this during the 1920s in Stockton:

But Saturday night how much drink men got I've no idea. It was traditional, and I think it was true, that Teesside beer was strong beer. And you were supposed to be a man if you could down your beer. And the big test was . . . with the buzzer, and if you could pick up your pint when it started, and if you'd downed it by the time it ended you were a man. And until you could do that you weren't really a man. But on Saturday nights they would go out, and 'they' didn't really apply to my family, and get boozed up in the pubs, and almost every other place in Stockton High Street was a pub in those days, and the place was alive with songs. Quite often noisy fights, but from half-past ten to half-past eleven onwards the place was alive with songs.[40]

Many of the contemporary surveys of unemployment mention cinema-going as a cheap and popular entertainment for the unemployed. Few of the respondents in this study mention the cinema as a pastime, except as an occasional luxury. One man had an aunt who worked in the local cinema, and was smuggled in from time-to-time, which saved him from paying 6d.[41] Again, the fact that cinema-going was rarely mentioned may be a reflection of the fact that the majority of respondents were from the 'respectable classes' and so concentrated almost all their income into basic necessities.

There were some attempts from within the community of unemployed to start clubs which met the specific need of unemployment. In Section I, the work of some shelters for the unemployed was discussed; similar schemes were set up by the unemployed themselves. The Darlington scheme, which was sponsored by the Mayor, was run by a committee of unemployed men. Mrs Natrass, who worked for the Personal Service League in

Stockton, also mentioned a shelter run entirely by unemployed men where people could learn handicrafts. The various unemployed associations, which were at their peak of activity in the early thirties, had a social as well as a political function, and some had a social function only. They organised discussion groups and concerts, which were reported in the local press as being very successful. Of course these associations, although they were at times quite strong, never represented more than a small minority of the Teesside unemployed.[42] They appear to have been the work of an enterprising and clubbable minority, men who were prepared to organise and to belong to an unemployed group.

Many unemployed people spent at least some of their time thrown back on their own resources. In her study of Edwardian Middlesbrough Lady Bell found that a substantial minority of people liked to read, and such people read a good deal while they were out of work.[43] 'When I was first unemployed I used to read a library book a day. In those days you were only allowed two books, and you could only keep them out for one week. One was fiction and the other non-fiction. Of course you got round this by using other people's tickets.'[44] The reference library was very popular because it provided entertainment and warmth, and a number of people mentioned the fact that they provided a shelter for the unemployed, something which is borne out by the reports of the Stockton and Middlesbrough Librarians.[45]

A few men, with an unusual degree of inventiveness, managed to spend their time very creatively. The daughter of a long-term unemployed man described his work:

He could make marvellous things with his hands. He once made a church from about five thousand to ten thousand match sticks. He used to collect boxes of matchsticks, and everyone was glued together and he made a model church . . . I think it took him two years. Then he made a ship in a bottle; and of course everyone used to say 'How did you get the ship inside the bottle?' It had every detail. It had a deck, the sails on it . . . He was always having to invent something. In those days he hadn't such a thing as an alarm clock that was a thing of the past you know, and he sat for weeks and weeks . . . he was fiddling with his tools and pieces of metal and we had a cuckoo clock . . . it occupied his mind for weeks.[46]

The son of an unemployed man told how his father spent five years making two full-size gypsy caravans from scrap metal and wood from closed shipyards in Stockton.[47] On a more modest level, many men did some jobs to save money in the home; mending shoes or cutting hair. A number of interviewees mentioned allotments; there were no special schemes to provide allotments for the unemployed on Teesside, but it seems that there, as in many other depressed areas, the allotment provided an important source of activity and food for many an unemployed man and his family.

A mixture of these kinds of activities kept many of the Teesside unemployed occupied, as they did the unemployed in other depressed areas, for much of their time. However, for a great many there was little to do when they were out of work. The response of many men appears to have been quite passive. Several people described the way in which large groups of men appeared to do nothing at all: 'They wore cloth caps and got greyer and greyer and greyer. They used to sit on the kerb and smoke woodbines, one woodbine would be broken in half; they did nothing.'[48]

Standing at street corners, passing a cigarette around. Albert Park was full, because at least they could sit. Even in the winter they would sit with their overcoats on. At St Georges there was a shelter, and you could go anytime and see a whole gang of them hanging about in the shelter.[49]

This response of passive acceptance was very common, and coloured the whole of Teesside's response to the depression. It is reminiscent of the descriptions of certain contemporaries; such as Walter Greenwood's fictional account of a depressed North Western town, or J. B. Priestley's description of Jarrow: 'Whenever we went there were men hanging about, not scores of them but hundreds of thousands of them. The whole town looked as if it had entered some penniless bleak Sabbath.'[50]

While the unemployed men spent their time as best they could, it was left to their wives to maintain the standards and continuity of home life. Many women worked exceptionally hard to see that family life did not alter too much.

Normally this meant carrying the burden of all the usual hard work in the home with less money to do it with. Few men helped much in the home if they were unemployed. Although a few looked after the children, the idea of what was men's and what was women's work was too entrenched in people's minds for either to seek change.

I would say that when I was young the womenfolk in those polished little houses, although they were supposed to be downtrodden, wouldn't have welcomed any interference from the men. My father would not have been allowed to touch anything, I can assure you, at home. On the other hand he would not have pushed a pram – not that we had a pram – but from other folk it would certainly have been ungentlemanly behaviour.[51]

A whole variety of observers, including the families of unemployed men, and people from outside, commented on the way in which housewives kept up their standards of cleanliness, order, and food, as far as they could.

There were some houses where beer got the better of people, and this was usually on a Saturday night . . . but those side streets, those terraces were very definitely polished, and once a week, at least once a week, towards the end of the week you'd see all the women on their knees in front of the doorstep but they washed as far out on the pavement as they could reach, therefore there was a semi-circle of washed pavement in front of them. The little windows were bright and shiny, so were the curtains and inside everything was blackleaded.[52]

Cleanliness was very important to the good housewife, and it was not just because they were house-proud; most of the dwellers in Teesside street houses fought a continual battle against vermin: 'The houses were bug-ridden. Beetles, black-locks, and the yards had to be swilled out on account of the awful middens that they had in the yards which smelt, and the yards invariably smelt all the time of this strong disinfectant.'

Most important of all, though, to keep up standards was economy. It was the first priority of every good housewife with an unemployed husband to provide the best they could with the cheapest foods. Mrs Bell, from Stockton, explained the significance of this: 'If you didn't manage you didn't eat did you? If you wasted your money you'd probably eat one day, but you'd probably go two days without eating. So you had to make your money go round.'

This often meant working hard, and shopping late at night or early in the morning to get the cheapest food. Mrs Bell again:

There was all sorts of different dodges the housewife did; for instance on a Saturday evening a lot of women, my mother did, used to save half her dole money and go to the market on a Saturday evening. But she would never go until about nine or ten at night . . . When the market was closing down, and of course in those days there wasn't such a thing as freezing . . . so a lot of market people had to sell off, and my mother would probably get a piece of meat to last us the weekend, that would probably have been marked 1s in the morning and by the evening it would probably be going for 4d . . . and she'd buy cooking apples . . . she'd ask at the stall if they'd any bruised apples, and he'd probably give her a large bag of bruised apples for maybe a penny.

People like the Bells are reminiscent of the families of Crook and the Rhondda described by the Pilgrim Trust, who managed well through the depression. Of course not all Teesside people were like this; some were more like those the Pilgrim Trust found in Liverpool, where there was already a 'culture of poverty' where unemployment only continued for longer than a normal habitual period of poverty. These people lacked the resilience and tradition of good management to cope with long-term unemployment. Few of the people interviewed came from this category of people, but Mrs Chilvers described what it was like to come from a family where the mother was a poor manager, albeit for an unusual reason:

My mother was a middle-class woman and she didn't adjust, as I look back now, to the conditions she was living under. She hadn't much pride in washing and cleanliness, in her own self she had, but not in her children. I had vermin in my hair, I had lice on me, just things were very very bad.

In this family they often used to go hungry: 'I've seen us just eat turnip, mashed turnip, with a bit of bread.'

Mr Hush, a retired pawnbroker from Middlesbrough described the life led by some of his customers: 'Some people lived absolutely hand-to-mouth, they pawned every day. One woman who lived absolutely on the poverty line, she was very poor, and she used to pawn for almost every meal.'

Most of the interviewees who described those less able to cope with poverty mostly seemed to think that the responsibility lay with one or other of the parents of a family. 'A lot of them did [drink] and that's why there were so many children who were just dragged up. It was nothing for a man to spend whatever he had coming in, in drink and gambling, and that was prevalent without a doubt.'[53] However, in view of the difficult struggle which the 'respectable' families had, it would seem that only a slight inadequacy, or misfortune could result in the sort of problems described by Mrs Chilvers and Mr Hush. This was probably especially true in the twenties. The effects of the higher cost of living in the twenties have already been described in Chapter 2; the conditions of Teesside then were similar to those of the York of Rowntree's first study, or the London surveyed by Charles Booth, where both found that most people fell into poverty through misfortune, rather than mismanagement.[54]

In a great many cases, though, families were held together, and continued to live relatively normal lives because of the individual effort of the parents. Even though the father was displaced from his normal role, and the mother was under great strain, the life of the family unit continued. Of course, it was not the case that each family relied entirely on its own members; one of the factors which helped the people of Teesside to withstand the strains of the depression was the close-knit community strength. Almost all interviewees commented on the help provided by neighbours and friends during times of trouble; the whole street would rally round to help someone. Even those people who regretted little of the inter-war years felt that this attitude was the most positive thing they remember from those days. Typical statements were: 'This was the most marvellous part about things. People used to help each other, because you do get that in street houses.'[55] Or, 'There was a tremendous community philosophy in those days.'[56] Of course these enthusiastic statements may be the products of a rosy attitude to the past; Robert Roberts, writing of his childhood in a poor part of Salford claimed that the 'cosy gregariousness' of slum dwellers has been exaggerated: 'Close propinquity, together with cultural poverty lead as much to enmity as to friendship.'[57] He pointed out that closeness led to frequent quarrels, to prying and interfering, and to people being subjected to the will of their family, especially the dominant members of it long after they were capable of being independent. However, as Chapter 4 showed, the kind of support system which operated on Teesside, as in other poor areas was essential. If a member of a family (especially the mother) was sick, or confined, then only the help of neighbours and family could ensure that the other members were looked after. Many families worked a system of sharing as much as they could: 'My uncle would bring this stuff (coal mixed with oil to burn on the fire) to our house and my mother would give him in return, for his family, some loaves she had baked.'[58]

Mrs Chilvers described how if anyone won a bet they would share it out amongst the neighbours so that all would share in the money and the pleasure, something which also occurs in Walter Greenwood's, *Love on the Dole*.[59] Relatives as well as friends were very important, indeed probably the most important source of help.[60]

There were many ways in which the people of Teesside used to combat the problems of poverty. One which was very frequently mentioned was credit. Some people eschewed credit of all kinds and had a rule that 'nothing should come into the house unless it is paid for', but most people relied on some kind of credit.[61] Clothes that were not bought second hand (and some that were) were bought on credit, as were any large household goods. The corner shop often gave goods 'on the slate'. It was always possible to get short-term cash loans from some independent operator who would provide a small sum of money for a few weeks on a fixed rate of interest. The most often mentioned form of credit was the pawnbroker. Again, this was beneath the dignity of a few, but many 'respectable' people had recourse to this form of loan. Many people remembered taking Sunday clothes in to the pawnbroker on a Sunday night, and redeeming them on the next Saturday. The only thing which people would not pawn were pans and hats.[62] Mr Hush, the retired pawnbroker, told of the great variety of goods which people would pledge to get some cash. One customer used to bring in her kitchen table, which fetched 1s. It was kept in the yard because it was too big for the shop. It was only redeemed 'for births, marriages and funerals'. Mr Hush related, 'Well we took all kinds in. We took a wooden leg in once, and the woman said, "The old man won't give me any money, so I've pawned his leg to stop him going out drinking . . ." ' Depending on their financial status they would use the pawn shop once a week, month, or even every day.

In some cases credit was a way of managing, and in others it did no more than to stave off financial ruin. The family who bought groceries on credit but always paid up on Friday evening were helped by credit, not so others: 'You'd go to a shop . . . you'd buy, say a pair of blankets, we'll say for 10s. Well you put 6d down you see, and 6d a week. Well what some of these people would do, once they had the blankets, they would pawn them and get say 8s or 9s.'[63]

The reverse of credit was insurance. A man who had been an insurance agent in the centre of Middlesbrough in the mid-thirties explained that nearly everybody had a minimum of insurance: 'It was to the unemployed, as well as to the employed, essential to have insurance. They wouldn't have big insurance . . . of course in those days the main thought was sufficient to cover funeral expenses and, well, the wife and family would have to take their chance after that.'[64]

This concurs with the findings of the Pilgrim Trust, that people had to be very demoralised before they gave up insurance against funeral expenses.[65] In most households, all money matters were left to the wife, and depending on her, some extra insurance might be taken out. Many interviewees described the doctor's 'club' to which people paid a penny or so a week to cover a minimum of medical care when members of the family were sick. Again, even the long-unemployed tried to keep this up.

If the chief sources of moral support came from families and neighbours, some people looked outside the immediate environment for solace in depression. Some people, as we saw in Chapter 5, were interested in politics. Other turned to religion, for either practical or spiritual support. These were invariably people who had belonged to a church beforehand. One interviewee put it like this: 'If they were religious to start with their faith seemed stronger.'[66] Of course churches had a social side to them; they had fetes and outings, and Sunday Schools for children. In Stockton and Middlesbrough there was a large Catholic community, which seemed to have a great appeal to the poor on a number of different levels. This is described by one Catholic interviewee:

Well of course religion was a soporific with regard to many people. Well perhaps that's the wrong word to use but it did play a very important part. Now in this town for instance I'd say that twenty-six to thirty per cent even now are Catholic, and of course it was this togetherness which meant that the Churches were full and so on. These missions would come and there was a certain amount of pomp and circumstance . . . strangely enough it gave a little bit of colour. And strangely enough it was poverty which increased the piety of the average person. One associated protestantism with the better off people, but the Methodists were extremely strong in this town. It seemed to appeal to the masses more than the Anglican, and I'm not decrying the Anglican Church of course. And I would also think, and again I might be wrong, that there was, with regard to Catholics (and I am a Catholic), a certain amount of fear. These people would shout and bawl from the pulpit 'hell or heaven forever' . . . but there was a certain amount of joy . . . and I can remember just before the war playing the organ at the Cathedral and it was nothing to have, on occasions which were special, ten thousand people. So religion played a great part in people's lives because it was an outlet to the mundane humdrum existence.[67]

For other people the social aspect of churchgoing could be a barrier during the depression. Mrs Chilvers said that only families with one child could afford to go to church, because only they could afford the right clothes. She described her own experience of being one of a poor family in church: 'What struck me when I left was that the first four pews were for the notables of your town . . . and if you were mucky and you had no shoes and your hair was full of lice nobody wanted to know you. They didn't ask why you had lice. I never remember a vicar coming to my mother's house. Never.'

Both Mrs and Mr Chilvers left their church as they formulated their left-wing convictions. Mr Chilvers described it thus: 'My attitude changed from a Bible-reading sailor wearing a crucifix on a chain on my wrist . . . and through attendance at meetings became a collector of "Thinkers Library" pocket volumes . . . Reluctantly and slowly I reached atheistic conviction.'

The weight of the evidence about the community response to unemployment suggests that large sections of the working class population in each town maintained a family and community strength despite the problem of poverty and unemployment. However great the sum of individual depression and anxiety (something which will be discussed in the next chapter) communities and families survived. There were other sections of the community, elusive even from oral testimony, who were less resilient and certainly suffered great hardships from the poverty of unemployment. But these homes were usually used to poverty (often the father had previously been employed on casual work) and so were at least able to accept the misfortunes of the depression. The information available about the political response in the depression, and the effects of unemployment on crime confirms this impression of a stable and resilient community. A number of interviewees commented directly on this fact, but they fall into two camps. Some said that the people of Teesside were stoical, that they 'just got on with it' and others felt that the acceptance of unemployment was due to a passivity, a feeling of demoralisation.

Those in the former camp, was commented on the stoicism of the Teesside unemployed, attributed it to the fact that unemployment was happening to everybody, that 'you were all in the same boat' and also to the fact that most people had had to cope with periods of poverty even before the depression, so it was something people knew how to cope with. These factors were brought out by the contemporary investigators, who often found that people who were unemployed in depressed areas adjusted much more easily than those in more prosperous places. The stigma of unemployment was reduced, there was no need to keep up with the neighbours, and all around were able to give help and support. The depressed areas were also isolated, and few people living there realised how well off people in the Midlands and South were: 'The biggest part of people were all in the same boat. If they were skint next door, and they were skint next door, and the other people skint like that it didn't make no difference . . . But today there's so many people got so much and so many got nothing.'[68]

However, another interviewee saw differently. 'I am of the opinion that there were a lot of people that were unemployed that long a time that they became demoralised. It became a way of life for them. At the end of the day I don't think they realised they were unemployed because they had been out of work that long.'[69]

These conflicting attitudes seem to be in part a difference of perception, and in part reality. Perhaps whilst some of the unemployed carried on, like those of Crook where the Pilgrim Trust found a 'determination not to give into unemployment and not to subsist on self pity', others were more like those George Orwell observed in North Western England, 'In the back streets of Wigan and Barnsley I saw every kind of privation, but I probably saw much less conscious misery than I would have seen ten years ago.'[70]

There were exceptions to this rule of acceptance, and some of them have been discussed already, but the most striking was certainly the reaction to the Means Test. This was so strong, and a point so often made by interviewees that it is worthy of separate consideration. Of course political opposition to the Means Test is well-attested, but the Teesside interviewees described their own personal reactions to it.

When asked about the Means Test, the initial reaction of many was 'Well it split up families'. Young men who were earning, and so would have been expected to keep their fathers, or who were unemployed themselves, were almost universally farmed out to relations or lodging houses, so that they could draw their dole, or allow their father to draw his. Many people were at pains to explain this, and to point out the fact that the home was broken up. The Pilgrim Trust found that this practice rarely alienated sons from the family, but it was nonetheless a practice which could not be forgiven by the Teesside interviewees. Mr Chilvers described his feelings about it:

Mr first hand experience was with a knock at the door when I was ostensibly 'farmed out' (supposed to be living with an aunt). A loud knock at the door sent me scurrying into a back kitchen and gritting my teeth. I had to listen to a Mr Bumble browbeating my mother about a guitar on the wall.

The obligation to sell possessions was also a major source of resentment. Relief from the Guardians had been Means Tested from the mid-twenties, but most of the people who were subjected to the Means Test in the thirties had previously been in receipt of unemployment benefit, and this had not affected them. 'Nobody had much in those days, see. Even the wireless was only after the war . . . and if you had anything you were told to sell it. Anything valuable. And people resented it, because maybe someone had bought it you, and you had to sell it.'[71]

Often the possessions that people had to sell were of sentimental value, or were symbols of their respectability (like a piano) or were bought from money saved over a long period of time. One interviewee, an old man of ninety whose memory was fading, could only remember from the inter-war years the bitterness and resentment he had felt (and still felt) about the Means Test. This man, Mr Vipond, offered to be interviewed chiefly because he wished to communicate this feeling. He was a Methodist, who had always been brought up to work hard, to save, and to be self-sufficient, and he bitterly resented the intrusion of the Means Test officer into his home. A similar case was related by another interviewee, of a man, a 'staunch presbyterian', who had had a good job and had managed to save and buy a small house. When he applied to the PAC he was forced to sell this house, and 'vowed never to save anything again'.[72]

It is this seemingly universal response to the Means Test, which shows that the acceptance of the unemployed on Teesside was not entirely passive and demoralised. Certainly many men do seem to have become dispirited, but there were still issues which could rouse universal indignation. This Means Test was a cause of lost dignity; and the outrage it caused shows that many people still had a great deal of dignity left to be conscious of. However, the overall resilience of the Teesside community, like those of the other depressed areas, was remarkable.

Chapter 8

The individual response to unemployment

Although most types of community within Teesside appeared to withstand the depression with remarkable resilience, they contained within them a large amount of individual suffering and anxiety. It is the purpose of this chapter to examine these effects on individuals to see how differently people with different experiences of unemployment reacted. This will include unemployed people of different ages and conditions, and their wives and children.

Various modern studies on the psychology of unemployment explain why the loss of work causes suffering to individuals, for so many aspects of a person's life are bound up in the work they do. Hayes and Nutman summarise the reasons why people place a high value on work thus: work is a source of income, a form of activity, a source of creativity or mastery, a source of identity, it structures time and gives a person a sense of purpose.[1] Of course not all these things will apply to every working person; for example, a person who does not find his or her work satisfying would probably not find it a source of creativity or mastery, and a casual worker would probably not so easily see work as a source of identity as someone with a permanent job. Almost certainly the fewer of those aspects of work quoted above that apply to an individual, the less likely he or she is to suffer in unemployment. However, they are all important in explaining why the psychological effects of being out of work are some of the most difficult to cope with. One correspondent wrote to the author: 'I am of the opinion that the one thing you will never measure is the stress on the nerves and minds of both men and women.'[2]

The contemporary investigators also drew attention to the factors which affected the individual response. According to the Pilgrim Trust the most telling feature in whether or not people were prepared to accept being out of work was their previous job.

Skilled men, whose whole life had often been involved in their job, and who derived a good deal of status from doing their work well, found being unemployed very hard, whereas unskilled men who derived less satisfaction from their work, and who in any case were probably used to having short spells out of work from time to time, found it much easier to adjust. They found that skilled men, even if they were out of work for months or years, might refuse to accept unemployment.[3] This was not only something which applied to older men who had been used to the routine of work for some time. The Carnegie Trust, in their study of young unemployed men, found that those who had served apprenticeships, and had high ambitions found it far more difficult to accept being out of work. They said that whereas educated young men often became very depressed when unemployed, the unskilled 'did not expect so much from life, even when in employment. Consequently their disillusionment and personal distress were not felt so keenly.'[4]

Age, itself, was another important factor in accepting unemployment. The Carnegie Trust found that young men were likely to be quite happy if they were only out of work for a short time, but were likely to become very demoralised if their efforts to find work were continually in vain. They concluded that 'young life demands recognition in the form of success and, when existence presents little else than a series of failures, even the most ardent and adventurous spirit begins to doubt its own capabilities'.[5] This applied to unskilled men as well as to skilled; even though they came to terms with being out of work more easily 'he has, at least, one thing in common with the young man more fortunately situated, and that is the idealism of youth'.[6] The Pilgrim Trust, however, in their sample found a number of 'workshy' young men who had never known regular work and had become quite used to life out of work. They cited one case of a young man who had never worked and 'had now evidently settled down on the allowance, eked out quite generously by less reputable sources of income, and expressed himself as quite contented'.[7] These cases were clearly a great worry to contemporaries, for all the studies done in the interwar years consider this question of the 'workshy', those who lost any taste for work, but they all found these cases to be a minority.

By contrast, some older men found an acceptable alternative lifestyle in unemployment. If they were in any case near retiring age, and were given a sum of money they could live on, and were able to find some alternative pursuit, such as working in an allotment, then they might be reasonably content. This of course, was very much dependent on individual character, and some older men found this adjustment easier than others.

The adjustment of men in middle years was more difficult. They had long been used to working and gave up hope less easily. According to the Pilgrim Trust their acceptance depended very much on their family responsibilities:

It is easier for the single man to acquiesce in unemployment than it is for the married man who has no children or only one, but in families where there is more than one child it becomes progressively likely that the unemployed man who is head of the family will be able to reconcile himself to becoming out of work.[8]

This was because a man with a large family might be no better off working than on the dole.[9] This might for some, though, be a purely academic proposition, if there was no work available.

Another crucial factor in an individuals attitude to unemployment was its duration. E. Bakke, in his study of unemployment explained this best when he pointed out that the feelings of an unemployed person would go through various stages; at first optimism that more work could be found, and perhaps a holiday feeling; then depression and anxiety if no work was forthcoming; and finally acceptance, and a feeling that unemployment was a normal way of life.[10] Also important was the experience of others around; all the contemporary surveys point out that unemployment was much easier to bear in the depressed areas, where communities of unemployed people developed, and the stigma of unemployment lessened as everyone around was shown to be in a similar situation. Individual character, also, undoubtedly played an important part, something which is demonstrated best by the contemporary oral history of the unemployed by Beales and Lambert.[11] The difference between the unemployed colliery banksman interviewed who said that unemployment had made him a selfish person 'closely examining, sometimes even suspecting, friendly gestures, seeing, whether it exists or not, selfishness behind all striving for position in politics or trade unions or co-operative societies', and the out of work London fitter who was also interested in politics, but used his unemployment to involve himself more, to join the WEA and read, was a difference not so much of circumstances as of individual attitude.[12]

All these factors appear in the Teesside sample. Of those interviewed it was those who were unemployed as young men who appeared to have taken the actual experience of unemployment most easily. This was because unemployment for a youth of fourteen to eighteen was almost always of a temporary nature. Most young men managed to get some kinds of part-time jobs for most of the time before they were eighteen; selling newspapers, being an errand boy, or a junior in a firm, and although they might often be out of work it was usually not for long. It was common for a young man to be paid off at the age of eighteen or twenty-one, but even this might not be too depressing an experience. One man, who had worked at temporary jobs since the age of eighteen, found unemployment, at least at first, something of a relief from hard work: 'Well, speaking from a single point of view, I was a single man, we learned to live with it . . . It didn't hit us so bad, we didn't realise it so much. But after a while it became boring, the repetition, doing the same thing all the time. That's why I joined the army.'[13]

This man explained that having never had a holiday, it was in some ways pleasant to be able to do what he liked for a short time, to explore the countryside and spend time in the company of friends. However, the holiday feeling wore off, and he was fortunate in being accepted for the army. This man could certainly not be described as lazy or workshy, because apart from a few months in his late teens he had worked hard all his life; as a young boy, then in the army and subsequently in the steel industry of Teesside, it was just that unemployment provided him with a brief respite.

Various testimonies suggest that young men were the most happy to spend time playing games outdoors, walking and mushrooming, swimming. They were on the whole more gregarious, and were happy to indulge in these activities. They were also more hopeful, (initially at least) and in many ways actually had more chance of finding work, which made their position more bearable. Many left Teesside either temporarily or permanently, something which was rare for a middle-aged man with a family to attempt. Young men were eligible to join the services, provided they were sufficiently tall and healthy, and many did join; although also many were turned down. One man recalled that when he joined the army in the thirties there were seven men from his class at school in the same regiment.[14] Others went to sea, although in the depression years this was not always easy.

It was more difficult, though, for a young man to find a job in the steelworks, or engineering works on Teesside. These jobs were obtained through the 'market', going to stand outside the works gates and trying to attract the attention of the foreman. The market operated on seniority, for the foreman would always choose someone who had some experience of the job rather than a young recruit.

Some young men and women attended the Junior Instruction Centres in each town, which provided them with something to do, but these were a minority because only the insured unemployed were required to attend.

The majority of Teesside youths did only casual work before they were eighteen, but the two interviewees who had had an apprenticeship before becoming out of work had a markedly different attitude to unemployment. As the Carnegie Trust found in their sample of young men, the thwarting of their youthful ambitions had a profound affect on them. One, although he managed to get a job with status and responsibility, said that always, until he retired, he had worried that he might become unemployed again, and might not be able to look after his family. This man had clearly been deeply unhappy about being unemployed, and found it a painful subject even years afterwards, and after a long and successful career.[15]

Young men who did not find work, after a long time of looking, could also become very depressed. The Carnegie Trust found that young men were more optimistic when they were first out of work, but gave up hope if their efforts to find it were always in vain. One interviewee described the plight of young men like this: 'Some young lads hardly worked . . . it was soul destroying for them. And you see they'd accept almost anything, take things lying down because they'd never known any better.'[16]

There were, as well, special problems for the young unemployed to face. One of the most difficult was the fact that they were less likely to qualify for Unemployment Benefit, and before 1934 only people over sixteen were entitled to benefit, although most children left school at fourteen. This meant that they became a drain on their families just at the time when they would normally expect to contribute to the family income, and to have some money of their own. After 1931, many young men were affected by the household Means Test, and had to leave home so that they could continue to draw their dole (if they were out of work) for otherwise their father would be expected to support them. The more fortunate stayed as lodgers with relatives, others went into lodging houses. Although these young men came home whenever they could, they had to be careful not to appear to be living at home. One interviewee described having to hide when he was at home when the Means Test officer came.[17] This, more even than the fact of unemployment, aroused the indignation of the people interviewed. In most cases the young man left home by mutual agreement with his family, but occasionally difficulties over money meant that a boy was turned out of his home. One man described this: he was assessed for dole against the earnings of his stepfather, who felt no obligation to keep him and turned him out of the house.[18]

Occasionally, also, a young man would stay at home and accept the Means Test rulings, and this brought its own problems. One man, who was earning, stayed at home even though his father's dole was stopped. He said that his father felt 'dreadful' about being kept by his son's income, but: 'I thought, rightly or wrongly, it would be opting out, a confession of failure sort of thing. But I knew quite a lot of fellows who did, and I didn't think any the less of them because they did but I thought I'm staying here, this is my home.'[19]

Another man described the responsibility he had felt to his own family, as a young out of work man: 'I wasn't married or anything like that, I had no responsibility, but I used to feel so guilty. I felt I should be giving more money at home, and yet when I look back on it I was at least paying my way out of my dole money.'[20]

This sense of responsibility probably did not weigh as heavily as that of a man with children to support, but it was the custom for young people to stay at home until they married, and before then to contribute money to the home, and so some people were very conscious of not being able to do this. Some contemporary reports describe family acrimony against a member of the family who was not 'paying his way' which caused trouble at home, or the feelings of defensiveness of the unemployed family which was very 'touchy' and took criticism as a reflection of their unemployment.[21]

Many young people who were unemployed and wanted to get married just went ahead, in an attempt to carry on a normal life, or sometimes in a bid for independence:

Well if they wanted to get married, and they had no prospect of a job a lot of them just went ahead, because somehow the dole managed to provide sufficient money for at least a room, and yes I wouldn't say that it influenced the rate of marriage, the frequency of marriage, a tremendous lot at all ... and they could often live with their parents, that often happened.[22]

However, some people, especially those from 'respectable' families, found it hard to imagine marrying on the dole. Jack Singleton, who became unemployed after serving an apprenticeship said: 'Madge and I were courting then, and I used to think we'd never get married, we'd never have enough money. If I got a job it would take years and years to save up and I'd be an old man. However, circumstances altered.'

Burdens of a different kind fell upon unemployed family men, and from the evidence of Teesside interviewees it seems that this category of people suffered most from being out of work. They had to give up a job which had often been important to them (it must be remembered that many of the interviewees were skilled people) and they keenly felt the fact that their families relied on them for financial support. When describing the feelings of men in this category interviewees often talked of them being very depressed. A typical comment came from the daughter of an unemployed man: 'My father went back to sea, he was so, you know, depressed. He didn't get much more money going back to sea, but he went.'[23]

This man felt the loss of the status and the occupation of work very keenly, and the fact that he could get almost as much money for his family from the dole as from wages made little difference. Another man described the difference between being made unemployed from casual work at eighteen, and later after he had spent some time in regular employment, and had a family to support. His first experience of being out of work had been in the 1926 strike as a boy, which had seemed like a holiday, and had given him the kind of new-found sense of freedom already described, though he said that he had not realised how difficult things had been for his parents. But losing a permanent job for a few months in 1930, and then from 1932 to 1933, had been completely different. He felt depressed, because 'when you were in work you felt you were doing something'. He then looked back to his 'proudest days' in 1924 when his company had been making steel for the Sidney Harbour Bridge.[24]

Other men, when describing what it was like to be an unemployed man with a family, concentrated on the problems of keeping their children. For one man it was a source of bitterness and anger that, because of a Means Test ruling that his father should support him and his family, 'I hadn't a ha'penny to keep my wife and kids.'[25]

The same story is told by the children of long-term unemployed men. They nearly all talk of their fathers being 'depressed' and in some cases this meant that their father did very little while he was out of work, because he could not summon the enthusiasm to be active in any way. Others were more enterprising, and found plenty to occupy themselves, but this was no substitute for working. To some the prospect of work dominated their whole lives. One woman, who could remember the depression from her very early years, said, 'The first thing I remember was that we were waiting for a green card. This would mean that a job had come his way.'[26] The most extreme case of depression described was that of Mr Chilver's father, who had his dole stopped one day and tried to commit suicide. The fact that he could no longer do anything at all for his family, and he believed that they would starve, was what finally decided him into this most desperate course of action.

Not only did married men find unemployment more difficult than a lot of single men, but it was less easy for them to move to more prosperous areas. Few of those interviewed could remember a whole family moving away from Teesside, and only very occasionally did a married man go away on his own. This would have seemed too big a step for many families, in times when communications were less good and even the cost of stamps was a great deal for the unemployed. Many worked on allotments and grew food, which provided an interest and occupation as well as a useful supplement to the family income. Some kept up a social life in clubs, or by playing sport, walking or gambling, although gregarious activities seemed easier for the younger men. One interviewee described how unemployment had ruined her parents social life: her father would not accept invitations to visit friends.

This attitude seems to have been the exception rather than the rule, because most interviewees described the friendly neighbourliness of the street, where people called informally without waiting to be invited, and where all were 'in the same boat' so that it did not matter what hospitality was offered. Nonetheless, this may not have been untypical of a certain kind of 'respectable' person. The father described here was the product of a strict non-conformist home, he was a teetotaller, refused ever to buy goods on credit, and had in everything the very high standards typical of the strictist of the 'respectable' class. The Pilgrim Trust discusses the idea of respectability in some detail, and pointed out that one of the corner-stones of it is the idea of 'keeping oneself to oneself' which would presumably include only having people into the house by invitation.[27]

As has been said before, most of the interviewees, although not as rigid in their standards as the man mentioned above, came from families with some pride in their work, and a strong sense of responsibility towards their own families. The kind of people described by the Pilgrim Trust, who settled down to unemployment reasonably happily because they had never expected much from life, were hardly represented in the survey for this study. Such people are described by some interviewees, who often commented that the children of such people suffered: this may be to a certain extent a reflection of their own values. Another type of unemployed man, described but (not surprisingly) not interviewed was the man who took out his feelings of frustration and anger on his family. Mrs Chilvers was convinced that this often happened:

They talk about battered wives . . . I remember men beating their wives up, which was a most distressing thing for me. One that I lived opposite, he was a very very bad-tempered man in drink, and I've seen his wife black and blue from head to foot, and screams in the middle of the night, and things like that, and that was on the increase during the unemployed, definitely.

It is difficult to know what truth there is in this statement, because wife-beating undoubtedly happened before the days of the depression (before Mrs Chilvers was old enough to understand such a thing) and her statement that it was on the increase is therefore not something that she could really substantiate from her own experience. If, as she suggested, it was related to drunkenness it may even have decreased, because the extent of drunkenness declined during the depression.[28] However, Mrs Chilvers' point was that the demoralisation of unemployment turned many men to violence, at least within their own homes, which at least seems plausible.

One category of men who were not included at all in the survey for this study were the long-term older unemployed men described by the Pilgrim Trust; those men who were a few years off retiring age when they lost their jobs, and had no chance of finding another in the depression. Men who were in their fifties or sixties in even the late thirties are most unlikely to be alive now. The Pilgrim Trust described how many of these men settled down to a sort of early retirement, and found themselves other occupations.[29] Doubtless this was also done by the older unemployed of Teesside, but those who remembered them felt, in retrospect, a special sympathy for them. These were, to those interviewees who described them, the men 'who never worked again'. While other men they knew had recovered from their period of unemployment, and perhaps if they had been young during the depression had prospered afterwards, these older men were seen as those who did not survive the hard times, and therefore deserved a special pity.

One very elusive category of unemployed is unemployed women. Although the official figures show that there were a substantial minority of women registered as unemployed, only one of the women interviewed had been without a job. This interviewee had served an apprenticeship as a seamstress but had then been unable to find work. She spent her time helping with housework at home, until she married. Although she said that she would have liked to use her needlework skills, she did not seem to have regarded herself as 'unemployed' in the same way that the men were.[30] Helping with housework was an acceptable occupation for a young girl, which may have meant that some unemployed women were not recognised as such. Both Beales and Lambert and the Pilgrim Trust found cases of unemployed women who reacted to being out of work in much the same way as men; feeling the loss of the company, of occupation, and of money, leaving a feeling of depression.[31] Although few Teesside women expected to work full-time after they married, as the women of Lancashire did, any unemployed women who were unmarried, or widowed must have suffered similar problems to those of the men described.

One effect of the depression which was spoken of by some of the women interviewed was the limitation it made on the choice of employment for young unmarried women. Several women said that they took jobs in service which they would not otherwise have chosen to do, and many young women travelled far away from

Teesside to do these jobs, although they would have preferred to stay in the area. Of course this was nothing new, traditionally there had been little choice of occupation for either men or women, but in other parts of the country there were opportunities opening up which would have been welcomed by many of the women of Teesside. Shop work was much preferred to service, but in a depressed area the opportunities were few. Some girls would have chosen factory work in favour of service, because of the greater freedom allowed; but there was only one factory providing employment for women on Teesside, Price's clothing factory in Middlesbrough which opened in the thirties.

The other effect of the depression on the employment of women was that many married women took on part-time jobs if their husbands were out of work. Again this was not entirely new; Lady Bell refers to married women doing part-time work to eke out the family income in Edwardian Middlesbrough. But the need became more pressing during the depression.[32] One woman described how her mother did this, although she would not otherwise have expected to work: 'She had to go to work. She worked nearly all the time . . . She was just an ordinary housewife with a large family, and she had to take whatever was going to make a little money.'[33]

The kinds of jobs that these women did were traditional 'women's work', jobs which unemployed men would almost certainly not have considered doing, or being offered if they had. Some took in washing from wealthier families, others did sewing. Some baked bread or pies and sold them. The mother of one interviewee used to ice cakes for special occasions, although there was little call for this kind of work during the depression.[34] Others went out to work, often cleaning and washing. This kind of work was hard and poorly paid, and put a great strain on a mother who had to work hard to look after a home and several children. One woman, Mrs Bell, said that her worst memory of the thirties was not her father's seven year unemployment, but the stress on her mother who had to do extra work:

She eventually got a job in a laundry, which was very hard, not only on my mother but on all the women who worked there. It was terribly hard. I only caught a glimpse of it one day [she had to take a mug of tea to her mother] and my mother came, and I could see her through the steam, and it upset me so much, she looked about a hundred, and at that time she must have been, say about forty-five. So old you know. And she took the tea from me, and told me to go back home and help my father. And she went back to the table. And there was this very long table and there were all these women scrubbing, and that was their job. There were about twelve of them. And they had to scrub the dirtiest clothes before they went in the wash. And literally all you could see was steam and soap suds and all this washing. . . . I shall always remember I cried all the way home.

Mrs Bell's father was somewhat unusual in that he did some housework while his wife was out at work: he did some cleaning and provided meals for the children, but as has already been said, many unemployed men would not have thought of spending their extra time doing housework, and many wives would not have allowed it.[35] This meant that the burden placed on the wives of unemployed men of having to manage on less money, and perhaps to work herself, was a heavy one. A number of contemporary surveys pointed out that women suffered physically more from unemployment than men, and the evidence for Teesside bears this out.[36]

Several interviewees volunteered the information that inter-war Teesside was a 'male-dominated society', something which it had in common with other parts of the country. By this they seemed to mean that most women were reliant on, and subservient to, their husbands, but they did carry a great deal of responsibility. One man explained how they were responsible for the family finances:

Well I think the women of this area were responsible mainly for the laying out of the cash, most of the household expenses were turned over to the wife. The men turned over what dole money they'd got, and kept a little, but as far as running the home was concerned, feeding the family, it was all left to the woman.[37]

All expenses incurred by the family which were not her husbands personal spending were administered by the wife. She would pay the rent (one man interviewed did not know how much rent his family paid, because his wife had always paid it) and the insurance money, as well as buying any new capital goods, clothes for all the family, food, and in better days, saving money. This meant that when the family income dropped because of unemployment the role of the wife was crucial: 'The women, the wives of the unemployed, their life was just the same, except that they had less money to do it on. They did exactly what they would have done before, but cutting down as much as they could.'[38]

Economising often in itself involved extra work. A number of people described how women went to the market late on a Saturday night to buy left-over food very cheaply.[39] Other ways of getting cheap food involved getting up early: 'I've seen us leave our house at 7.30 in the morning, and walk all the way to Hinton's in South Street, and wait for bacon bones, and mostly you were lucky, sometimes you weren't. And our mothers tried, didn't they, well.'[40]

Of course the success of the wife of an unemployed man, as has previously been suggested, was ultimately dependent on her husband; for she relied on him to bring home money each week. One interviewee said that the well-being or otherwise of the family depended 'on the selfishness of the men'.[41]

As has already been shown, many women did manage to provide an adequate diet for their families in the thirties. However, the nutritional analysis contained in Chapter 2 showed that those people most likely to suffer from poor nutrition in the thirties were expectant and nursing mothers; another strong indication that the contemporary reports that the health of women suffered during the depression were justified. How they managed in the twenties, when scales of relief were low, and the cost of living high, is difficult to determine. Contemporary reports suggested that many women deprived themselves of food in order to feed their family, but the task of catering adequately for any member of the family was exceptionally hard.

Despite all these problems, many women, at least in retrospect, were proud of the way they managed during the depression. They could point to the fact that they had brought up a healthy family, who were usually a great source of pride to them. Whilst the men often looked back on the inter-war years as a time of depression and demoralisation, many women appeared to feel those times were a battle which had been won. In very rough contrast, unemployed men were taken away from the hardships, but also the satisfaction of work, while their wives had extra work, extra responsibility, which was extremely difficult at the time but satisfying to look back on.

Interviews with the children of the unemployed were, for the most part, almost left out of the contemporary studies because, of course, they were then so much younger, but they were an important part of this study. Many of the people interviewed had been children of unemployed men and often they also had been unemployed in their turn. Almost without exception, the people interviewed who had been children of an unemployed man, even if they spoke of great hardships at home, spoke about their childhoods as a time when they had been secure and happy. Most in retrospect felt grateful for the efforts and sacrifices their parents had made on their behalf. This is perhaps not surprising, for it is common for people to remember good things of their childhood, but it is still significant. Again, though, it is very important to remember that nearly all these people survived the depression to live at least generally contented lives. This is not to say that they are unrepresentative, but they probably represent only one section of Teesside society.

Many people described the games they played as children, and the fun they had within their families. In some cases having the father at home could even mean that they were given more attention, because of all the spare time father had: 'He spent hours playing with me on the mat . . . He would read to me by the hour, and he always taught me "never pass a word", (he showed me the dictionary) never pass a word without knowing its meaning.'[42]

Mrs Bell's father also played with the children:

He made a board and played ludo with us, and he had patience and we were happy playing. And we played dominoes, he used to sing with us, he used to invent games, he used to say 'I'm going to put so many things in a matchbox and you guess how many articles are in it.' And he'd put a dried pea and all sorts of little things – you'd probably think there would be only three or four things but he'd probably manage to get fifty things in it. A tiny bit of rice you know. He always used to do things to make us happy, you know.

Mrs Chilver's father took his children for walks, and even to political meetings, so that they became involved with his interests. These fathers may have been unusual, and certainly from the fuller descriptions of each of them by each daughter it is clear that they were very concerned for the well-being of their families and conscientious people, but it is unlikely that they were exceptional. They are reminiscent of some men described by the Pilgrim Trust, who found it easier to adjust to long-term unemployment because of the satisfaction provided by their families. 'A further factor which doubtless makes it easier to adjust to unemployment is that many of those who have large families can do a useful job if they stay at home and help bring up the children.' They cited the case of one man with eight children 'his chief interest was evidently his family, and he had not much use for any amusements and interests which he could not share with them. He found that looking after them was practically a full-time job for himself and his wife.'[43]

Of course in some cases an unemployed man might find the home environment annoying, and his children suffer as a result. The Pilgrim Trust also cited the case of the woman who said about her husband, 'when he was out of work we were always having rows over the children. He will never let them do anything. It is much better now he is at work.'[44]

Some Teesside interviewees described children who were 'dragged up' during the depression: underfed, poorly clothed, dirty and lousy. Sometimes this state of affairs came from pure neglect, othertimes from financial stringency (especially in the twenties) or from parents who were less intelligent or adequate than the average. Most interviewees agreed that family size was very important to the well-being of children, something which is clearly borne out in Chapter 2.[45] An only child (there were two interviewed) would be quite well provided for even if their fathers were out of work. They would be better than averagely clothed, might have toys bought for them, better food, and perhaps an iced cake for their birthday.

Under these conditions even children from caring homes could suffer from the problems of unemployment. This might manifest itself in many ways. The schoolteacher in the study pointed out that many children were prevented from being educated after the age of fourteen because of financial stringency at home, something which did not begin with the depression but was sustained by it. Most children from poor homes had to be very resilient, and often learn to fend for themselves in many ways. Many young boys had to try to earn extra money for the family, even before they left home at fourteen. One man described his early attempts to find a job for himself: 'I used to pop into this cafe and sit around, and then I took it into my head, I thought "I'll collect a few pots" (I wasn't fourteen then) and the fellow said to me "you might as well work for me" and he gave me a job.'[46]

Other boys ran errands and sold newspapers, in the evenings and at weekends. Mrs Bell described a family where the job of all the children was to collect firewood, make it into bundles, and sell it on the streets.

It was traditional for children to run errands for their parents, but if the family was poor they had to learn to strike a hard bargain. Mrs Bell told how she used to go to the pawn shop, and had to make sure that she got the right amount of money for the goods she took in, a job she hated doing. Similarly she had to learn to be firm when shopping:

I'd stand there and say, 'I want twopennyworth of potstuff.' And I'd stand there and watch what she was putting in the bag . . . I would say, 'You haven't put a turnip in.' She'd say, 'You've got quite sufficient for tuppence.' And I'd say, 'My Mum says I have to have a turnip, we need a turnip today.' And I'd sort of stand there and in the end she'd say, 'Give her one of those small turnips, there we are.' And I would invariably get it you know.

A more extreme example of children having to cope for themselves was the case already described of the boy turned out of his family home by his stepfather.[47] He left Middlesbrough then to look for work, and confessed that he was homesick when he had to go away while still in his early teens.

No member of a family, therefore, could escape some kind of hardship. Few interviewees remembered their individual experience of the depression with any rosy glow of hindsight, although most of them coped remarkably well. This record of individual hardship re-enforces the strength of the communities, which was shown in the previous chapter and those on crime and politics. When seen in the context of the sufferings of so many individuals, the way in which communities stayed with most of their old values intact is impressive.

Conclusion

Some interesting results arose from each subject examined. The unemployment figures for Teesside showed that it was an area of persistently heavy unemployment, which adversely affected most sections of the working population. The inquiry into living standards amongst the Teesside unemployed produced some of the most important results of the study. It showed that the living standards of the unemployed in the twenties were considerably worse than in the thirties. This acts as a reminder that although the popular idea of the hardships of the inter-war unemployed focuses on the thirties, the large number of people who were out of work in the 1920s faced a much harsher existence. Their experience was probably closer to that of people unemployed in Edwardian or late nineteenth-century England. A budget and cost of living index for the thirties was constructed, and this was subjected to a nutritional analysis, on the basis of modern nutritional standards. This was a new piece of work, for all previous historians who have considered the question of the nutritional standards of the unemployed of the inter-war years have relied on the out-of-date studies of the early nutritional scientists. This study showed that in an area like Teesside, where the cost of living was low, the unemployed and their families could usually be adequately fed, provided that they took care over their housekeeping, and denied themselves any luxuries; something which many people interviewed clearly did. However the food which could be bought from an unemployed man's income would have been inadequate for pregnant and nursing mothers; an important section of the population. Whilst it was not possible to construct an accurate budget for the twenties, it was clear from the study that the unemployed of the twenties would have been far worse off, and in many cases almost certainly undernourished. The related area of health was an extremely problematic field. There were a number of indications that the effects of unemployment did hold back the improvements in health which were a feature of this period, but the extremely complex nature of the question made it difficult to draw any really firm conclusions in this area. The study of crime showed little real correlation between any changes in the crime rate and unemployment, except in the case of juveniles. An investigation into popular attitudes to crime on Teesside suggested some possible reasons for this: the Teesside code of ethics was already geared to a life which was hard, standards of behaviour were normally enforced by other members of the community as well as by the police. Whilst the experience of the depression did weaken these cultural values a little, and this can be seen in the rise of juvenile crime, in general they held up well. There was seemingly little political response from the Teesside electorate. Many people appeared to believe that the problems of unemploy-ment were not susceptible to a political solution. However, the continually strong support for the Labour Party, even in times when nationally the party fared ill, was typical of depressed areas. Also, there were short-lived protest movements in the early twenties and early thirties which attracted a good deal of popular support, although this was not sustained. The response of the politicians, though, was quite marked. All candidates for election on Teesside believed that unemployment was an important issue, and some of them developed a special interest in the subject. The story of the local administrative reaction to the problems of unemployment is that of institutions not designed to cope with such large-scale problems, at times retreating to recommend tried and tested methods of help, such as voluntary aid, and at other times calling for changes in administration which were surprisingly radical. There was much information on the response of the Teesside community, and it is difficult to summarise. Generally, unemployed communities held together well, kept up their old values and relied on traditional supports. The record of the response of the unemployed and the employed shows them reacting as they might to a natural disaster; accepting what they saw to be inevitable, and struggling in a number of *ad hoc* ways to cope with the problems it caused. However, the individual response emphasises the extent of suffering and anxiety felt by the unemployed, and the fact that the whole families of the unemployed were affected.

Notes

Introduction

1 The Pilgrim Trust, *Men Without Work*, Cambridge, 1938. E. W. Bakke, *The Unemployed Man*, London, 1933. H. L. Beales and R. S. Lambert, *Memoirs of the Unemployed*, London, 1934.

2 (i) Bede, *Opera Historica*, 3rd edition, Cambridge, 1962. (i) B. S. Rowntree, *op. cit.* (ii) C. Booth, *op. cit.*

3 Oral History, I, 4, 1973, p. 1–47.

4 P. Thompson, *The Edwardians*, London, 1975, p. 6.

5 Mr Vipond, interview.

6 Some parish records of Stockton and Middlesbrough contain lists of the weekly numbers of communicants, but these are an insufficient guide.

7 H. Macmillan, *Winds of Change*, London, 1966, p. 160–1.

8 G. A. North, *Teesside's Economic Heritage*, Margate, 1975, p. 60.

9 *Ibid.*, p. 60.

10 Darlington MOH report, 1931.

11 S. Constantine, *Unemployment in Britain Between the Wars*, London, 1980, p. 2–4.

12 See S. Pollard, *The Development of the British Economy 1914–1967*, 2nd edition, London, 1969. P. Mathias, *The First Industrial Nation*, London, 1969. R. S. Sayers, *Economic Change in England 1880–1939*, Oxford, 1967.

13 J. Stevenson and C. Cook, *The Slump*, London, 1979, p. 55.

14 Pilgrim Trust, *op. cit.*, p. 15.

15 *Ibid.*

16 S. Constantine, *op. cit.*, p. 24.

17 J. B. Priestley, *English Journey*, 2nd edition, London, 1977, p. 321.

18 G. A. North, *op. cit.*, p. 59.

19 *Ibid.*, p. 63–64.

21 *Ibid.*, p. 67. See also D. Dougan, *A History of North East Shipbuilding*, London, 1962, Appendix II, for detailed figures on launches in Middlesbrough and Stockton yards in the inter-war years.

22 G. A. North, *op. cit.*, p. 65.

23 *Ibid.*, p. 66.

Chapter 1 The extent of unemployment

1 S. Glyn and J. Oxborrow, *Inter-War Britain: A Social and*

Economic History, London, 1976, p. 144, and R. McKibbin, 'The economic policy of the second Labour Government', *Past and Present*, 1975, no. 78.

2   Pilgrim Trust, *op. cit.*, pp. 173–6 and Carnegie UK Trust, *Disinherited Youth*, Cambridge, 1943, pp. 74–5.

3   According to B. B. Gilbert, *British Social Policy 1914–39*, 2nd edition, London, 1973, p. 56 out of work donation was also to prevent revolutionary disturbances.

4   W. Garside, *The Measurement of Unemployment: Methods and Sources in Great Britain*, London, 1980, p. 32.

5   S. Glyn and J. Oxborrow, *op. cit.*, p. 144.

6   W. Garside, *op. cit.*, p. 32.

7   A full explanation of the difficulties of measuring juvenile unemployment can be found in W. Garside, 'Juvenile unemployment between the wars', *Economic History Review*, 1977, vol. 87.

8   The 1921 and 1931 censuses give an indication of how many people worked in insurable occupations in each town. The exact numbers of people insured against unemployment in the UK is also available in each census.

9   The chief variations in the relationship between the numbers entitled and not entitled to unemployment benefit come after 1924 and 1931. For figures see Table 6.

10   As the exact number of insured workers in each town is not available, unemployment has been calculated as a percentage of the total workforce. This means that the percentage figure is an underestimate.

11   The figures given in the first column in 1921 and 1922 are an estimate, based on an incomplete set of figures.

12   Even a very large error in these figures would make very little difference to the over-all numbers of unemployed. An error of 100 per cent in the numbers of women unemployed would add no more than four per cent to the figure for the total workforce.

13   Carnegie Trust, *op. cit.*, p. 14.

14   Mr Barrett, interview.

15   J. J. Astor *et al.*, *The Third Winter of Unemployment*, London, 1922, p. 241.

16   A. A. Hall, 'Working class living standards on Teesside', C.N.A.A. Ph.D. thesis, Teesside Polytechnic, 1979, Chapter 4.

17   Most unemployment, though, even in depressed areas, was for periods of less than a year. See S. Constantine, *op. cit.*, pp. 6–9.

18   J. Stern, 'Who bears the burden of unemployment', in W. Beckerman (ed.), *Slow Growth in Britain*, Oxford, 1979, pp. 62–84.

19   Ted Leesson, interview.

20   Like the Rhondda, Stockton relied heavily on one source of employment which shut down in the inter-war years. In Crook there was only one source of employment which also closed.

21   It was rare for a town to have an unemployment rate which coincided with the national average, because most towns in Britain had a rate either much higher or much lower than average.

Chapter 2 Living standards of the unemployed

1 Boards of Guardians had a virtual autonomy over scales of relief, but the Ministry of Health could refuse permission for them to increase their borrowing under the Local Authority (Financial Provisions) Act of 1921. This could be used to keep expenditure of Guardians to a level desired by National Government. In practice few Guardians broke the principle of less eligibility. The Public Assistance Committees were under government control, and although they had a degree of liberty to fix their own scales they could be replaced by central government if their actions displeased.

2 The first two unemployment insurance acts in Britain (1911 and 1920) were passed when unemployment was estimated at around four per cent and was mostly of a casual nature. They were intended to provide temporary relief only.

3 See J. Macnicol, *The Movement for Family Allowances*, London, 1980, pp. 104–107.

4 See Pilgrim Trust, *op. cit.*, pp. 118–120.

5 The rules for the provision of relief are given repeatedly in the Minutes of the Middlesbrough Board of Guardians.

6 Middlesbrough MOH report 1922.

7 Mrs Bell, interview.

8 F. Bell, *At the Works*, 2nd edition, 1911, p. 50.

9 Mrs Bell, interview.

10 This pattern is mentioned by several social investigators, going back to B. S. Rowntree, *The Human Needs of Labour*, 2nd edition, London, 1957.

11 See Chapter 1.

12 Mr Parker, interview.

13 For a comparison of wage rates in different parts of the country see A. Chapman, *Wages and Salaries in the UK*, Cambridge, 1953, Chapter 2.

14 See J. Stevenson and C. Cook, *The Slump*, 1977, p. 17.

15 See *Ministry of Labour Gazette*, 1919–39.

16 Pilgrim Trust, *op. cit.*, p. 204.

17 G. C. M. McGonigle and J. Kirby, *Poverty and Public Health*, London, 1937. H. Tout revealed in *The Standard of Living in Bristol*, 1938, pp. 44–56, that in inter-war Bristol unemployment was the greatest single cause of poverty. It is not part of this study to look at relative causes of poverty or to fix a poverty line for Teesside, but the evidence given in this chapter suggests that unemployment was not as potent a cause of poverty on Teesside as it was in Bristol. This is backed up by the findings of the Pilgrim Trust, *op. cit.*, which found that the greatest rate of poverty amongst the unemployed in the towns they studied was in the prosperous town of Leicester.

19 Mrs McCart, interview.

20 Pybus Bros were a subsidiary of Hintons, a multiple retailer which sold goods to both middle class and working class customers. See D. Taylor, 'How to be a successful grocer in nineteenth century Middlesbrough', *Cleveland and Teesside Local History Society Bulletin*, no. 42.

21   Frequent references to overcrowding are made in the Middlesbrough and Darlington MOH reports of the early 1920s.

22   Further work is needed to make firm comparisons of the situation of the unemployed before and after the war, but it is clear that their financial position *vis à vis* the employed changed considerably during the thirties.

23   See S. Constantine, *op. cit.*, pp. 28–29.

24   G. Orwell, *The Road to Wigan Pier*, 2nd edition, London, 1962, p. 85.

25   B. S. Rowntree, *Poverty and Progress*, London, 1941; and J. B. Orr, *Food, Health and Income*, 1936.

26   Stockton MOH reports, written by Dr McGonigle, mention this view persistently. See also J. B. Priestley, *op. cit.*, p. 326.

27   Most of the contemporary surveys mention this. See especially Pilgrim Trust, *op. cit.*, pp. 128–33.

28   Mrs Chilvers, interview.

29   Mr O'Connell, interview.

30   Mr J. Singleton, interview.

31   Elizabeth Roberts, 'Working class living standards in Barrow and Lancaster 1890–1914', *Economic History Review*, 1977, vol. 87.

Chapter 3 The effects of unemployment on health

1   For a fuller account see J. Macnicol, *op. cit.*, p. 55f.

2   *Ibid.*

3   *Ibid.*, p. 57.

4   Kathleen Vaughn, 'Maternal mortality and its relation to the shape of the pelvis', *Proceedings of the Royal Society of Medicine*, No. 23, 1916.

5   J. Macnicol, *op. cit.*, p. 50.

6   *Ibid.*

7   J. Hadfield, *Health in the industrial North East 1919–30*, Sheffield Ph.D., 1979, p. 286.

8   See for example the report in the *Guardian*, 14.6.1982.

9   M. H. Brenner, 'Mortality and the national economy. A review in the experience of England and Wales 1936–76', *The Lancet*, Sept. 1979.

10   There have been a number of criticisms of Brenner's methods on the grounds that they manipulate data to explain relationships. S. Kasl's reply to Brenner in, 'Mortality and the business cycle', *American Journal of Public Health*, 1979, is one such. Kasl writes:

The unemployment data . . . shows a pattern which bears no relationship to the infant mortality data. However, though the image of detrending the high rates . . . become low rates and the slight elevation of 1960 now becomes a low rate. Then with a little lag thrown in and some manipulations the link with the unemployment cycle is beginning to merge. It is hard to know what it all means.

11   See A. A. Hall, *op. cit.*, ch. VIII.

12   See for example G. Kitson-Clark, *The Making of Victoria England*, London, 1966, Chapter 3.

13   Oral testimony for Teesside suggests that most people drank condensed instead of fresh milk, irrespective of its cleanliness, because condensed milk was cheaper.

14   The rents for Corporation houses were normally between 7s and 10s and for privately let homes between 3s and 7s.

15   This type of scheme was enlightened by contemporary standards, although they have since been criticised.

16   Nine hundred families amounted to between three and five per cent of the total population.

17   See J. Stevenson and C. Cook, *op. cit.*, pp. 42–3.

18   Accurate figures of the number of mothers in Middlesbrough are not available.

19   Most of the interviewees in this study belonged to a 'doctor's club' which ensured basic medical care in return for a weekly payment. They normally only consulted the doctor, though, if a member of the family was decidedly ill.

20   The minutes of the maternity and child welfare committees give accounts of milk and Glaxo supplied by them.

21   Oral testimony related that these services were available, but the minutes of the education committee do not give details.

22   MOH reports warn of the heavy death toll to infants from diarrhoea and enteritis.

23   Middlesbrough MOH report.

24   *North Eastern Daily Gazette*, 31.10.1928 and 7.11.1928.

25   Middlesbrough MOH report 1925.

26   McKeown, *Medicine in Modern Society*, pp. 48–50 quoted in J. Hadfield, *op. cit.*, p. 11.

27   The rents of Stockton corporation houses were between 8s and 10s.

28   J. Hadfield, *op. cit.*, p. 378.

29   Articles in local newspapers helped to publicise the clinics, and the MOH reports testify to the fact that they won the confidence of local mothers.

30   As the popularity of the clinics was reported to have increased, by 1930 the numbers attending in Stockton would almost certainly have been greater than in Middlesbrough despite the difference in the size of the two towns.

31   See p. 77.

32   J. Stevenson and C. Cook, *op. cit.*, p. 80.

33   Stockton MOH Report 1934.

34   See Pilgrim Trust, *op. cit.*, p. 139.

35   Stockton MOH Report 1935.

36   Stockton MOH Report 1934.

37   Stockton MOH Report 1934.

38   This cannot be proved, but as McGonigle was renowned for setting high standards in health it seems a reasonable conclusion. For variations in assessments in school inspections see N. Branson and M. Heineman, *Britain in the Nineteen Thirties*, 1971, p. 226.

39   G. McGonigle and J. Kirby, *op. cit.*

40 Darlington MOH report 1938.
41 Darlington MOH report 1923.
42 *Ibid.*, 1934.
43 Pilgrim Trust, *op. cit.*, pp. 136–8.
44 H. Beales and R. S. Lambert, *op. cit.*, Appendix B.
45 Pilgrim Trust, *op. cit.*
46 Mr Tom Chilvers, interview.
47 Mr Jack Singleton, interview.

Chapter 4 Unemployment and crime

1 H. L. Beales and R. S. Lambert, *op. cit.*, p. 235 and Pilgrim Trust, *op. cit.*, pp. 161–2.
2 See J. Stevenson and C. Cook, *op. cit.*, p. 87.
3 *Loc. cit.* and *Darlington and Stockton Times*, 2 May 1920, *North Eastern Daily Gazette*, 23 March 1925.
4 H. Mannheim, *Social Aspects of Crime in England Between the Wars*, London, 1940, p. 147.
5 For a ful explanation see A. K. Bottomley, *Criminology in Focus*, London, 1979.
6 A full explanation of the problems of dealing with crime figures can be found in N. Walker, *Crimes, Courts and Figures*, 1971.
7 H. Mannheim, *op. cit.*, pp. 72–3.
8 V. Gatrell and T. Hadden, 'Criminal statistics and their interpretation', in E. Wrigley (ed.), *Nineteenth Century Society*, 1972, p. 351 and N. Walker, *op. cit.*, Chapter 1.
9 V. Gatrell and T. Hadden, *op. cit.*, p. 351.
10 H. Mannheim, *op. cit.*, p. 80.
11 V. Gatrell and T. Hadden, *op. cit.*, p. 369.
12 S. Ruck, 'The increase of crime in England', *Political Quarterly*, vol. 3, 1932.
13 H. Mannheim, *op. cit.*, p. 157.
14 *Ibid.*, p. 147.
15 *Ibid.*, p. 282.
16 Middlesbrough Chief Constable's Annual Report 1922.
17 *Ibid.*, 1923.
18 *Ibid.*, 1933.
19 H. Mannheim, *op. cit.*, p. 282.
20 *North Eastern Daily Gazette*, 15 January 1921.
21 Mr Jack Singleton, interview.
22 Mrs McCart, interview.
23 Mr McCart, interview. Another aspect of this can be seen in R. Roberts, *The Classic Slum*, 2nd edition, London, 1973, p. 156, who talks about violence between rival gangs in Edwardian Salford.
24 Mr McGee, interview.
25 Mr Tom Sowler, interview.
26 Mr Basil Reid, interview.
27 Mr Settle, interview.

28 Mr Tommy Chilvers, interview.
29 Mrs Winifred Chilvers, interview.

Chapter 5 Politics on Teesside

1 The 1929–31 Labour Government fell because of economic pressures, but these were directly linked with the world-wide slump rather than reflecting the Government's handling of the unemployment problem. For a fuller account see R. Skidelsky, *Politicians and the Slump*, London, 1967.

2 The Unemployment Insurance Act of 1911 covered workers in the engineering, building and shipbuilding trades. The Act of 1920 extended the scheme to cover anyone earning less than £250 p.a. except agricultural labourers, domestic and civil servants.

3 For changes in the rates of unemployment benefit see Chapter 2.

4 C. Mowat, *op. cit.*, p. 127.

5 *Ibid.*, p. 471.

6 Tariffs were approved by some sections of industry but were popularly associated with high food prices.

7 For a full explanation see R. Skidelsky, *op. cit.*, and D. Winch, *Economics and Policy*, 2nd edition, London, 1972.

8 Both Ramsay MacDonald, the Prime Minister and Philip Snowden, Chancellor of the Exchequer held this view.

9 J. Stevenson and C. Cook, *op. cit.*, p. 63.

10 D. Winch, *op. cit.*, Chapter 6.

11 When Mosley created his New Party only four MPs, including his wife, left their old party to join him.

12 D. Winch, *op. cit.*, Chapters 6 and 7.

13 J. Stevenson and C. Cook, *op. cit.*, p. 107.

14 In 1931 a National Liberal was returned for Middlesbrough West.

15 See C. Cook, *A Short History of the Liberal Party*, London, 1976.

16 Minutes of Middlesbrough Conservative Association, 10 January 1936.

17 *North Eastern Daily Gazette*, 4 December 1923.

18 *North Eastern Daily Gazette*, 4 December 1923.

19 *North Eastern Daily Gazette*, 28 October 1924, 2 May 1929, 22 October 1931, and the collection of Ellen Wilkinson Press Cuttings in the Labour Party Library.

20 See A. Edwards press cuttings, Teesside Polytechnic Library, Middlesbrough.

21 Mostly in the *Darlington and Stockton Times*.

22 D. Winch, *op. cit.*, pp. 226–8.

23 Macmillan was interested in Keynesian ideas, and in the idea of a regional development policy, and other MPs advocated a socialist state.

24 Mr McGee, interview.

25 Mr A. Darlington, interview.

26 Carnegie UK Trust, *Disinherited Youth*, Cambridge, 1943, pp. 78–9.

27   Mr Basil Reid, interview.
28   Mr O'Connell, interview.
29   Mrs Bell, interview.
30   Mr A, (Darlington), interview.
31   Mr C, (Middlesbrough), interview.
32   J. Stevenson and C. Cook, *op. cit.*, p. 269.
33   W. Hannington, *Unemployed Struggles*, 3rd edition, 1977.
34   J. Stevenson and C. Cook, *op. cit.*, p. 265.
35   *Darlington and Stockton Times*, 21 November 1931.
36   *North Eastern Daily Gazette*, 22 September 1931.
37   This is discussed further in Chapter 7.
38   H. Macmillan, *Winds of Change*, London, 1966, p. 288.
39   J. Stevenson and C. Cook, *op. cit.*, p. 265.
40   The rate was raised to 12*s* in due course, and keepers agreed not to raise their rents accordingly.
41   *North Eastern Daily Gazette*, 7 October 1931.
42   Minutes of Stockton Unionist Labour Advisory Committee, 29 November 1931.

Chapter 6 The administrative reaction to unemployment

1   See Chapter 2.
2   *Ibid.*
3   Information provided by J. J. Turner, author of 'Poor relief and unemployment in Middlesbrough 1914–1926', M.A. thesis, C.N.A.A., 1982.
4   See Chapter 2.
5   Middlesbrough Guardians Minutes, 18 May 1922.
6   See Chapter 2, Table 15.
7   Middlesbrough Guardians Minutes, 18 March 1926. Relief for these men was increased after a meeting with lodging house keepers, who refused to lower their rates.
8   Minutes of Middlesbrough Guardians, 15 April 1922.
9   B. J. Elliot, 'The social and economic effects of unemployment in the coal and steel industries of Sheffield between 1925 and 1935', University of Sheffield M.A., 1969, p. 34.
10   Minutes of Middlesbrough Guardians, 19 September 1922.
11   *Ibid.*, 22 June 1927.
12   *Ibid.*
13   This is explained fully in Chapter 5.
14   Minutes of Middlesbrough Guardians, October 1922.
15   *Ibid.*, 12 May 1924.
16   Middlesbrough Council Minutes, February 1931.
17   *Ibid.*
18   *Ibid.*, 19 May 1930.
19   Minutes of Middlesbrough PAC, 23 February 1931.
20   For a full explanation see Chapter 2.
21   See Chapter 2, Table 15.

22 See Chapter 4.
23 *North Eastern Daily Gazette*, 27 April 1931.
24 Middlesbrough Council Minutes, October 1923.
25 *Ibid.*
26 Normally from the Labour Party or Trades Council.
27 *North Eastern Daily Gazette*, 12 November 1921.
28 *Ibid.*, 11 January 1922.
29 J. J. Turner, *op. cit.*, p. 59.
30 Mr Basil Reid, interview.
31 J. J. Turner, *op. cit.*, p. 58.
32 Mr Basil Reid, interview.
33 See Chapter 5.
34 Minutes of Stockton Public Assistance Committee, 5 October 1931.
35 *Darlington and Stockton Times*, 11 June 1925.
36 There are financial reports given regularly in the Minutes of the Town Council.
37 Mrs Natrass, interview.
38 Minutes of Stockton Town Council, April 1936.
39 Minutes of Juvenile Employment Committee, May 1932.
40 *Darlington and Stockton Times*, 18 May 1925.
41 *North Eastern Daily Gazette*, 23 November 1922.
42 *Darlington and Stockton Times*, 18 July 1925.
43 *North Eastern Daily Gazette*, 14 September 1931.
44 *Ibid.*
45 Minutes of Stockton Town Council, September 1923.
46 Minutes of Middlesbrough Town Council, March 1934.
47 *Ibid.*, 29 May 1923.
48 *Ibid.*, 7 February 1935.

Chapter 7 The community response to unemployment

1 *North Eastern Daily Gazette*, 23 November 1922.
2 Mrs O'Connell, interview.
3 *North Eastern Daily Gazette*, 17 June 1931.
4 *Darlington and Stockton Times*, 7 May 1931.
5 Mr A, (Middlesbrough), interview.
6 Mr Ted Leesson, interview.
7 This was also found by J. Stevenson when looking at the *Consett Guardian* for the inter-war years.
8 See also *Darlington and Stockton Times*, June 1919.
9 *North Eastern Daily Gazette*, 28 December 1921.
10 See D. Winch, *op. cit.*, p. 84.
11 *North Eastern Daily Gazette*, 21 February 1921.
12 *Ibid.*, 4 January 1921.
13 *Ibid.*, 23 February 1923.
14 *Ibid.*, 1 September 1931.
15 See Chapter 1.

16 This practice started in 1924. It was something which only happened in areas of very heavy unemployment. See J. J. Turner, *op. cit.*, p. 39.
17 Mr and Mrs McCart, interview.
18 Mr Jimmy Finegan, interview.
19 Mr B, (Middlesbrough), interview.
20 Mrs Bell, interview.
21 Mr McGee, interview.
22 Mrs Bell, interview.
23 Miss Brenda Anderson, interview.
24 Mr A, (Middlesbrough), interview.
25 Pilgrim Trust, *op. cit.*, p. 342.
26 Mr Jack Feeney, interview.
27 S. Constantine, *op. cit.*, p. 342.
28 Pilgrim Trust, *op. cit.*, p. 342.
29 *Ibid.*
30 Mr McGee, interview.
31 Mr Ted Leesson, interview.
32 Mr McCart, interview.
33 Mr Tom Sowler, interview.
34 Radio Cleveland Interviews on the Thirties, Cleveland County Archive Department.
35 Mr Tom Sowler, interview.
36 R. McKibbin, 'Working class gambling in Britain 1881–1939', *Past and Present*, 1979, No. 82.
37 *Ibid.*, p. 157. This is backed up by oral testimony for Teesside.
38 Mrs Winifred Chilvers, interview.
39 Mr Tom Sowler, interview.
40 Mr Tom Sowler, interview.
41 Mr A, (Darlington), interview.
42 See Chapter 5.
43 Lady Bell, *At the Works*, 2nd edition, London, 1911, p. 144. Lady Bell's teams estimated that one half of all workmen read books and papers, and one quarter newspapers only.
44 Mr A, (Middlesbrough), interview.
45 Council Minutes of Stockton and Middlesbrough.
46 Mrs Bell, interview.
47 Mr Tom Chilvers, interview.
48 Mrs Pat Wilson, interview.
49 Mrs Winifred Chilvers, interview.
50 J. B. Priestley, *op. cit.*
51 Mr Tom Sowler, interview.
52 *Ibid.*
53 Mr O'Connell, interview.
54 B. S. Rowntree, *op. cit.*, and C. Booth, *op. cit.*
55 Mrs Winifred Chilvers, interview.
56 Mr O'Connell, interview.
57 R. Roberts, *The Classic Slum*, 4th edition, 1977, p. 47.

58 Mr Ellenor, interview.
59 W. Greenwood, *Love on the Dole*, 7th edition, 1978, Part II, Chapter 7.
60 See M. Anderson, 'Household structure in the industrial revolution', in *Household and the Family in Past Times*, ed. P. Laslett, London, 1972, for a detailed study of kinship ties of working people in nineteenth century Britain.
61 Miss Brenda Anderson, interview.
62 Mrs Winifred Chilvers, interview.
63 Mr O'Connell, interview.
64 Mr Jack Singleton, interview.
65 Pilgrim Trust, *op. cit.*, pp. 182–4.
66 Miss Brenda Anderson, interview.
67 Mr O'Connell, interview.
68 Mr McGee, interview.
69 Mr C, (Middlesbrough), interview.
70 G. Orwell, *op. cit.*, p. 78.
71 Mrs McCart, interview.
72 Mr Ted Leesson, interview.

Chapter 8 The individual response to unemployment

1 J. Hayes and P. Nutman, *Understanding the Unemployed*, London, 1981, Chapter 4.
2 Mr D. Raby, letter to the author.
3 Pilgrim Trust, *op. cit.*, p. 153.
4 Carnegie Trust, *op. cit.*, p. 67.
5 *Ibid.*, p. 70.
6 *Ibid.*, p. 67.
7 Pilgrim Trust, *op. cit.*, p. 173.
8 *Ibid.*, p. 165.
9 This is also true of Teesside, see Chapter 4.
10 E. W. Bakke, *The Unemployed Man*, London, 1933.
11 H. Beales and R. Lambert, *op. cit.*
12 *Ibid.*, p. 91.
13 Mr B, (Middlesbrough), interview.
14 *Ibid.*
15 Mr Jack Singleton, interview.
16 Mr C, (Middlesbrough), interview.
17 Mr Tom Chilvers, interview.
18 Mr McGee.
19 Mr O'Connell, interview.
20 *Ibid.*
21 Carnegie Trust, *op. cit.*, p. 66.
22 Mr Jack Singleton, interview.
23 Mrs McCart, interview.
24 Mr Lee, interview.
25 Mr Vipond, interview.

26 Miss Brenda Anderson, interview.
27 Pilgrim Trust, *op. cit.*, pp. 188–93.
28 See Chapter 4.
29 Pilgrim Trust, *op. cit.*, p. 172.
30 Mrs A, (Darlington), interview.
31 Pilgrim Trust, *op. cit.*, p. 238 and H. Beales and R. Lambert, *op. cit.*, p. 269.
32 Lady Bell, *op. cit.*, p. 50.
33 Mrs Bell, interview.
34 Mrs Winifred Chilvers, interview.
35 See Chapter 6.
36 See especially M. Spring-Rice, *Working Class Wives*, 2nd edition, London, 1981.
37 Mr Jack Singleton, interview.
38 *Ibid.*
39 See Chapter 6.
40 Mrs McCart, interview. Hinton's 'bone rush' was a notable feature of the depression. See D. Taylor's interview with Kirkland Hinton, 12 March 1980.
41 Miss Brenda Anderson, interview.
42 *Ibid.*
43 Pilgrim Trust, *op. cit.*, p. 171.
44 *Ibid.*, p. 147.
45 See Chapter 2.
46 Mr McGee, interview.
47 *Ibid.*

Bibliography

Primary Sources

Middlesbrough

Minutes of Middlesbrough Conservative Association 1932–9. Held by the Association, 314 Linthorpe Road, Middlesbrough.

Annual reports of Middlesbrough Chief Constable 1919–39. Cleveland County Archive Department.

Annual reports of Middlesbrough Medical Officer of Health 1919–39. Cleveland County Archive Department.

Minutes of Middlesbrough Board of Guardians 1919–39. Cleveland County Archive Department.

Minutes of Middlesbrough Public Assistance Committee 1931–9. Cleveland County Archive Department.

Minutes of Middlesbrough Town Council 1919–39. Cleveland County Archive Department. (Special attention was paid to minutes of: Unemployment Committee, Health Committee, Maternity and Child Welfare Committee, Museum and Public Library Committee, Finance Committee.)

Parish records of Church of St Oswald, Marton Grove 1923–39, Church of St Hilda 1921–38, Church of St Aidan the Martyr 1920–35. Cleveland County Archive Department.

Minutes of Middlesbrough Trades Council 1919–77. Cleveland County Library.

Ellen Wilkinson Press Cuttings. Labour Party Library.

Arthur Edwards Press Cuttings. Teesside Polytechnic Library.

Election addresses of Henry Williams, Trevelyan Thompson, Kingsley Griffith, and Ernest Young. University Library, University of Bristol.

Stockton-on-Tees

Annual reports of Medical Officer of Health 1919–39. Cleveland County Archive Department.

Minutes of Stockton Juvenile Employment Committee 1925–39. Cleveland County Archive Department.

Minutes of Town Council 1919–39 (with special attention to various committees; see above). Cleveland County Archive Department.

Durham Joint Standing Committee Minutes 1919–39. Durham County Archive Department.

Minutes of Stockton Constitutional Association 1920–37. Durham County Archive Department.

Minutes of Stockton Unionist Labour Advisory Committee 1925–33. Durham County Archive Department.

Parish records of Church of St Cuthbert 1919–39. Durham County Archive Department.

Stockton Conservative Association Press Cuttings. Durham County Archive Department.

Election addresses of Strother Stewart and Cecil Hayes. University Library, University of Bristol.

Darlington

Darlington Outdoor Relief Lists 1919–30. Darlington Public Library.

Election addresses of Herbert Pike Pease. Darlington Public Library.

Minutes of Town Council 1919–39. Darlington Public Library.

Annual reports of Darlington Medical Officer of Health. Held by Durham Area Health Authority.

Durham Joint Standing Committee Minutes 1919–30. Durham County Archive Department.

Arthur Edwards Press Cuttings. Held by Teesside Polytechnic Library.

British Steel File on Employment.

Census abstracts.

Darlington and Stockton Times.

Labour Gazette.

Labour Party File on Unemployment. Labour Party Library.

North Eastern Daily Gazette.

Northern Echo.

Oral testimony.

Published sources

J. J. Astor, *et al.*, *The Third Winter of Unemployment*, London, 1922.

E. W. Bakke, *The Unemployed Man*, London, 1933.

H. L. Beales and R. S. Lambert, *Memoirs of the Unemployed*, London, 1934.

W. Beckerman (ed.), *Slow Growth in Britain: Causes and Consequences*, Oxford, 1979.

F. Bell, *At the Works*, 2nd edition, London, 1911.

W. H. Beveridge, *Unemployment: A Problem of Industry*, London, 1909.

C. Booth, *Life and Labour of the People of London*, New York, 1970.

A. K. Bottomley, *Criminology in Focus*, London, 1979.

A. Bowley, *Wages and Incomes Since 1860*, London, 1937.

J. Boyd Orr, *Food, Health and Income*, London, 1936.

M. Bragg, *Speak for England*, London, 1976.

N. Branson and M. Heineman, *Britain in the Nineteen Thirties*, London, 1971.

N. Branson, *Britain in the Nineteen Twenties*, London, 1975. *Popularism*, London, 1979.

M. H. Brenner, 'Mortality and the national economy: a review in the experience of England and Wales 1936–76', *The Lancet*, September 1979.

A. Briggs, *Victorian Cities*, London, 1968.

M. Bruce, *The Coming of the Welfare State*, 4th edition, London, 1968.

D. Burn, *Economic History of Steelmaking 1867–1939*, Cambridge, 1940.

J. Burnett, *A History of the Cost of Living*, London, 1969.

Carnegie UK Trust, *Disinherited Youth*, Cambridge, 1943.

A. Chapman, *Wages and Salaries in the UK*, Cambridge, 1953.

G. D. H. and M. Cole, *Conditions of Britain*, London, 1937.

M. Colledge, *Unemployment and Health*, North Tyneside Community Health Council, 1980.

S. Constantine, *Unemployment in Britain Between the Wars*, London, 1980.

C. Cook, *Sources in British Political History 1900–1951*, London, 1975.

C. Cook, *A Short History of the Liberal Party*, London, 1976. (See also Stevenson; Peele.)

R. C. Davison, *The Unemployed*, London, 1929. *British Unemployment Policy since 1930*, London, 1938.

D. Dougan, *A History of North East Shipbuilding*, London, 1962.

E. Durkheim, *Suicide: A Study in Sociology*, London, (1897), 1952.

B. J. Elliot, 'The social and economic effects of unemployment in the coal and steel industries of Sheffield between 1925 and 1935', MA University of Sheffield, MA thesis, 1969.

G. Ewart Evans, *Where Beards Wag All*, London, 1970.

D. Fraser, *The Evolution of the British Welfare State*, London, 1973.

W. R. Garside, *The Measurement of Unemployment: Methods and Sources in Great Britain, 1850–1979*, Oxford, 1980. 'Juvenile unemployment between the wars', *Economic History Review*, 1977, 87.

V. Gatrell and T. Hadden, 'Criminal statistics and their interpretation', in E. Wrigley (ed.), *Nineteenth Century Society*, London, 1972.

B. B. Gilbert, *British Social Policy 1914–39*, 2nd edition, London, 1973.

S. Glyn and J. Oxborrow, *Inter-War Britain: A Social and Economic History*, London, 1976.

J. Gollan, *Youth in British Industry*, London, 1937.

R. Graves and A. Hodge, *The Long Weekend*, London, 1940.

W. Greenwood, *Love on the Dole*, 7th edition, London, 1978.

M. le Guillot, *A History of the River Tees*, Middlesbrough, 1978.

J. Hadfield, 'Health in the industrial North-East 1919–30', University of Sheffield PhD thesis, 1979.

A. A. Hall, 'Working class living standards on Teesside', CNAA PhD thesis, Teesside Polytechnic, 1979.

A. H. Halsey (ed.), *Trends in British Society Since 1900*, London, 1972.

W. Hannington, *Unemployed Struggles*, 3rd edition, London, 1977.

R. H. C. Hayburn, 'The responses to unemployment in the 1930s with particular reference to South-East Lancashire', University of Hull PhD thesis, 1970.

J. Hayes and P. Nutman, *Understanding the Unemployed*, London, 1981.

R. Hoggart, *The Uses of Literacy*, London, 1957.

A. Hutt, *The Condition of the Working Class in Britain*, London, 1933.

S. Kasl, 'Mortality and the business cycle', *American Journal of Public Health*, 1979.

G. Kitson-Clark, *The Making of Victorian England*, London, 1966.

P. Laslett (ed.), *Household and the Family in Past Times*, London, 1972.

P. Lillie, *History of Middlesbrough*, Middlesbrough, 1968.

H. Macmillan, *Winds of Change*, London, 1966.

J. Macnicol, *The Movement for Family Allowances*, London, 1980.

H. Mannheim, *Social Aspects of Crime in England Between the Wars*, London, 1940.

P. Mathias, *The First Industrial Nation*, London, 1969.

A. Marwick, *Britain in the Century of Total War*, London, 1968.

A. McCanse and E. Widowson, *The Composition of Foods*, HMSO, London, 1978.

N. McCord, *North East England: A Social and Economic History*, London, 1979. (See also Thane.)

G. C. M. McGonigle and J. Kirby, *Poverty and Public Health*, London, 1937.

R. McKibbin, 'The economic policy of the second Labour Government', *Past and Present*, 1975, 78. 'Working-class gambling in Britain 1881–1939', *Past and Present*, 1979, 82.

C. Mowat, *Britain Between the Wars*, London, 1955.

M. Muggeridge, *The Thirties*, 2nd edition, London, 1971.

G. A. North, *Teesside's Economic Heritage*, Margate, 1975.

D. Oddy, 'Working class diets in late nineteenth century Britain', *Economic History Review*, 1970, vol. 23.

J. B. Orr, *Food, Health and Income*, London, 1936.

G. Orwell, *The Road to Wigan Pier*, 2nd edition, Harmondsworth, 1962.

G. Peele and C. Cook (eds.), *The Politics of Reappraisal*, London, 1975.

H. Pelling, *A Short History of the Labour Party*, London, 1965.

Pilgrim Trust, *Men Without Work*, Cambridge, 1938.

S. Pollard, *The Development of the British Economy 1914–1967*, 2nd edition, London, 1969. *The Gold Standard and Unemployment Policies Between the Wars*, London, 1970. *A History of Labour in Sheffield*, London, 1959.

J. B. Priestley, *English Journey*, 2nd edition, London, 1977.

P. Reeves, *Round about a Pound a Week*, London, 1913.

H. W. Richardson, *Economic Recovery in Britain 1932–39*, London, 1967.

E. Roberts, 'Working class living standards in Barrow and Lancaster 1890–1914', *Economic History Review*, 1977, vol. 87.

R. Roberts, *The Classic Slum*, 4th edition, London, 1977.

B. S. Rowntree, *The Human Needs of Labour*, 2nd edition, London, 1957.

S. Ruck, 'The increase of crime in England', *Political Quarterly*, 1932, vol. 3.

R. S. Sayers, *Economic Change in England 1880–1939*, Oxford, 1967.

R. Skidelsky, *Politicians and the Slump*, London, 1967.

M. Spring-Rice, *Working Class Wives*, 2nd edition, London, 1981.

J. Stern, 'Who bears the burden of unemployment?' in W. Beckerman (ed.), *Slow Growth in Britain*, Oxford, 1979.

J. Stevenson and C. Cook, *The Slump*, London, 1977.

D. Taylor, 'How to become a successful grocer in nineteenth-century Middlesbrough', *Cleveland and Teesside Local History Society Bulletin*, No. 42, 1979.

P. Thompson, *The Edwardians*, London, 1975.

H. Tout, *The Standard of Living in Bristol*, London, 1938.

J. J. Turner, Poor relief and unemployment in Middlesbrough 1914–1926, CNAA MA thesis, 1982.

K. Vaughn, 'Maternal mortality and its relation to the shape of the pelvis', *Proceedings of the Royal Society of Medicine*, No. 23, 1916.

N. Walker, *Crimes, Courts and Figures*, London, 1971.

Index